D0810199

THE WORKS OF SHAKESPEARE

EDITED FOR THE SYNDICS OF THE
CAMBRIDGE UNIVERSITY PRESS
BY
JOHN DOVER WILSON

THE FIRST PART OF
THE HISTORY OF
HENRY IV

THE FIRST PART OF
THE HISTORY OF
HENRY IV

CAMBRIDGE
AT THE UNIVERSITY PRESS
1971

PUBLISHED BY
THE SYNDICS OF THE CAMBRIDGE UNIVERSITY PRESS

Bentley House, 200 Euston Road, London, NW1 2DB
American Branch: 32 East 57th Street, New York, N.Y. 10022

ISBNs:

0 521 07532 7 *clothbound*

0 521 09475 5 *paperback*

First edition 1946
Reprinted 1949

Reprinted as Pocket Edition 1958
Reprinted as First Edition 1958, 1964

First Paperback Edition 1968
Reprinted 1971

First printed in Great Britain at the University Press, Cambridge
Reprinted in Great Britain by Hazell Watson & Viney Ltd,
Aylesbury, Bucks

CONTENTS

In
MEMORY
of
Q

INTRODUCTION

I. *Two Parts but one play*

As with *Hamlet* so with 1 and 2 *Henry IV* the commentary has much exceeded the limits of this edition,
and I have found myself obliged to contrive two supple-
mentary volumes for the overplus. *The Fortunes of
Falstaff,* published in 1943, deals with the much
debated character and career of the fat knight, and so
allows me to concentrate here upon *Henry IV* as a
chronicle-play, which was after all what Shakespeare
set out to write. A second excursus, concerned with
the sources and textual history of the double play and
its sequel *Henry V*, and including a discussion of the
reasons for the change from 'Oldcastle' to 'Falstaff'
(see below, p. xxix), is being prepared in collaboration
with Dr Duthie; and I have contributed to the Greg
Presentation Number of *The Library* (June 1945) a
tentative outline of my conclusions as regards *Henry IV*,
references to which will be found in the Notes below.
Meanwhile, the present Introduction[1] and the Stage-
history are concerned with both Parts, which, issued
separately for convenience, each with its own notes and
glossary, have in fact been envisaged and edited as one
drama.

Dr Johnson wrote:

These two plays will appear to every reader, who shall
peruse them without ambition of critical discoveries, to be
so connected that the second is merely a sequel to the first;
to be two only because they are too long to be one[2].

But very few have since subscribed to, or even noticed,
this judgement; and whatever modern actors, critics or

[1] Which, it should perhaps be stated, was written before
the appearance of Dr Tillyard's *Shakespeare's History Plays.*
[2] Johnson's *Shakespeare*, 1765, iv. 235.

editors may say on the matter—most of them say
nothing at all—they seem agreed to treat the two Parts
as independent, if serially related, plays[1]. The only
exception I know of is Quiller-Couch[2], formerly captain
of this adventure, to whose memory the following
edition, of what was I think, after *The Tempest*, his
favourite play, is inscribed.

Of the serial character there is of course no question.
Second and third of a tetralogy on the rise of the house
of Lancaster, they are linked by *Henry V* with another,
earlier written, tetralogy on the fall of the same house,
while in *Henry VIII* we have a kind of pendant to the
chain, in which the twilight of the Civil Wars and the
night of Crookback's tyranny are offset by a picture of
the blessed day of a Protestant king, uniting the 'roses'
in one stem, from which springs the infant Elizabeth,
whose baptism at the hands of Archbishop Cranmer
brings the play and its eight predecessors to an appro-
priately 'Elizabethan' conclusion. Furthermore, as
hinted at the end of the Introduction to *Richard II* and
argued more fully in the volume on the sources to
follow, it seems at least possible that the series which
begins with *Richard II* and ends with *Henry V* once
existed in a pre-Shakespearian form as three, not four
plays, and that it only became four through the expansion, at Shakespeare's hands, of a single *Henry IV* into
a two-part play. In a word, the two parts proceed,
I believe, from an underlying textual unity. That does
not necessarily mean that the unity persists in their
present state; for one cannot, or should not, argue from
textual premises to aesthetic conclusions[3]. Falstaff was
originally called Oldcastle, and his character, difficult

[1] G. L. Kittredge writes, in the latest edition from
America (p. viii): 'The two Parts of *Henry IV* are not two
halves of a single play. Each part is complete in itself.'
[2] *Shakespeare's Workmanship*, p. 134.
[3] v. *Modern Language Review*, xxv. 404-6.

as it is to credit the fact, was certainly distilled by some
strange alchemy of popular legend and ecclesiastical
defamation from that of a fine soldier and a stalwart
martyr for conscience' sake. But Lollardry has nothing
dramatically to do with the knight of Eastcheap, and
is irrelevant alike to our enjoyment and our criticism
of him. Similarly, to prove, as I think is possible, that
the two parts grew out of one is not to prove that they
are one still. It has, however, this negative bearing on
the question: it rules out a different textual diagnosis,
which has been widely accepted or assumed, and from
which other critics have not hesitated to draw aesthetic
conclusions of their own.

It is commonly held that *2 Henry IV* was an afterthought on Shakespeare's part, or, as one writer puts
it, like *2 Tamburlaine* 'an unpremeditated addition,
occasioned by the enormous effectiveness of the by-
figure of Falstaff'[1]. And the following from the Arden
edition of the play is a good illustration of the kind of
criticism that flows from such assumptions:

The Second Part of *Henry IV* is unquestionably inferior
to the First Part as a work of dramatic art....[It] is faulty
in construction, and occasionally feeble in execution. For
the greater part of four acts the poet is occupied with a
theme, of which the interest had been exhausted in the
previous play, and which grows stale by repetition[2].

I am far from sharing this editorial boredom; but I admit at once that *1 Henry IV*, which was probably being
acted on Shakespeare's stage while *2 Henry IV* was still
in the process of composition and rehearsal, exhibits a
certain unity that its sequel lacks. Neither, however,
is in any true dramatic sense complete or self-contained,
as are for instance *Richard II* and *Henry V*, the first
and fourth of the same series; and the comparison with

[1] C. F. Tucker Brooke, *Tudor Drama*, 1911, p. 333.
[2] *2 Henry IV* (Arden Shakespeare), pp. xxiii–xxiv.

Marlowe's *Tamburlaine* only serves to bring out the fundamental distinction between the two cases. *1 Tamburlaine* is a play, rounded off and clearly written without thought of a second part, which was only added in the hope of repeating the harvest reaped from Part 1. *1 Henry IV*, on the contrary, is as patently only part of a whole, inasmuch as at its close all the strands of the plot are left with loose ends. The rebels, Northumberland and Archbishop Scroop, are still at large after the battle of Shrewsbury; and the Archbishop is introduced and given a scene to himself in 4. 4 in order to prepare the audience for the expedition of Prince John in Part 2. The relations of the Prince with his father, eased by the interview in 3. 2 and his brilliant conduct in battle, still await that final clarification which, as Elizabethan auditors acquainted with the merest outline of the life of Henry of Monmouth would know, belonged to the death-bed scene in the Jerusalem chamber. Most striking of all perhaps is that stone of stumbling to modern interpreters, the soliloquy at the end of the second scene of Part 1, which looks forward not only to the coronation of Henry V but also to the rejection of Falstaff, neither of which occurs until the very end of Part 2. If Part 1 be an integral drama, and Part 2 a mere afterthought, the soliloquy is inexplicable; indeed, the failure of critics to explain it is itself largely due to their absorption in the first part and their neglect of, or contempt for, the second. In short, the political and dynastic business of this history play, which is twofold, the defeat of the rebels and the repentance of the Prince including his reconciliation with his father, is only half through at the end of Part 1. As for the comic underplot, by treating the drama as two plays critics have unwittingly severed and so overlooked all sorts of subtle threads of character and action belonging to it. In particular, as I have shown elsewhere, Falstaff's false claim to the *spolia*

opima of Harry Hotspur, though the key to his character
in Part 2, seems nothing more than a farcical incident
unless the last scenes of Part 1 and the opening scenes
of Part 2 are considered as belonging to the same play[1].

On the other hand, think of the two parts as one,
and the structure of the whole is revealed in its proper
proportions. The normal dramatic curve, so to say,
in Shakespeare is one that rises in intensity up to the
middle of the play, e.g. in the trial scene of *The Merchant*, the play scene of *Hamlet*, the deposition scene
of *Richard II*; relaxes during act 4, partly in order to
gather up loose secondary threads of the plot, partly
to give the principal actors a much-needed rest, and
partly to relieve the strain upon the attention of the
audience; and mounts again for the second and final
climax of act 5, which we call catastrophe in tragedy
and solution in comedy. Such and no other is the shape
of *Henry IV*, in which the battle of Shrewsbury is the
nodal point we expect in a third act, while the political
scenes of minor interest, which in Part 2 round off the
rebellion and dismiss the old king's troubles before the
auspicious accession of his son, are just the kind of
hang-over we get in a Shakespearian fourth act. And
the curve, so plain to the eye in the rebellion plot, is
to be traced as surely, if less obviously, in other plots
also, all of which, it may be noted, find their acme or
turning-point in the battle of Shrewsbury. There Prince
and King, as I said, come to a temporary understanding,
to drift asunder again for most of Part 2, only to reach
harmony in the moments before death separates them
for ever. There Falstaff, as the accepted slayer of
Hotspur, attains the height of his credit and his fortunes,
which then fluctuate during the first half of Part 2,
take an upward turn (which deludes him but not us),
with his prospects of a loan from Justice Shallow and

[1] Cf. *The Fortunes of Falstaff*, pp. 90–1.

of becoming chief favourite at the court of the young
King, and finally come crashing to the ground outside
the Abbey. There, too, the Prince's friendship for him
finds its tenderest expression in the epitaph over his vast
corpse on the stricken field, is obscured for the next
four acts (because Shakespeare deliberately keeps the
two characters apart except for the brief and, from
Falstaff's point of view, doubtful meeting in the presence
of Doll Tearsheet), and once again reaches finality at
their second meeting, after the coronation. Yet another
indication of planning is the symbolic arrangement,
which excludes the Lord Chief Justice from Part 1,
though there are indications that he appeared early
in the pre-Shakespearian version[1], restricts that part to
the theme of the truant prince's return to Chivalry,
and leaves the atonement with Justice, or the Rule of
Law, as a leading motive for its sequel. In short, when
the Queen of the blue-stockings remarks, 'I cannot help
thinking that there is more of contrivance and care in
Shakespeare's execution of this play than in almost any
he has written'[2], one cannot help thinking she is right.

The whole series of events, with all the moral forces that
are brought into collision, are directed to a single end. The
action as it advances converges on a definite point. The
thread of purpose running through it becomes more marked.
All minor effects are subordinated to the sense of an ever-
growing unity. The end is linked to the beginning with
inevitable certainty, and in the end we discern the meaning
of the whole.

The words are taken from S. H. Butcher's well-known
summary of Aristotle's views on drama in the *Poetics*[3],
and every one of them is applicable to the play before

[1] v. notes 1. 2. 63–4, 83–6; 3. 2. 32–3.
[2] Elizabeth Montagu, *An Essay on the Writings and
Genius of Shakespeare*, 1769.
[3] *Aristotle's Theory of Poetry and Fine Art* (4th ed.),
pp. 284–5.

us. Yet this end—τὸ τέλος μέγιστον ἁπάντων—
the crown and meaning of the whole, is the Repentance
of the Prince and his Rejection of Falstaff, which almost
all the commentators since Hazlitt have themselves
rejected. Taking the play as two and not one, they have
never seen it as a whole, nor guessed that it might have
been planned as a single structure, and probably intended when completed to be acted by the Lord
Chamberlain's men on alternate afternoons. Until it
be thus thought of, it will continue to languish in the
undeserved neglect into which it has fallen since the
eighteenth century. Once its unity is accepted by
readers and producers, it will stand revealed as one of
the greatest of dramatic masterpieces.

II. 'The History of Henrie the Fourth'

Henry IV is Shakespeare's vision of the 'happy breed
of men' that was his England. Here he meets Chaucer
on his own ground, and stretches a canvas even wider
and more varied than that of *The Canterbury Tales*.
True, he was to paint vaster worlds still in *King Lear*
and *Antony and Cleopatra*; but those worlds, despite
the animation of the titans which inhabit them, are of
necessity remote and somewhat indistinct, whereas in
the great expanse of *Henry IV* every incident and per-
sonage, whether tragic or comic, momentous or trivial,
bears the hall-mark, not merely of poetic genius, but of
pure English gold, standard and current in the realm of
Her Majesty Queen Elizabeth. True, also, its political
theme, together with the historical setting and design,
interests the subjects of King George VI less than it
did hers; but that again simply attests its supreme
excellence as an Elizabethan history play. Nothing
dates like political issues; and generally speaking the
more keenly they are felt by one generation the less
likely are they to be understood by another. Historians

and scholars, however, should be proof against such
changes in the climate of opinion, and it is strange to
find Sir Edmund Chambers writing:

In *Henry IV* chronicle history becomes little more than
a tapestried hanging, dimly wrought with horsemen and
footmen, in their alarms and their excursions, which serves
as a background to groups of living personages, conceived
in quite another spirit and belonging to a very different
order of reality[1].

The distinction here drawn between the political and
comic groups is sadly misleading. *Henry IV*, at both
social levels, was written by an Elizabethan called
William Shakespeare; that is to say, it is at once 'for
all time' and of its own age, through and through and
from top to bottom. If we are to see it in correct
perspective, and enjoy it as its creator meant it to be
enjoyed, we must appreciate alike the medieval elements in the 'reverend vice' Falstaff and the modern
appeal of the 'truant to chivalry' Prince Hal. Above
all, we must recognize that its history was as relevant
and fascinating to Elizabethan and Jacobean English-
men as the history in Hardy's *Dynasts* and Scott's
Antiquary and Tolstoy's *War and Peace* is to English-
men, Scots, and Russians in 1945. By 1600, indeed,
it had become so exciting that the authorities would
only permit Part 2 to be printed after a drastic purge,
which robbed the political scenes of some 170 lines,
and then, apparently repenting of even that concession,
thought best to suppress it altogether[2].

But that the political and comic scenes in *Henry IV*
should seem in modern eyes to belong to 'different
orders of reality' is due as much to a disproportionate
attention paid to the latter as to things gone out of
mind in the former. 'Sir John, Sir John', exclaims

[1] E. K. Chambers, *Shakespeare: a Survey*, p. 118.
[2] See Note on the Copy, *2 Henry IV*, pp. 119–23.

the Lord Chief Justice, 'I am well acquainted with your manner of wrenching the true cause the false way.' And had Maurice Morgann and nineteenth-century critics taken a hint from these words they might themselves have preserved a 'level consideration' of the play. In the little book above mentioned I have attempted to restore Shakespeare's balance, and do not need to repeat my arguments here. Yet Falstaff was certainly extraordinarily popular in Shakespeare's own day, was even perhaps the most captivating figure that ever lured Elizabethan and Jacobean crowds to the playhouse. The very prentice boys who paid their pennies to stand about the stage stopped cracking nuts, we are told, when he appeared[1]. From the other end of society, we have the legend, more plausible than most, that the great Queen could not have enough of him; and, on hearing of his unexpected death in *Henry V*, commanded his resuscitation in a new play which should show him in love. Yet it is also certain that his vast form did not then appear to dwarf the rest of the characters and make the scenes in which he was not present look faded and outmoded. On the contrary, it is safe to say that those scenes, political and military for the most part, were so full of interest in themselves that Shakespeare could make the comic under-plot as fascinating as he liked without fear of disturbing the balance of the play.

More, indeed, is involved than *Henry IV*. For if Hal be the cad and hypocrite that many modern readers imagine, or even if he seem merely 'dimly wrought' by the side of his gross friend, then the whole grand scheme of the Lancastrian cycle miscarries, since it is the person and reign of King Henry V which gives the bright centre to that dark picture, a brightness that by contrast makes the chaos that follows all the more

[1] v. *Stage-History*, p. xxxi, below.

ghastly. When Shakespeare set forth along the road
which begins with *Richard II*, he had the whole
journey in view; had, indeed, already traversed the
second half of it; and envisaged the road immediately
before him, which stretched from the usurpation of
Bolingbroke, through the troubles of his reign, to the
final triumph of his son over the French, as a great
upward sweep in the history of England and the
chapter of that history which the men of his age found
more interesting than any other. How lively was this
interest is shown, on the one hand, by the otherwise
puzzling identification, in the private letters of states-
men and courtiers and in her own words, of Elizabeth
with King Richard, coupled with the evident touchi-
ness of the authorities on the subject of Henry IV's
accession, which came in 1600–1 to be associated
with the Essex crisis[1]; and on the other by the fact
that the anniversary of Agincourt was still a day of
national rejoicing in the sixteenth and seventeenth
centuries.

> And Crispin Crispian shall ne'er go by,
> From this day to the ending of the world,
> But we in it shall be rememberéd,

seemed very truth to those who first heard the lines,
though to-day St Crispin has been long since forgotten
and Agincourt is but a name in the history books. To
understand, then, what Shakespeare attempted in
Henry IV, and to see Falstaff within the dramatic frame
to which he belongs and from which modern criticism
has improperly released him, we must do what we can
in the twentieth century to recapture the political
significance of the play.

First then, *respice finem*; everything leads up to the
coronation of the Prince. Little as it has been observed

---

[1] v. Introduction to *Richard II* (New Shakespeare),
pp. xxx–xxxiv, and *2 Henry IV*, pp. 120–3.

during the past two hundred years, this last scene is the inevitable finale, as inevitable and as much foreseen by the audience from the very beginning as the death of the hero in a tragedy. Everything that goes before is coloured by its approach. Harry Monmouth is heir apparent: how will he behave when he comes to the throne? Even the comic under-plot turns on the answer to this question; it is the theme of the very first conversation that Hal and Falstaff hold in our hearing. And inseparable from the coronation scene is that which foreruns it, the great accord with Justice, wherein the young King, his wildness buried in his father's grave, makes his peace with the old judge who had previously committed him to prison. 'There', he declares, 'is my hand';

> You shall be as a father to my youth,
> My voice shall sound as you do prompt mine ear,
> And I will stoop and humble my intents
> To your well-practised wise directions[1].

In speaking thus Henry exhibits the spirit of the true 'governor' as distinct from that of the tyrant. For, as Hooker observes,

By the natural law, whereunto he [God] hath made all subject, the lawful power of making laws to command whole politic societies of men belongeth so properly unto the same societies, that for any prince or potentate of what kind so ever upon earth to exercise the same of himself, and not either by express commission immediately and personally received from God, or else by authority derived at the first from their consent upon whose persons they impose laws, it is no better than mere tyranny[2].

We are so apt, in this 'democratic' age, to be taken up with the prerogatives, exercise of power, and high

[1] *2 Henry IV*, 5. 2. 118–21.
[2] *Laws of Ecclesiastical Polity*, I, x, par. 8.

handed ways of the Tudors with their parliaments, as to forget that, though themselves the representatives and embodiment of

> The majesty and power of law and justice[1],

this law was not their dictates, or Diktate, but the Common Law of England derived from ancient usage, or, as the formula ran, 'the laws of Edward the Confessor'. We forget too how keenly conscious the best of them were of the duties and responsibilities to which they were called both 'by express commission immediately and personally received from God' and 'by authority derived at the first from their consent upon whose persons they impose laws'. 'To be a king and wear a crown', declared the aged Elizabeth to her turbulent last parliament, in the very spirit of the speech on the Burden of Kingship which Shakespeare had given to his Henry V a couple of years before, 'is more glorious to them that see it, than it is pleasure to them that bear it'. And again,

> I was never so much enticed with the glorious name of a king, or royal authority of a queen, as delighted that God hath made me His instrument to maintain His truth and glory, and to defend this kingdom from peril, dishonour, tyranny, and oppression[2].

More surprising perhaps to some will it be to read of her unhappy sister, Mary Tudor, falling upon her knees at a meeting of her Council before her coronation, and speaking

> very earnest and troubled, of the duties of kings and queens, and how she was determined to acquit herself in the task God had pleased to lay before her, to his greater glory and service, to the public good and all her subjects' benefit[3].

---

[1] *2 Henry IV*, 5. 2. 78.
[2] J. B. Black, *The Reign of Elizabeth*, p. 194.
[3] H. F. M. Prescott, *Spanish Tudor*, pp. 243-4.

It is in such a mood we are to imagine Shakespeare's Prince going to his own coronation; it is with such parallels in mind that we should interpret his 'conversion', which is not so much a moral reformation or repentance for sin in the theological sense—Hal has very little 'sin' about him—as a dedication to public service. Yet the conversion is complete and deeply religious. He too falls upon his knees, not like Mary in the presence of her Council, but by the bedside of his dead father, as he believes him to be, in a scene which is one of the finest that Shakespeare ever wrote[1]. And the anointed king who emerges from the Abbey is a different *man* from the prince who entered:

> Presume not that I am the thing I was[2].

Any discussion in print or on the stage of the constitutional position of Henry IV and of his heir would have been dangerous during Elizabeth's reign; but I suppose that something like the following more or less tallies with contemporary opinion on the subject. King Richard had been weak, capricious, tyrannical. Such defects tend to upset the balance of the monarchical state, since they encourage the planetary nobles, who revolve about the sovereign, to start from their spheres in pursuit of personal ambition, and if the worst befalls 'chaos is come again', as it came during the reign of the *roi fainéant* Henry VI. Bolingbroke saved England from this fate by imposing his will upon her; but, in so doing, he sinned. Richard II, for all his instability and evil deeds, was the Lord's anointed; and in lifting up his hand against him, Bolingbroke had struck at God himself. In the Shakespearian Addition

[1] *The Fortunes of Falstaff*, pp. 77–80.
[2] *2 Henry IV*, 5. 5. 57.

to *Sir Thomas More*, the great Lord Chancellor thus
instructs a crowd of rioters:

> For to the king God hath his office lent
> Of dread, of justice, power, and command;
> Hath bid him rule and willed you to obey;
> And to add ampler majesty to this,
> He hath not only lent the king his figure,
> His throne and sword, but given him his own name,
> Calls him a god on earth. What do you then,
> Rising 'gainst him that God Himself enstalls,
> But rise 'gainst God; what do you to your souls,
> In doing this, O desperate as you are?[1]

In like manner Bolingbroke has put his soul in jeopardy
by the sin of usurpation, sees one consequence of it in
the wayward son God has given him,

> That, in his secret doom, out of my blood,
> He'll breed revengement and a scourge for me[2],

and seeks to expiate it by undertaking a crusade to the
Holy Land. Other members of the state are also conscious of his plight. The rebel barons feel themselves
peers of the man they have set upon the throne and
resent the exercise of authority they have helped him to
usurp; and Hotspur, afire for glory, eaten up with ambition, is the spokesman of their point of view. For
a weak title in the monarch is only less dangerous to
the realm than a weak character, and the disorder that
flows from such weakness is one of the chief political
themes of *Henry IV*. But Shakespeare lived in an age
when men were becoming increasingly aware that above
the interests of nobles, however brilliant and attractive,
was the cause of

> this little world,
> This precious stone set in the silver sea...
> This blessed plot, this earth, this realm, this England;

[1] ll. 98–107 (with spelling and punctuation modernized).
See Pollard and others, *Shakespeare's Hand in 'Sir Thomas
More'*, 1923.   [2] *1 Henry IV*, 3. 2. 6–7.

and that above the very throne itself sat Justice. They knew too that the only security for England against internal strife and the 'envy of less happier lands' was a Prince who, with divine right on his side, that is, with a clear title to the throne and the sceptre firmly in his grasp, could be the leader of a united and harmonious common weal, in which noble, merchant, yeoman, and peasant worked together for the good of the whole. Such a Prince was Queen Elizabeth; such is Shakespeare's Harry Monmouth[1].

The blessing, then, which rested upon Henry V during his all too brief reign, was denied his father; and the contrast between their dispositions and prospects forms yet another leading theme of the play. Shakespeare deliberately reshapes the historical data derived from Holinshed in order to bring it out. Henry IV actually reigned from 1399 to 1413; *Henry IV* begins a 'twelve month' after his coronation and compresses the fourteen years into a period of not more than a year and a half[2]. Condensation of this kind was greatly to the advantage of dramatic art; it also does much to quicken our sense of the reign's brevity and inquietude[3]. In history again, Henry's main difficulties were solved by the Battle of Shrewsbury, fought on 21 July 1403, ten years before his death; the rising of the Archbishop of York in 1405, the final defeat of

[1] The foregoing paragraph is repeated, with variations, from *The Essential Shakespeare*, pp. 93–5.

[2] P. A. Daniel (*Time-Analysis of Shakespeare's Plays*) reckons that Part 1 takes 'three months at the outside' and fancies that for Part 2 'a couple of months would be a liberal estimate'. As Part 2 opens within a few days of the Battle of Shrewsbury, the two parts comprise not more than five months of dramatic time, which gives us 17 months from the end of *Richard II* to the end of *2 Henry IV*.

[3] Hall heads his chapter on Henry IV 'The Vnquiete Tyme of Kyng Henry the Fourthe', and that on Henry V 'The Victorious Actes of Kyng Henry the Fifth'.

Northumberland and Lord Bardolph in 1408, and the
death of Glendower (which Holinshed dates 1410,
though it actually took place c. 1416) being so to speak
minor sequels to the crushing of Hotspur. By bringing
all these events into the same year, and dwelling at considerable length upon the second and third, Shakespeare gives an impression of the usurper struggling
with a hydra, which but for his sons he could never
have overcome and only succeeds in overcoming
within an hour of his death.

And this impression is further accentuated by other
devices. Henry IV, though only 36 years of age at
Shrewsbury and dying in his 46th year, is represented as a sick, care-worn, and old man throughout
the play. He strikes the note in the very first words
of Part 1:

> So shaken as we are, so wan with care—

words which must be taken as referring both to his
realm and to himself. At the opening of Part 2 he has
become gravely ill; in the first scene of its act 3 we
have a glimpse of him in his bed-chamber at Westminster, vainly seeking the slumber that comes so easily
to the peasant and the ship-boy; and brooding, as ever,
on the past, on his guilt, on Richard, the despised victim
who had prophesied that these troubles would pursue his
supplanter, that the Percies would revolt yet again, that

> The time will come, that foul sin, gathering head,
> Shall break into corruption.

And though on this occasion he avers, to Warwick and
Surrey,

> Then, God knows, I had no such intent
> But that necessity so bowed the state
> That I and greatness were compelled to kiss[1],

[1] *2 Henry IV*, 3. 1. 72–7. I now think that I overstressed
the sincerity of these words in my Introduction to *Richard II*,
p. xxi.

he calls God to witness a different story, when speaking
to Harry in a later scene:

> God knows, my son,
> By what by-paths and indirect crookt ways
> I met this crown, and I myself know well
> How troublesome it sate upon my head[1].

The disease that lays him low is apoplexy; but, as
Falstaff expounds his Galen, apoplexy has its original
'from much grief, from study [i.e. brooding] and
perturbation of the brain'[2]; a diagnosis corroborated
by Prince Thomas, who shortly before his father's
death declares:

> Th' incessant care and labour of his mind
> Hath wrought the mure, that should confine it in,
> So thin that life looks through and will break out[3].

Shakespeare leaves his audience in no doubt that the
root of the king's sickness is sickness of soul.

And this brings me to the other device for under-
lining the usurpation; not only is Henry haunted by
Richard, and constantly speaking of him, but Shakespeare is plying us with suggestion on the source of
Henry's cares from beginning to end of the drama.
Here, and not poverty of subject-matter, is the chief
explanation of that 'repetition' which the 'Arden'
editor finds so boring[4]. The dramatist desires both to
make the issue clear to spectators who have not seen
his *Richard II* on the stage, and to keep it continuously
before the minds of all. Hotspur first broaches it in
the third scene, where he taxes father and uncle with
having helped

> To put down Richard, that sweet lovely rose,
> And plant this thorn, this canker, Bolingbroke.

---

[1] *Ibid.* 4. 5. 183–6.   [2] *Ibid.* 1. 2. 113–14.
[3] *Ibid.* 4. 4. 118–20.   [4] v. *supra*, p. ix.

Bolingbroke gives us his own picture of Richard, 'the skipping king', in the first interview with Prince Hal; and in the parleys before Shrewsbury, Worcester reminds him, in turn, of the oath he had taken, shortly after landing at Ravenspurgh, that he 'did nothing purpose 'gainst the state'. In Part 2, again, besides the references by the sick king already spoken of, we have at 1.1.187–209 the account of the archbishop's crusade against Richard's sacrilegious murderer, and at 1.3.87–108 his scorn for the fickleness of the common people, who after rejecting Richard for Bolingbroke, are now, like a dog returning to his vomit, 'become enamoured' of the dead man's grave; while in the talk between the rebels and Westmoreland at Gaultree (4.1.113–39), the presence of Mowbray, son of the Mowbray whose quarrel with Bolingbroke furnished the occasion of the latter's banishment by Richard, leads to a discussion of that episode, which had been the beginning of all the trouble. Thus, constant allusion to Richard and his fate is combined with skilful variation in the incidents referred to, so that by the time the play is finished the whole story has been recalled. There is, in truth, no repetition; only insistence upon the circumstances of Bolingbroke's accession, upon the weakness of his title, the illegality of his usurpation, the inexpiable crime of Richard's murder.

Moreover, this harping upon Richard's tragic end had its bearing upon the character and actions of the Prince as well as on those of his father. When the King sees his Harry conducting himself like Richard and treading the path that leads to deposition and death, we wonder that he should understand his son so little. Yet the career of Richard was undoubtedly a warning to the prodigal Prince, and Shakespeare reminds us of it, again and again, in order that we may the more appreciate the wisdom and rightness of the reformation when it comes. Whether he ever turned over the pages

of Hall's *Chronicle* we do not know; but if he did, the
following passage from the opening paragraphs of the
chapter on Henry V influenced his shaping of the play:

For what can bee more shame or reproche to a prince,
then he whiche ought to gouerne and rule other shall by
cowardnes, slouth and ignorance, as a pupille not of viii or
x yeres of age, but beyng of xx or xxx yeres and more,
shalbe compelled to obey and folowe the willes of other,
and be ruled and beare no rule, like a ward and not like
a gardē, like a seruant and not like a Master. Suche a
gouernour was kyng Richarde the seconde, whiche of hym-
self beeyng not of the most euill disposicion, was not of
so symple a mind, nor of suche debilite of witte, nor yet
of so litle herte and corage, but he might haue demaunded
and learned good and profitable counsaill, and after aduise
taken, kept, retayned and folowed the same: But how-
soeuer it was, vnprofitable counsailers wer his confusion
and finall perdicion. Suche another ruler was kyng
Edwarde the seconde, whiche two before named kynges fell
from the high glory of fortunes whele to exstreme misery
and miserable calamittee. By whose infortunate chance (as
I thynke) this kyng Henry beying admonished, expulsed
from hym his old plaie felowes, his preuie Sicophantes
and vngracious gard as authors and procurers of al
mischifes and riot, and assigned into their places men of
grauitee, persons of actiuitee, and counsaillers of greate
witte and pollicie [1].

Nor is the theme relinquished with *Henry IV*. The
crowning proof of its importance for Shakespeare and
his audience is that it recurs in *Henry V*, and at the
most solemn moment of that play. Listen to the hero-
king's prayer before Agincourt:

O God of battles, steel my soldiers' hearts,
Possess them not with fear: take from them now
The sense of reck'ning, or th'opposéd numbers
Pluck their hearts from them. Not to-day, O Lord,
O not to-day, think not upon the fault

[1] Hall's *Chronicle*, p. 47 (ed. 1809).

My father made in compassing the crown!
I Richard's body have interréd new,
And on it have bestowed more contrite tears,
Than from it issued forcéd drops of blood.
Five hundred poor I have in yearly pay,
Who twice a day their withered hands hold up
Toward heaven, to pardon blood: and I have built
Two chantries, where the sad and solemn priests
Sing still for Richard's soul. More will I do:
Though all that I can do is nothing worth;
Since that my penitence comes after all,
Imploring pardon[1].

The prayer is granted, and the victory won. But it is
written that the sins of the fathers shall be visited upon
the children unto the third and fourth generation, and
the terrible curse pronounced by the Bishop of Carlisle
in *Richard II*[2] remained to be fulfilled in the Wars
of the Roses, of which 'continuall discension for the
croune of this noble realme' King Henry the Fourth was
by his crime 'the first aucthor'[3], as Shakespeare reminds
us yet again in each of the Three Parts of his *Henry VI*[4].
To us, who do not shrink from crowning a younger
brother in place of his elder, when it suits the country's
convenience, and for whom a king is no longer

> the figure of God's majesty,
> His captain, steward, deputy-elect[5],

all this makes but slight appeal, if it does not pass
altogether unnoticed; in days when absolute monarchy,
legitimacy, and 'the divinity that doth hedge a king'
were pillars of the social system, it touched the central
nerve of political thought and feeling. Had Shake-

---

[1] *Henry V*, 4.1.285 [306] ff. [2] *Richard II*, 4.1.136 ff.
[3] v. title of Hall's *Chronicle*, cited pp. xxv–vi of my
Introduction to *Richard II* (New Shakespeare).
[4] *1 Henry VI*, 2.5.64–71; *2 Henry VI*, 2.2.19–31;
3 Henry VI, 1.1.104–42; *Richard III*, 3.3.9 ff.
[5] *Richard II*, 4.1.125–6.

speare not insisted upon it, his gorgeous historical tapestry would have lacked the scarlet thread that, dyed in the blood

Of fair King Richard, scraped from Pomfret stones[1],

runs through the eight plays.

III. *Falstaff's 'day's service' in 1942*

'This is a play', Mrs Elizabeth Inchbald tells us, 'which all men admire and which most women dislike. Many revolting expressions in the comic parts, much boisterous courage in the graver scenes, together with Falstaff's unwieldy person, offend every female auditor; and whilst a facetious Prince of Wales is employed taking purses on the highway, a lady would rather see him stealing hearts at a ball'[2]. If one did not know that was written in 1817, the last words would almost betray the date. Yet I am not without evidence that modern women are still much of the same mind; and the comparatively infrequent appearances of *Henry IV* in the nineteenth-century theatre may well be due to an increase in the female portion of the audience. Of the play's abiding popularity with men, on the other hand, there has never been any question; and Johnson speaks both for the eighteenth century and for his sex when he declares: 'None of Shakespeare's plays are more read than the first and second parts of *Henry IV*. Perhaps no author has ever in two plays afforded so much delight'[3]. It is even reported that this delight has been turned to military account in the

[1] *2 Henry IV*, i. 1. 205.
[2] Cited by Hemingway, *1 Henry IV*, New Variorum Shakespeare, p. 395.
[3] Johnson's *Shakespeare*, iv. 355. For the play's 18th-century popularity v. pp. xxxiii ff.

present war. Scene: the Headquarters of the newly formed 'X' Division, stationed in a village near the south coast. Time: February 1942. Atmosphere: 'sticky'— no comradeship, low morale, the members of the large Mess imbued with an initial dislike for each other that seemed to grow upon further acquaintance; and the General in despair. As a last resort, fifteen copies of *Henry IV* having been procured at the suggestion of a Jewish artillery officer, the various colonels, majors, etc., are detailed by public notice to attend a play-reading upon a certain evening. They arrive embarrassed and resentful. Notwithstanding, the parts are distributed and the play starts; Falstaff being taken by a large Colonel of the Tanks. And presently, as the beer flows freely and the house becomes filled with smoke, one man after another gradually begins to 'warm up'. 'We read the whole play right through for several hours', my informant tells me, 'and by the end the whole company were roaring and gesticulating. I can still see "Falstaff" sitting on the edge of his chair, almost kneeling forward, his khaki tunic unbuttoned, the sweat of his zeal running down his temples, as he fairly exploded his way through the part, relishing every word. All reserve was gone. The atmosphere in the Mess was transformed. It was astonishing; and long since that bold company has marched to glory overseas.'

J. D. W.

1944

xxix

THE STAGE-HISTORY OF
KING HENRY IV

The stage-history of *Henry IV* begins in the inn-yards, perhaps before Shakespeare came to London. Tarlton, who died in 1588, and was the Clown of the Queen's Company, is reported to have taken part in performances, 'at the Bull at Bishopsgate', of a play in which a madcap Prince Hal struck the Lord Chief Justice with his fist[1]; and this play, of which the first half of the extant *Famous Victories of Henry V*, 1598, is obviously a 'maimed and deformed' report, was as obviously in some way related to Shakespeare's twin-drama. In *The Famous Victories* the chief of the Prince's companions is called Sir John Oldcastle and, as all the world knows, was also called so by Shakespeare, until descendants of Oldcastle's widow, powerful at Court, put pressure upon him to change the name[2]. Yet the old name persisted. Falstaff is Falstaff in the printed texts of *1* and *2 Henry IV*, but traces of his former title remain in both (v. notes 1. 2. 41-2, 156; 2. 1. 2. 118; Ep. 30-1), and he reappears as Oldcastle in an account of the first recorded performance of the play, a private one given at the instance of the Lord Chamberlain for the entertainment of the Flemish ambassador in 1600; while Oldcastle recurs in documents, plays, and books down to 1651[3], though Falstaff is more frequent and triumphs in the end.

Late 1597 is the usually accepted date of the earliest public production of Shakespeare's *1 Henry IV*,

[1] *Tarltons Jests*, 1611, ed. Shakespeare Society, 1844, p. 24.   [2] Cf. *The Library*, XXVI, pp. 2-16.
[3] E. K. Chambers, *William Shakespeare*, i. 382.

with 2 *Henry IV* following shortly after. But, apart from the command one of 1600 just mentioned, no actual performance can be traced before the winter of 1612–13, when among twenty plays enacted by the King's men during the wedding festivities of the Princess Elizabeth and the Elector Palatine, appear the titles *The Hotspurre* and *Sir John Falstaffe*, which Sir Edmund Chambers claims as *1* and *2 Henry IV*[1]. On New Year's night, 1625, again, *The First Part of Sir John Falstaff* was played at Whitehall, 'the prince only being there'; and on 29 May 1638, 'the princes berthnyght', *Ould Castel* was acted by the King's men at the Cockpit in Court. There is nothing to show whether the performances in 1600 and 1638 labelled *Oldcastle* were of Part 1 only, Part 2 only, or of both; or even of a conflated drama composed of the principal Falstaff scenes of both, such as has been preserved in the so-called Dering MS., belonging to the decade 1613–23, which is described elsewhere[2]. In this MS., it may be noted, most of the scenes come from Part 1, the Falstaff of which has always been more popular than the Falstaff of Part 2.

Such are the meagre records of performances before the Civil Wars. That they reflect the facts most inadequately is proved by contemporary references of various kinds which testify to an immense vogue[3]. Leonard Digges, for instance, in lines prefixed to the 1640 edition of Shakespeare's *Poems*, after stating that Ben Jonson's wittiest plays were often acted to half-empty houses, continues:

> when let but Falstaffe come,
> Hall, Poines, the rest, you scarce shall have a roome
> All is so pester'd.

[1] *Elizabethan Stage*, ii. 217; iv. 180.
[2] v. Note on the Copy, p. 107.
[3] cf. Introduction, p. xv.

Among the commendatory poems in the folio edition
of Beaumont and Fletcher, 1647, was one by Sir
Thomas Palmer, which begins:

> I could prayse Heywood now; or tell how long
> Falstaff from Cracking Nuts hath kept the throng.

And whatever be the provenance of the 'select pieces
of drollery' published by Henry Marsh in 1662, and by
Francis Kirkman in 1672, under the title of *The Wits,
or, Sport upon Sport*, yet another witness to the popularity of *Henry IV* is furnished by the first of these
'drolls', entitled *The Bouncing Knight*, and made up,
with some compression and alteration, out of the
Falstaff scenes at the Boar's Head; while in the frontis-
piece to the 1662 edition, which shows an artificially
lighted stage in a roofed-over building, the two most
prominent figures out of seven there seen are Falstaff
and the Hostess. It may be noted, for what it is worth,
that this Falstaff is only comfortably, not grossly, fat.

Of the original cast for *Henry IV* we know nothing.
Malone wrote that he remembered reading in some
tract that the original actor of Falstaff was Heminges;
but nothing survives to confirm the statement. Nor is
there any external evidence that Kempe ever took the
part, or that the Prince was played by Burbage, though
the first is possible and the second very probable. In
Historia Histrionica (1699) Truman is made to say:
'in my time, before the Wars, Lowin used to act, with
mighty applause "Falstaff" and other parts'. And if
Lowin was able to show Davenant how Shakespeare
had taught him to play King Henry VIII, and thus
pass the lesson on to the Restoration theatre, he may
have done the same for Falstaff.

Certainly Falstaff was one of the first of Shakespeare's
family to triumph home with the Merry Monarch; for
1 Henry IV was among the plays acted at the Red Bull,
Clerkenwell, immediately upon (or even before) the

Restoration by a company of old players from the days
of King Charles I. These old players were taken by
Killigrew for the basis of his King's Company formed
under the patent of 21 August 1660, and this was the
play with which the company opened their new theatre,
Gibbons's tennis-court in Vere Street, Clare Market,
on 8 November 1660. There Pepys saw it on 31
December 1660. On the way to the theatre he had
bought a copy of the play. There is no evidence now
what edition it was that he bought, but the Quarto of
1639 was the most recent. 'My expectation being too
great', he writes, 'it did not please me...and my
having a book, I believe did spoil it a little.' At his
second visit, on 4 June 1661, he found it 'a good play'.
On 2 November 1667, at the King's Company's playhouse between Brydges Street and Drury Lane, he,
'contrary to expectation, was pleased in nothing more
than in Cartwright's speaking of Falstaffe's speech about
"What is Honour?"'—a speech which the age of the
heroic tragedy was peculiarly fitted to enjoy.

King Henry IV, with Hotspur among the characters,
is the only play of the name known to Downes, the
contemporary chronicler (in *Roscius Anglicanus*) of the
Restoration stage; and it seems likely that Part 2 was
not revived until the reign of Queen Anne. According
to Downes, *King Henry IV* was one of the 'principal
old stock plays' belonging to the King's Company; and
he gives a few names out of the cast. He does not
mention Walter Clun; yet Clun must have been a very
early actor of Falstaff in his day, because it is mentioned among his parts in the elegy (printed by G.
Thorn-Drury in *A Little Ark*, 1921) which was composed after his murder by a robber in August 1664. In
Downes's list Cartwright is the Falstaff; Burt acts the
Prince, Hart is Hotspur, Wintersel the King and
Shotterel Poins. As all these had been among the old
Red Bull players, it is probable that the cast at Vere

Street had been the same as it was at the theatre off
Drury Lane. Another successful actor of Falstaff, even
during the life of Cartwright, was John Lacy. After
Wintersel the most famous player of the King was
Kynaston, whose 'real majesty' in the part drew long
and glowing praise from Colley Cibber in his *Apology*.
In 1682, when the King's Company and the Duke's
were combined, Betterton came into the part of Hotspur.
He played it, says Cibber, with 'wild impatient starts'·
and 'fierce and flashing fire.' But he was forty-seven
years old when he first undertook it, and it seems probable
that he had dropped the play out of the repertory for
some years before he revived it at the Little Theatre in
Lincoln's Inn Fields in the season of 1699–1700, and
himself appeared as Falstaff. According to a letter
written from Bond Street on 28 January 1700, and first
printed, from the manuscript in the British Museum,
by Malone in his *Dryden*, this 'revived humour of Sir
John Falstaff' had drawn all the town, 'more than any
new play that has bin produced of late...and the
criticks allow that Mr Betterton has hitt the humour of
Falstaff better than any that have aimed at it before'.
He kept the play in his repertory and continued to
play Falstaff during at least eight of his remaining ten
years of life.

Hitherto there has been no evidence of any alteration
or adaptation; the play appears to have been acted as
Shakespeare wrote it, though probably with cuts. And
Betterton's new version, which he published in 1700,
was in no sense an adaptation or revision. His text he
took almost unchanged from the Fourth Folio, and his
alterations were confined to cuts. By stopping act 3,
sc. 1 at the end of the dispute about the division of the
kingdom, on Hotspur's line, 'Are the indentures drawn,
shall we be gone?', he robbed Hotspur, Mortimer and
Worcester of some first-rate lines, and the play of one of
the best and truest love scenes in all Shakespeare, the

mock wrangling between Hotspur and his wife. Act 4,
sc. 4 is cut out, and act 5 goes straight from the Prince's
discovery of Falstaff's bottle of sack to the entrance of
Hotspur to fight him. Of single speeches the most
heavily cut are Lady Percy's in act 2, sc. 3, the
King's first speech, which lacks all mention of the
Crusade, and his 'God pardon thee!' speech in act 3,
sc. 2. He also pruned, but did not omit, the 'play extempore' in act 2, sc. 4. Later acting versions were
to cut out much more than that; but Betterton's pruning
set the fashion that was followed until recent years, the
principle being to exalt the Falstaff scenes at the expense
of the historical part of the play.

Meanwhile, the popularity of Part 1 naturally led
to a revival of interest in Part 2. Of this last a printed
acting version has survived with the title: 'The Sequell
of Henry the Fourth: with the Humours of Sir John
Falstaffe and Justice Shallow. As it was Acted by His
Majesty's Company of Comedians at the Theatre-
Royal in Drury Lane. Alter'd from Shakespeare by the
late Mr Betterton.' The performance referred to
probably took place on 17 December 1720; but the
attribution to Betterton is doubtful, since the high-
handed tampering with Shakespeare's diction leaves an
impression quite different from that which Betterton's
comparatively respectful treatment of Part 1 conveys.
The original has been severely shortened by the cutting
of the dialogue as well as by the omission of Induction,
the first scene, Northumberland's farewell, act 3, sc. 1
(out of which a mangled version of the King's speech
on Sleep is lifted to be worked in just before the great
death-bed scene), the before-supper scene at Shallow's,
and the arrest of Doll and the Hostess. The piece ends
with matter taken from *Henry V* — the challenge brought
by the French Ambassador, and the condemnation of
Cambridge, Scroop, and Grey. The cast included
Barton Booth as King, Wilks as Prince, Mills as

Falstaff, Bowman as the Lord Chief Justice, and Colley Cibber as Shallow.

When Genest declared that Betterton himself revived Part 2, he was probably misled by the title-page of this printed version[1]. Yet there is little doubt that his success with Part 1 was responsible for the revival of Part 2 by others. Falstaff had come to stay once more. During Betterton's life-time George Powell and Richard Estcourt also impersonated the fat knight of Part 1, and that Part lost none of its popularity after his death in 1710. Indeed, the vogue of *Henry IV* reached its zenith in the eighteenth century. Our records[2] for the first half give us no fewer than two hundred and twenty performances of Part 1 in London, 1704–50 and eighty of Part 2 for the shorter period, 1720–50; Drury Lane between the winter of 1710–11 and September 1747, when Garrick took command, claiming seventy-eight of the former and forty-five of the latter. It is interesting to note, too, that *2 Henry IV* was chosen in May 1734 as a benefit for 'the editor of Shakespeare', Lewis Theobald. In these performances the favourite Falstaff in both Parts was at first Harper; but presently a serious rival to Betterton appeared in James Quin.

Quin had played Hotspur at Lincoln's Inn Fields in 1718–19. Two seasons later he played the King. Two seasons later again he made his first appearance as Falstaff. And from then onwards he frequently played that part in *1 Henry IV* until his retirement in 1751, and less often the Falstaff of *2 Henry IV*, which he chose for his benefit on 11 March 1736, at which

[1] v. Hazelton Spencer, *Shakespeare Improved*, 1927, p. 359.
[2] v. *A Calendar of performances of '1 Henry IV' and '2 Henry IV' during the first half of the eighteenth century* by A. H. Scouten and Leo Hughes (Journ. English & Germanic Philology, xliii, 23–41).

performance he spoke, apparently in character as the Ghost of Shakespeare, 'a Prologue by Mr Betterton representing the part of Falstaffe Forty years ago, at the Revival of the Play'. Quin was not as merry as Harper, and 'his supercilious brow, in spite of assumed gaiety, sometimes unmasked the surliness of his disposition'; but none was held to equal him, and that 'superciliousness', which helped to give his Falstaff an air of breeding and intellectual power, was missed in later performers. Quin appears to have made his own version of the play, of which his manuscript part of Falstaff is now in the Folger Shakespeare Library. We may learn from the New Variorum edition of *1 King Henry IV* (p. 502) that Quin followed Pope for his text rather than Betterton; that he considerably reduced Falstaff's participation in the highway robbery; that he was the first of many to omit the whole of the 'play extempore' in act 2, sc. 4, and that he opened Falstaff's speech at 2. 4. 264 with 'Ha, ha, ha! d'ye think I did not know ye?'—a gag which survived as late as Beerbohm Tree's production in 1896.

Garrick took little interest in *1 Henry IV*, though he played Hotspur on five occasions in 1746–7. He took still less in *2 Henry IV*, though he also staged it at Drury Lane on 13 March 1758 and played the King in it four times, while what appears to be his acting version may now be seen at the Folger Library. Part 2 again made its contribution to contemporary history in 1761–2, when Covent Garden found in it a vehicle for a coronation spectacle appropriate to the coronation of King George III, and cut out the parts of Shallow and Silence to make room for the show.

After Quin the best Falstaff was Henderson, who played it first in *1 Henry IV* at the Haymarket in July 1777 and for the last time in October 1785. He also appeared as the Falstaff of *2 Henry IV* on several occasions between 1777 and October 1784, after which that play drops out for twenty years until it was restored to the Covent Garden stage by J. P. Kemble. But the vogue of *1 Henry IV* continued; and the last two decades of the century saw plenty more Falstaffs— Palmer, Ryder, King, Fawcett, Cooke (something of a Falstaff off the stage), who modelled his performance on Henderson's, besides others who chose to try the part at their own benefit performances. Falstaffs, in fact, are so many as to suggest that the part was to the stage of those days what Hamlet is to ours—a part which no actor can be satisfied without attempting. At least one actress tried it also, Mrs Webb.

It has been suggested that it was an eighteenth-century custom to give the two Parts close together. But of the performances of Part 2 in London during the whole period only a small proportion can be shown as being staged within a week of the much more frequently acted Part 1. The general attitude of theatre and public to *Henry IV* may be seen from Francis Gentleman's comments on Part 1 in Bell's edition of the play in 1773. The speeches of the King, he tells us, are 'much too long, though in general fine'; and in act 3, sc. 2, the fine scene between King and Prince, 'no actor could find breath to speak, nor any audience patience to hear his prolixity'. Lady Percy's speech to Hotspur is 'only rejected by the stage because Lady Percy is seldom personated by an actress fit to speak them'. The play extempore 'rather choaked and loaded the main business' and 'would be dreadfully tedious in representation'. Finally, act 3, sc. 1 is 'a strange, unmeaning wild scene...between Glendower, etc., which is properly rejected'. Just about the same time Davies was writing: 'No joke ever raised such loud and repeated mirth, in the galleries, as Sir John's labour in getting the body of Hotspur on his back.'

The nineteenth century opens with Stephen Kemble's Falstaff. This corpulent brother of John Philip Kemble and Mrs Siddons was able to play Falstaff without padding. When Hazlitt saw him in Part 1 at Drury Lane in October 1816, he wrote one of his wittiest and wickedest notices in *The Examiner*:

The town has been entertained this week by seeing Mr Stephen Kemble in the part of Falstaff, as they were formerly with seeing Mr Lambert in his own person. We see no more reason why Mr Stephen Kemble should play Falstaff, than why Louis XVIII is qualified to fill a throne, because he is fat, and belongs to a particular family. Every fat man cannot represent a great man. The knight was fat; so is the player: the Emperor was fat, so is the King who stands in his shoes. But there the comparison ends. There is no sympathy in mind—in wit, parts, or discretion. Sir John (and so we may say of the gentleman at St Helena) 'had guts in his brains.' The mind was the man. His body did not weigh down his wit. His spirits shone through him. He was not a mere paunch, a bag-pudding, a lump of lethargy, a huge falling sickness, an imminent apoplexy, with water in the head.

For all that, Stephen Kemble's Falstaff must have had its admirers, since, having played the part first in London at Drury Lane in 1802, he was still playing it in April 1820, and with no serious rival. His brother John had thoughts of playing it also and actually announced it for 22 May 1815. But either he fell ill, or, more probably, he was dissuaded. As Hotspur he was notable from November 1791 till May 1817, when he took the part for the last time, with Young acting Falstaff for the first time. Another good Hotspur, to the Falstaff of Stephen Kemble, was Elliston; and on 9 and 11 March 1819, and again on 20 April 1820, Stephen Kemble had for Hotspur no less an actor than Edmund Kean, who thereafter never acted Hotspur again. On 14 January 1804 John Kemble brought *2 Henry IV* back to Covent Garden in a version that transposed scenes 5. 3 and 5. 4 and concluded the latter with Falstaff's confident 'I shall be sent for soon at night'. He had a strong cast, in which he himself took the King; and the setting showed his care for beauty and fitness. Seventeen years later another coronation, that of George IV, recalled the play to Covent Garden. This time the audience was shown not merely the procession, but the ceremony in the Abbey, the procession to Westminster Hall, with the Banquet and even the entry of 'the Challenger'. The play thus staged, first on 25 June 1821 with Macready as the King and Charles Kemble as the Prince, was repeated on 19 July, the day of the coronation, when by Royal command the theatre was opened free, and again before an overcrowded house on 7 August.

Meanwhile Macready had continued to make Hotspur one of his best performances. He had won golden opinions when he first played it at Bath in 1815; and he went on playing it till December 1847. In his diary for 13 December 1833, he made a noteworthy comment: 'I found in the progress of the scene' (he means, no doubt, act 2, sc. 3) 'the vast benefit derived from keeping vehemence and effort out of passion. It is every thing for nature. The reading of the letter was not bad chiefly on that account.' Equally memorable was his King in Part 2, which he acted first in Park Theatre, New York, on 27 February 1827, then at Drury Lane on 14 May 1834 and other special occasions. Of these performances Lady Pollock remarks that he infused so much poetry into the death scene that 'the Second Part became a popular tragedy'.

The coronation performances of 2 *Henry IV* led on naturally to attempts to break new ground in the staging of Part 1. The first came from Charles Kemble, with Planché and George Scharf to back him up. In his splendid production at Covent Garden in May 1824, he did more than pay 'the same Attention to Costume which has been observed in the Revival of *King John* at this Theatre'. He had scenery, 'mostly new', by the Grieves, and tried to make it as archaeo-logically accurate as the costumes. He called particular attention to a few scenes, among them the King's Chamber in the old Palace of Westminster; the inn-yard at Rochester with the castle, by night; Hotspur's Camp; a distant view of Coventry; and Shrewsbury from the field of battle. A formidable list of 'in-disputable authorities'—including the sumptuary laws passed during the reign of King Henry IV—shows the pains taken to make sure that every character should 'appear in the precise habit of the period'.

The oddest production belonging to this time took place at Zürich on 20 January 1838, when the poet Beddoes hired the theatre, together with most of its actors, to present both Parts as a single drama in a condensed German version. He himself played Hot-spur, while the role of Falstaff was filled by another amateur, Dr Schmidt, an unusually stout man who had during the preceding months been specially fed up for the occasion[1].

Samuel Phelps in 1846 opened his third season at Sadler's Wells with 1 Henry IV, and himself made his first appearance as Falstaff, with Creswick (later to be a very popular Falstaff) as Hotspur. The play was much liked and was given again in several seasons before Phelps left the theatre in 1862. He began by putting back both the play extempore and the first part of act 3, sc. 1, but dropped both out again in 1856. His most notable appearance as Falstaff was in the revival at Drury Lane, under Falconer and Chatterton, on 28 March 1864, during the celebration of the tercentenary of Shakespeare's birth. Walter Montgomery played Hot-spur, Walter Lacy the Prince, and John Ryder the King. For the first time since the Restoration, act 3, sc. 1 was played complete, and the version as a whole was fuller than that which had been current in the theatre. The

[1] H. W. Donner, *Thomas Lovell Beddoes*, 312-16.

staging was sumptuous, with new scenery by Beverley; and the Battle of Shrewsbury, which included an ambush and a surprise, roused enthusiasm. Opinion had always differed about Phelps as Falstaff: to some he was 'the real successor of Henderson,' to others not so; but the production was very popular and ran for 'several months. There can be no doubt, however, about his triumph with 2 *Henry IV*, in which he played the double role of King and Shallow, first at Sadler's Wells (17 March to 13 April 1853, and again 14 September and 6 November 1861), later at Drury Lane on 1 October 1864, and at Manchester in September 1874 with Charles Calvert, who had staged 1 *Henry IV* at his Prince's Theatre in 1868 with himself as Falstaff. Writing on the production of 1861, John Oxenford describes Phelps's Shallow as 'a masterpiece of comic creation'.

Henry IV appears to have aroused little interest during the seventies and eighties. The year 1885, however, saw performances at both Oxford and Cambridge. The newly founded O.U.D.S. chose 1 *Henry IV* for its first production. Falstaff was acted by the second Lord Coleridge, Hotspur by Arthur Bourchier, the Prince by Alan Mackinnon, and Glendower by Holman Clark. Mrs (Margaret) Woods, the poet, wife of the then President of Trinity, acted Lady Percy, and also painted the scene of the Boar's Head Tavern; and Lady Mortimer was played by Lady E. Spencer Churchill, who sang a song in Welsh. The prologue, written by George Curzon, afterwards Lord Curzon of Kedleston, was spoken by C. Gordon Lang, the future Archbishop of Canterbury. In the autumn of the following year the play was acted at the A.D.C. in Cambridge. Their stage version, printed by the Cambridge University Press and sold by a Cambridge firm of booksellers, is worth notice because it preserves the only known English attempt to rearrange the order of the scenes. This, the first experiment of the A.D.C. in producing Shakespeare, was criticized at great length in *The Cambridge Review* by a writer who regretted that Glendower's part had been cut, but showed no sign of being aware that the play had been reshaped.

After the tercentenary performance at Drury Lane, there was no notable production of *1 Henry IV* in London until Beerbohm Tree staged it at the Haymarket on 8 May 1896, playing Falstaff himself, with Lewis Waller as Hotspur, and Mrs Tree as Lady Percy. The play, produced during the run of *Trilby*, in order to give Tree some escape from Svengali, was not on the scale of Tree's later 'magnoperations' at His Majesty's Theatre; but it was handsome, and included a tableau of the battle of Shrewsbury. The scene of the inn-yard at night was cut out—a sacrifice at variance with tradition. The scene between Gadshill and the Chamberlain disappeared soon after Betterton, but the professional theatre had always made much of the Carriers and assigned them to good comedians—Johnson, Bullock, Pinkethman, Macklin, Woodward, Moody, Quick, Munden, and many another. The Glendower scene was played entire, including the Welsh lady's singing, in which Miss Marion Evans made a hit. Play and acting alike were chastised with scorpions by Mr Bernard Shaw in the *Saturday Review*; but others were kinder, and Joseph Knight in *The Athenæum* welcomed the performance as the first to show the play in the new style of acting, not 'ladled out' in the tradition of the so-called tragic acting at the big houses. Tree played Falstaff again at His Majesty's Theatre during November 1914 with Matheson Lang for his Hotspur; but he preferred being seen as the Falstaff of *The Merry Wives of Windsor*.

Benson, on the other hand, for some reason preferred *2 Henry IV* to the usually more popular First Part, and was already playing it at Stratford in 1894. That, if one had to go, Part 1 should be omitted from his famous 'cycle' of the Histories in 1901 and 1906 is perhaps not strange, since Part 2 is essential as an induction to *Henry V*. W. B. Yeats was in Stratford during the 1901 performances and wrote in *The Speaker*: 'Partly because of the way play supports play, the theatre moved me as it had never done before'. Both Parts, however, were included in a different 'cycle' played at Stratford in 1905, and beginning with Marlowe's *Edward II*. Part 1 was performed again at the same place in 1909, with Louis Calvert and Lewis Waller as Falstaff and Hotspur respectively, while in 1913 Benson appeared once more in Part 2, this time as the King. Between 1894 and 1926 Part 2 was in fact played by the Benson company at Stratford on no fewer than fourteen separate occasions, not to mention those on which they played it elsewhere; G. R. Weir until his death in 1909 being the Falstaff, 'a Falstaff in his habit as he lived'. But the most memorable performance of *Henry IV* at Stratford was that of 23 April 1932, after the opening of the New Memorial Theatre by Edward, Prince of Wales, who flew directly from Windsor in his aeroplane for the ceremony, when the august audience were given the rare opportunity of seeing Part 1 in the afternoon and Part 2 in the evening. In this Birmingham, however, had led the way, when Sir Barry Jackson, who first staged Part 1 with a full text and no change in the order of the scenes on 11 October 1913, produced both Parts on the same day, 23 April 1921.

1 Henry IV came into the repertory of the Old Vic in 1920, and *2 Henry IV* at the end of October 1917, when Ben Greet produced it. Among interesting performances outside Stratford since then may be mentioned Part 2 produced at the Court Theatre by J. B. Fagan in February 1921, in a version from which, according to *The Times* review, 'most of what may be called the Holinshed element was discarded, and wisely', and, as a contrast, Part 1 produced in December 1922 at the Maddermarket by the Norwich Players in the Elizabethan manner; while on 28 February 1935 the experiment was made of giving the role of Falstaff in Part 1 to a master-comedian of the variety stage, Mr George Robey. He was found amusing, but rather as Robey than as Falstaff, his most Shakespearian moments being in the play extempore, a part within a part, which allowed him scope for his fancy. 'A diverting performance', said *The Times*, 'but not a comfortable one'; and the *New Statesman* found him 'the old soak rather than the fallen gentleman', and even at his best nothing more than 'a super-Bardolph'. Mr Robert Atkins's Falstaff in his production of Part 1 in October and Part 2 in November of 1942, at the Westminster Theatre, was held to restore the role to traditional lines after the incursion of Mr Robey. This, it was said, was a quiet, ruminative Falstaff, whose merriment betrayed that his thoughts were apt to linger over the days that were gone. Among amateur performances may be noted those of Part 1 by the Marlowe Society at Cambridge in 1909, by the Edinburgh University English Literature Society in 1929, and by the King's College (London) Musical and Dramatic Society in 1932; while Part 2 was given in March 1943 by the King's Scholars of Westminster School in their exile at Whitbourne Court, Worcestershire.

In America, as in England, the history of *Henry IV* lies mainly in the parts of Falstaff and of Hotspur. The first man to act Falstaff in America was David Douglass, who produced Part 1 at the Chapel Street Theatre, New York, on 18 December 1761, with the younger Lewis Hallam for Hotspur. Douglass and Hallam appeared in these characters again at the John Street Theatre on 25 February 1768, when Miss Cheer acted Lady Percy. The absence of Glendower and Lady Mortimer from the cast shows that act 3, sc. 1 was all cut out, as in England. In 1772–3 Douglass is found playing Falstaff at Philadelphia; and there, at the Southwark Theatre in 1778, Howe's Thespians— in other words, the British officers then occupying the city—gave two performances of this play (25 and 30 March), their scene-painter being the afterwards famous Major John André. Ten years later, in November 1788, the Old American Actors, under Hallam and Henry, got round the law prohibiting the theatre in Philadelphia very much as the managers of the un-licensed theatres in London used to get round the licensing laws; they pretended that it was not a play and staged it at the Southwark Theatre, then disguised as the Opera House. In 1796 there first appeared at the New Theatre in Philadelphia one of the famous American Falstaffs, William Warren, who had just come over from England. For Hotspur he had Thomas Abthorpe Cooper, who was to be the greatest of all the American Hotspurs, until, some forty years later (with Junius Brutus Booth as the Prince), he took up Falstaff, a part in which he was not happy, and which he played only a few times. In the 1796 production there was no Glendower, no Lady Mortimer and no Gadshill; but Francis and the Carriers were retained. Warren went on acting Falstaff until he was too old and too ill to get through the part. By this time John E. Harwood had come to be accounted the best Falstaff yet seen in America. His fame only went down before that of George Frederick Cooke, who appeared many times as Falstaff in this play during his American visit of 1810–11, which ended with his death at Providence. At some, at least, of his performances Cooke restored 'the original scene between the Prince and Falstaff,' which must mean the play extempore. On 4 February 1822, *2 Henry IV* was staged at the Park Theatre, New York, with a spec-tacular coronation pageant modelled on the Covent

Garden production of 1821; and the play was given on at least three other occasions in America before 1850, including the revival in 1827 with Macready as King, already mentioned.

May 13, 1828, at the Park Theatre, New York, first saw another eminent American Falstaff in James Henry Hackett, who went on playing the part in *1 Henry IV* until shortly before his death in 1871, and gave this play a run of two weeks in New York in 1869, while on 23 March 1841 he chose *2 Henry IV* for his benefit. Hackett was said to have the 'exclusive monopoly' of Falstaff; and during his long career he had, among many Hotspurs, John H. Clarke, Henry Wallack, his son J. W. Wallack, Charles Kean and Vandenhoff. Hackett had decided views about Falstaff, and in 1840 he published them in a pamphlet entitled *Falstaff*, in which he replied to the criticism of his performance in *The Times* of 5 November 1839. His main point is that Falstaff shows no sign of refinement, intellect, or breeding. Some held Hackett's performance to be perfect; others found his joviality shallow and not unctuous enough. It was even said that before the play was out he became boring and that the audience turned their attention away from him to Hotspur and the historical parts of the play. The list of eminent American Falstaffs ends with John Henry Jack in the eighteen-seventies. Augustin Daly intended to produce this play, and details of his version, which never saw the stage, may be found in the New Variorum edition, on p. 504. Ada Rehan was to have acted the Prince; and the news is said to have prompted Julia Marlowe to try the part. Her production took place at Palmer's Theatre, New York, on 19 March 1896, with William F. Owen as Falstaff and Robert Taber as Hotspur. The play was acted by the Yale University Dramatic Association in 1906 and in 1920, and by the Players Club of New York in 1926.

HAROLD CHILD.

June 1945

xlvii

TO THE READER

The following is a brief description of the punctuation and other typographical devices employed in the text, which have been more fully explained in the *Note on Punctuation* and the *Textual Introduction* to be found in *The Tempest* volume:

An obelisk (†) implies corruption or emendation, and suggests a reference to the Notes.

A single bracket at the beginning of a speech signifies an 'aside.'

Four dots represent a *full stop* in the original, except when it occurs at the end of a speech, and they mark a long pause. Original *colons* or *semicolons*, which denote a somewhat shorter pause, are retained, or represented as three dots when they appear to possess special dramatic significance. Similarly, significant *commas* have been given as dashes.

Round brackets are taken from the original, and mark a significant change of voice; when the original brackets seem to imply little more than the drop in tone accompanying parenthesis, they are conveyed by commas or dashes.

Single inverted commas (' ') are editorial; double ones (" ") derive from the original, where they are used to draw attention to maxims, quotations, etc.

The reference number for the first line is given at the head of each page. Numerals in square brackets are placed at the beginning of the traditional acts and scenes.

THE
HISTORY OF
HENRIE THE
FOVRTH;

With the battell at Shrewsburie,
betweene the King and Lord
Henry Percy, surnamed
Henrie Hotspur of
the North.

With the humorous conceits of Sir
Iohn Falstalffe.

AT LONDON,
Printed by *P. S.* for *Andrew Wise*, dwelling
in Paules Churchyard, at the signe of
the Angell. 1598.

The Scene: England

CHARACTERS IN THE PLAY

KING HENRY *the Fourth*

HENRY, *Prince of Wales*

LORD JOHN *of* LANCASTER } *sons to the king*

EARL *of* WESTMORELAND

SIR WALTER BLUNT

THOMAS PERCY, *Earl of Worcester*

HENRY PERCY, *Earl of Northumberland*

HENRY PERCY, *surnamed* HOTSPUR, *his son*

EDMUND MORTIMER, *Earl of March*

RICHARD SCROOP, *Archbishop of York*

ARCHIBALD, *Earl of Douglas*

OWEN GLENDOWER

SIR RICHARD VERNON

SIR MICHAEL, *of the household of the Archbishop of York*

EDWARD POINS, *gentleman-in-waiting to Prince Henry*

SIR JOHN FALSTAFF

GADSHILL

PETO

BARDOLPH

LADY PERCY, *wife to Hotspur, and sister to Mortimer*

LADY MORTIMER, *daughter to Glendower, and wife to Mortimer*

MISTRESS QUICKLY, *hostess of the Boar's Head tavern, Eastcheap*

Lords, Officers, Sheriff, Vintner, Chamberlain, Drawers, two Carriers, Travellers, and Attendants

THE FIRST PART OF THE HISTORY OF HENRY IV

[I. I.]   *London. The Palace*

*KING HENRY with SIR WALTER BLUNT,
meeting WESTMORELAND and others*

King. So shaken as we are, so wan with care,
Find we a time for frighted peace to pant,
And breathe short-winded accents of new broils
To be commenced in strands afar remote:
No more the thirsty entrance of this soil
Shall daub her lips with her own children's blood,
No more shall trenching war channel her fields,
Nor bruise her flowerets with the arméd hoofs
Of hostile paces: those opposéd eyes,
Which, like the meteors of a troubled heaven,   10
All of one nature, of one substance bred,
Did lately meet in the intestine shock
And furious close of civil butchery,
Shall now, in mutual well-beseeming ranks,
March all one way, and be no more opposed
Against acquaintance, kindred, and allies....
The edge of war, like an ill-sheathéd knife,
No more shall cut his master...Therefore, friends,
As far as to the sepulchre of Christ,
Whose soldier now, under whose blesséd cross   20
We are impresséd and engaged to fight,
Forthwith a power of English shall we levy,
Whose arms were moulded in their mothers' womb
To chase these pagans in those holy fields
Over whose acres walked those blesséd feet

Which fourteen hundred years ago were nailed
For our advantage on the bitter cross....
But this our purpose now is twelve month old,
And bootless 'tis to tell you we will go:
30 Therefore we meet not now. Then let me hear
Of you, my gentle cousin Westmoreland,
What yesternight our council did decree
In forwarding this dear expedience.
   Westmoreland. My liege, this haste was hot
        in question,
And many limits of the charge set down
But yesternight, when all athwart there came
A post from Wales, loaden with heavy news,
Whose worst was that the noble Mortimer,
Leading the men of Herefordshire to fight
40 Against the irregular and wild Glendower,
Was by the rude hands of that Welshman taken,
A thousand of his people butchberéd,
Upon whose dead corpse there was such misuse,
Such beastly shameless transformation,
By those Welshwomen done, as may not be
Without much shame retold or spoken of.
   King. It seems then that the tidings of this broil
Brake off our business for the Holy Land.
   Westmoreland. This matched with other did, my
        gracious lord,
50 For more uneven and unwelcome news
Came from the north, and thus it did import:
On Holy-rood day the gallant Hotspur there,
Young Harry Percy, and brave Archibald,
That ever-valiant and approvéd Scot,
At Holmedon met,
Where they did spend a sad and bloody hour;
As by discharge of their artillery,

And shape of likelihood, the news was told;
For he that brought them, in the very heat
And pride of their contention did take horse,   60
Uncertain of the issue any way.

   King. Here is a dear, a true industrious friend,
Sir Walter Blunt, new lighted from his horse,
Stained with the variation of each soil
Betwixt that Holmedon and this seat of ours;
And he hath brought us smooth and welcome news.
The Earl of Douglas is discomfited,
Ten thousand bold Scots, two and twenty knights,
Balked in their own blood did Sir Walter see
On Holmedon's plains. Of prisoners, Hotspur took   70
Mordake Earl of Fife, and eldest son
To beaten Douglas, and the Earl of Athol,
Of Murray, Angus, and Menteith...
And is not this an honourable spoil?
A gallant prize? ha, cousin, is it not?

   Westmoreland. In faith,
It is a conquest for a prince to boast of.

   King. Yea, there thou mak'st me sad, and mak'st
     me sin
In envy, that my Lord Northumberland
Should be the father to so blest a son...   80
A son who is the theme of honour's tongue,
Amongst a grove the very straightest plant,
Who is sweet Fortune's minion and her pride,
Whilst I by looking on the praise of him
See riot and dishonour stain the brow
Of my young Harry....O that it could be proved
That some night-tripping fairy had exchanged
In cradle-clothes our children where they lay,
And called mine Percy, his Plantagenet,
Then would I have his Harry, and he mine: 90

But let him from my thoughts....What think you, coz,
Of this young Percy's pride? The prisoners,
Which he in this adventure hath surprised,
To his own use he keeps, and sends me word,
I shall have none but Mordake Earl of Fife.

   Westmoreland. This is his uncle's teaching, this
      is Worcester,
Malevolent to you in all aspects,
Which makes him prune himself, and bristle up
The crest of youth against your dignity.

100 *King.* But I have sent for him to answer this;
And for this cause awhile we must neglect
Our holy purpose to Jerusalem....
Cousin, on Wednesday next our council we
Will hold at Windsor, so inform the lords:
But come yourself with speed to us again,
For more is to be said and to be done
Than out of anger can be utteréd.

   Westmoreland. I will, my liege.   *[Exeunt*

[1. 2.]   *London. A room in the house of the*
                    PRINCE OF WALES

SIR JOHN FALSTAFF *lies snoring upon a bench in a
corner. The* PRINCE OF WALES *enters and rouses him*

   Falstaff [*waking*]. Now, Hal, what time of day is
it, lad?

   Prince. Thou art so fat-witted with drinking of old
sack, and unbuttoning thee after supper, and sleeping
upon benches after noon, that thou hast forgotten to demand that truly which thou wouldest truly know. What
a devil hast thou to do with the time of the day? Unless
hours were cups of sack, and minutes capons, and clocks
the tongues of bawds, and dials the signs of leaping-

houses, and the blessed sun himself a fair hot wench in 10
flame-coloured taffeta, I see no reason why thou shouldst
be so superfluous to demand the time of the day.

Falstaff. Indeed, you come near me now, Hal, for
we that take purses go by the moon and the seven stars,
and not by Phœbus, he, 'that wandering knight so
fair'.... And, I prithee, sweet wag, when thou art king,
as God save thy grace—majesty I should say, for grace
thou wilt have none.

Prince. What, none?

Falstaff. No, by my troth, not so much as will serve 20
to be prologue to an egg and butter.

Prince. Well, how then? come, roundly, roundly.

Falstaff. Marry then, sweet wag, when thou art king
let not us that are squires of the night's body be called
thieves of the day's beauty; let us be Diana's foresters,
gentlemen of the shade, minions of the moon, and let
men say we be men of good government, being governed
as the sea is by our noble and chaste mistress the moon,
under whose countenance we steal.

Prince. Thou sayest well, and it holds well too, for 30
the fortune of us that are the moon's men doth ebb and
flow like the sea, being governed as the sea is by the
moon—as for proof now, a purse of gold most reso-
lutely snatched on Monday night and most dissolutely
spent on Tuesday morning, got with swearing 'lay by'
and spent with crying 'bring in'—now in as low an ebb
as the foot of the ladder, and by and by in as high a flow
as the ridge of the gallows.

Falstaff. By the Lord, thou sayst true, lad, and is
not my hostess of the tavern a most sweet wench?   40

Prince. As the honey of Hybla, my old lad of the
castle, and is not a buff jerkin a most sweet robe of
durance?

Falstaff. How now, how now, mad wag? what, in thy quips and thy quiddities? what a plague have I to do with a buff jerkin?

Prince. Why, what a pox have I to do with my hostess of the tavern?

Falstaff. Well, thou hast called her to a reckoning
50 many a time and oft.

Prince. Did I ever call for thee to pay thy part?

Falstaff. No, I'll give thee thy due, thou hast paid all there.

Prince. Yea, and elsewhere, so far as my coin would stretch, and where it would not, I have used my credit.

Falstaff. Yea, and so used it that, were it not here apparent that thou art heir apparent—But, I prithee, sweet wag, shall there be gallows standing in England when thou art king? and resolution thus fubbed as it is
60 with the rusty curb of old father Antic the law? Do not thou, when thou art king, hang a thief.

Prince. No, thou shalt.

Falstaff. Shall I? O rare! By the Lord, I'll be a brave judge!

Prince. Thou judgest false already. I mean, thou shalt have the hanging of the thieves and so become a rare hangman.

Falstaff. Well, Hal, well—and in some sort it jumps with my humour, as well as waiting in the court, I can tell you.
70 *Prince.* For obtaining of suits?

Falstaff. Yea, for obtaining of suits, whereof the hangman hath no lean wardrobe....'Sblood, I am as melancholy as a gib cat or a lugged bear.

Prince. Or an old lion, or a lover's lute.

Falstaff. Yea, or the drone of a Lincolnshire bagpipe.

Prince. What sayest thou to a hare, or the melancholy of Moor-ditch?

Falstaff. Thou hast the most unsavoury similes and art indeed the most comparative, rascalliest, sweet young prince....But, Hal, I prithee, trouble me no 80 more with vanity. I would to God thou and I knew where a commodity of good names were to be bought: an old lord of the council rated me the other day in the street about you, sir, but I marked him not, and yet he talked very wisely, but I regarded him not, and yet he talked wisely and in the street too.

Prince. Thou didst well, for wisdom cries out in the streets, and no man regards it.

Falstaff. O, thou hast damnable iteration, and art indeed able to corrupt a saint: thou hast done much harm 90 upon me, Hal—God forgive thee for it: before I knew thee, Hal, I knew nothing, and now am I, if a man should speak truly, little better than one of the wicked... I must give over this life, and I will give it over: by the Lord, an I do not, I am a villain. I'll be damned for never a king's son in Christendom.

Prince. Where shall we take a purse to-morrow, Jack?

Falstaff. 'Zounds, where thou wilt, lad, I'll make one, an I do not, call me villain and baffle me.

Prince. I see a good amendment of life in thee, 100 from praying to purse-taking.

Falstaff. Why, Hal, 'tis my vocation, Hal, 'tis no sin for a man to labour in his vocation.

POINS *enters*

Poins! Now shall we know if Gadshill have set a match. [*points*] O, if men were to be saved by merit, what hole in hell were hot enough for him? This is the most omnipotent villain that ever cried 'Stand' to a true man.

Prince. Good morrow, Ned.

Poins. Good morrow, sweet Hal. What says Monsieur

110 Remorse? What says Sir John Sack and Sugar? Jack,
how agrees the devil and thee about thy soul, that thou
soldest him on Good Friday last, for a cup of Madeira
and a cold capon's leg?

Prince. Sir John stands to his word, the devil shall
have his bargain, for he was never yet a breaker of
proverbs: he will give the devil his due.

Poins. Then art thou damned for keeping thy word
with the devil.

Prince. Else he had been damned for cozening the devil.

120 *Poins.* But, my lads, my lads, to-morrow morning, by
four o'clock, early at Gad's Hill, there are pilgrims going
to Canterbury with rich offerings, and traders riding to
London with fat purses....I have vizards for you all,
you have horses for yourselves, Gadshill lies to-night in
Rochester, I have bespoke supper to-morrow night in
Eastcheap: we may do it as secure as sleep. If you will
go, I will stuff your purses full of crowns; if you will not,
tarry at home and be hanged.

Falstaff. Hear ye, Yedward, if I tarry at home and
130 go not, I'll hang you for going.

Poins. You will, chops?

Falstaff. Hal, wilt thou make one?

Prince. Who, I? rob? I a thief? not I, by my faith.

Falstaff. There's neither honesty, manhood, nor good
fellowship in thee, nor thou cam'st not of the blood
royal, if thou darest not stand for ten shillings.

       [*Poins makes signals behind Falstaff's back*

Prince. Well then, once in my days I'll be a madcap.

Falstaff. Why, that's well said.

Prince. Well, come what will, I'll tarry at home.

140 *Falstaff.* By the Lord, I'll be a traitor then, when thou
art king.

Prince. I care not.

Poins. Sir John, I prithee, leave the prince and me alone, I will lay him down such reasons for this adventure that he shall go.

Falstaff. Well, God give thee the spirit of persuasion, and him the ears of profiting, that what thou speakest may move, and what he hears may be believed, that the true prince may (for recreation sake) prove a false thief, for the poor abuses of the time want countenance... 150 Farewell, you shall find me in Eastcheap.

Prince. Farewell, the latter spring! Farewell, All-hallown summer! [*Falstaff goes*

Poins. Now, my good sweet honey lord, ride with us to-morrow. I have a jest to execute that I cannot manage alone. Falstaff, Bardolph, Peto and Gadshill shall rob those men that we have already waylaid—yourself and I will not be there: and when they have the booty, if you and I do not rob them, cut this head off from my shoulders. 160

Prince. How shall we part with them in setting forth?

Poins. Why, we will set forth before or after them, and appoint them a place of meeting, wherein it is at our pleasure to fail; and then will they adventure upon the exploit themselves, which they shall have no sooner achieved but we'll set upon them.

Prince. Yea, but 'tis like that they will know us by our horses, by our habits, and by every other appointment, to be ourselves.

Poins. Tut! our horses they shall not see, I'll tie them 170 in the wood; our vizards we will change after we leave them; and, sirrah, I have cases of buckram for the nonce, to immask our noted outward garments.

Prince. Yea, but I doubt they will be too hard for us.

Poins. Well, for two of them, I know them to be as true-bred cowards as ever turned back; and for the

third, if he fight longer than he sees reason, I'll forswear
arms. The virtue of this jest will be the incomprehensible
lies that this same fat rogue will tell us when we meet at
180 supper, how thirty at least he fought with, what wards,
what blows, what extremities he endured, and in the
reproof of this lives the jest.

    Prince. Well, I'll go with thee. Provide us all things
necessary, and meet me to-morrow night in Eastcheap,
there I'll sup...Farewell.

    Poins. Farewell, my lord.   [*Poins goes*

    Prince. I know you all, and will awhile uphold
The unyoked humour of your idleness.
Yet herein will I imitate the sun,
190 Who doth permit the base contagious clouds
To smother up his beauty from the world,
That when he please again to be himself,
Being wanted he may be more wond'red at,
By breaking through the foul and ugly mists
Of vapours that did seem to strangle him.
If all the year were playing holidays,
To sport would be as tedious as to work;
But when they seldom come, they wished for come,
And nothing pleaseth but rare accidents:
200 So, when this loose behaviour I throw off,
And pay the debt I never promiséd,
By how much better than my word I am,
By so much shall I falsify men's hopes,
And like bright metal on a sullen ground,
My reformation, glitt'ring o'er my fault,
Shall show more goodly, and attract more eyes,
Than that which hath no foil to set it off.
I'll so offend, to make offence a skill,
Redeeming time when men think least I will.   [*he goes*

[1. 3.]   *Windsor. The Council Chamber*

Enter the KING, NORTHUMBERLAND, WORCESTER,
HOTSPUR, SIR WALTER BLUNT, *with others*

King. My blood hath been too cold and temperate,
Unapt to stir at these indignities,
And you have found me—for accordingly
You tread upon my patience. But be sure
I will from henceforth rather be myself,
Mighty and to be feared, than my condition,
Which hath been smooth as oil, soft as young down,
And therefore lost that title of respect
Which the proud soul ne'er pays but to the proud.

Worcester. Our house, my sovereign liege,   10
          little deserves
The scourge of greatness to be used on it,
And that same greatness too which our own hands
Have holp to make so portly.

Northumberland. My lord,—

King. Worcester, get thee gone, for I do see
Danger and disobedience in thine eye:
O, sir, your presence is too bold and peremptory,
And majesty might never yet endure
The moody frontier of a servant brow.
You have good leave to leave us. When we need   20
Your use and counsel, we shall send for you....
                              [*Worcester goes out*
You were about to speak.

Northumberland. [*bows*]   Yea, my good lord.
Those prisoners in your highness' name demanded,
Which Harry Percy here at Holmedon took,
Were, as he says, not with such strength denied
As is delivered to your majesty.

Either envy, therefore, or misprision
Is guilty of this fault, and not my son.
  Hotspur. My liege, I did deny no prisoners,
30 But I remember, when the fight was done,
When I was dry with rage and extreme toil,
Breathless and faint, leaning upon my sword,
Came there a certain lord, neat and trimly dressed,
Fresh as a bridegroom, and his chin new reaped
Showed like a stubble-land at harvest-home.
He was perfuméd like a milliner,
And 'twixt his finger and his thumb he held
A pouncet-box, which ever and anon
He gave his nose and took't away again—
40 Who therewith angry, when it next came there,
Took it in snuff—and still he smiled and talked:
And as the soldiers bore dead bodies by,
He called them untaught knaves, unmannerly,
To bring a slovenly unhandsome corse
Betwixt the wind and his nobility:
With many holiday and lady terms
He questioned me, amongst the rest demanded
My prisoners in your majesty's behalf.
I then, all smarting with my wounds being cold,
50 To be so pest'red with a popinjay,
Out of my grief and my impatience,
Answered neglectingly I know not what,
He should, or he should not, for he made me mad
To see him shine so brisk, and smell so sweet,
And talk so like a waiting-gentlewoman
Of guns, and drums, and wounds, God save the mark!
And telling me the sovereignest thing on earth
Was parmaceti for an inward bruise,
And that it was great pity, so it was,
60 This villainous salt-petre should be digged

Out of the bowels of the harmless earth,
Which many a good tall fellow had destroyed
So cowardly, and but for these vile guns
He would himself have been a soldier....
This bald unjointed chat of his, my lord,
I answered indirectly, as I said,
And I beseech you, let not his report
Come current for an accusation
Betwixt my love and your high majesty.

Blunt. The circumstance considered, good my lord,   70
Whate'er Lord Harry Percy then had said
To such a person, and in such a place,
At such a time, with all the rest retold,
May reasonably die, and never rise
To do him wrong, or any way impeach
What then he said, so he unsay it now.

King. Why, yet he doth deny his prisoners,
But with proviso and exception,
That we at our own charge shall ransom straight
His brother-in-law, the foolish Mortimer,   80
Who, on my soul, hath wilfully betrayed
The lives of those that he did lead to fight
Against the great magician, damned Glendower,
Whose daughter, as we hear, that Earl of March
Hath lately married...Shall our coffers then
Be emptied to redeem a traitor home?
Shall we buy treason? and indent with fears,
When they have lost and forfeited themselves?
No, on the barren mountains let him starve;
For I shall never hold that man my friend,   90
Whose tongue shall ask me for one penny cost
To ransom home revolted Mortimer.

Hotspur. Revolted Mortimer!
He never did fall off, my sovereign liege,

But by the chance of war. To prove that true
Needs no more but one tongue for all those wounds,
Those mouthéd wounds, which valiantly he took,
When on the gentle Severn's sedgy bank,
In single opposition, hand to hand,
100 He did confound the best part of an hour
In changing hardiment with great Glendower.
Three times they breathed and three times did
     they drink,
Upon agreement, of swift Severn's flood,
Who then affrighted with their bloody looks,
Ran fearfully among the trembling reeds,
And hid his crisp head in the hollow bank
Bloodstainéd with these valiant combatants.
Never did bare and rotten policy
Colour her working with such deadly wounds,
110 Nor never could the noble Mortimer
Receive so many, and all willingly.
Then let him not be slandered with revolt.
  King. Thou dost belie him, Percy, thou dost
     belie him.
He never did encounter with Glendower:
I tell thee,
He durst as well have met the devil alone,
As Owen Glendower for an enemy.
Art thou not ashamed? But, sirrah, henceforth
Let me not hear you speak of Mortimer:
120 Send me your prisoners with the speediest means,
Or you shall hear in such a kind from me
As will displease you....My Lord Northumberland,
We license your departure with your son.
Send us your prisoners, or you'll hear of it.
        [*King Henry, Blunt and other nobles*
        leave the chamber

Hotspur. And if the devil come and roar for them,
I will not send them: I will after straight
And tell him so, for I will ease my heart,
Albeit I make a hazard of my head.
  Northumberland. What, drunk with choler? stay and
      pause awhile,
Here comes your uncle.

WORCESTER returns

  Hotspur.   Speak of Mortimer!   130
'Zounds, I will speak of him, and let my soul
Want mercy if I do not join with him:
Yea, on his part, I'll empty all these veins,
And shed my dear blood drop by drop in the dust,
But I will lift the down-trod Mortimer
As high in the air as this unthankful king,
As this ingrate and cank'red Bolingbroke.
  Northumberland. Brother, the king hath made your
      nephew mad.
  Worcester. Who struck this heat up after I was gone?
  Hotspur. He will forsooth have all my prisoners,   140
And when I urged the ransom once again
Of my wife's brother, then his cheek looked pale,
And on my face he turned an eye of death,
Trembling even at the name of Mortimer.
  Worcester. I cannot blame him, was not
      he proclaimed,
By Richard that dead is, the next of blood?
  Northumberland. He was, I heard the proclamation:
And then it was when the unhappy king
(Whose wrongs in us God pardon!) did set forth
Upon his Irish expedition;   150
From whence he intercepted did return
To be deposed and shortly murderéd.

Worcester. And for whose death we in the world's
  wide mouth
Live scandalized and foully spoken of.
 Hotspur. But soft, I pray you, did King Richard then
Proclaim my brother Edmund Mortimer
Heir to the crown?
 Northumberland.   He did, myself did hear it.
 Hotspur. Nay, then I cannot blame his cousin king,
That wished him on the barren mountains starve.
160 But shall it be that you, that set the crown
 Upon the head of this forgetful man,
 And for his sake wear the detested blot
 Of murderous subornation, shall it be
 That you a world of curses undergo,
 Being the agents, or base second means,
 The cords, the ladder, or the hangman rather?—
 O, pardon me that I descend so low,
 To show the line, and the predicament,
 Wherein you range under this subtle king!—
170 Shall it for shame be spoken in these days,
 Or fill up chronicles in time to come,
 That men of your nobility and power
 Did gage them both in an unjust behalf
 (As both of you, God pardon it! have done)
 To put down Richard, that sweet lovely rose,
 And plant this thorn, this canker, Bolingbroke?
 And shall it in more shame be further spoken,
 That you are fooled, discarded, and shook off
 By him for whom these shames ye underwent?
180 No, yet time serves wherein you may redeem
 Your banished honours, and restore yourselves
 Into the good thoughts of the world again:
 Revenge the jeering and disdained contempt
 Of this proud king, who studies day and night

To answer all the debt he owes to you,
Even with the bloody payment of your deaths:
Therefore, I say—

  Worcester.　　　　　Peace, cousin, say no more.
And now I will unclasp a secret book,
And to your quick-conceiving discontents
I'll read you matter deep and dangerous,　　　　　190
As full of peril and adventurous spirit
As to o'er-walk a current roaring loud
On the unsteadfast footing of a spear.

  Hotspur. If he fall in, good night! or sink or swim.
Send danger from the east unto the west,
So honour cross it from the north to south,
And let them grapple: O, the blood more stirs
To rouse a lion than to start a hare!

  Northumberland. Imagination of some great exploit
Drives him beyond the bounds of patience.　　　　　200

  Hotspur. By heaven, methinks it were an easy leap,
To pluck bright honour from the pale-faced moon,
Or dive into the bottom of the deep,
Where fathom-line could never touch the ground,
And pluck up drownéd honour by the locks,
So he that doth redeem her thence might wear
Without corrival all her dignities:
But out upon this half-faced fellowship!

  Worcester. He apprehends a world of figures here,
But not the form of what he should attend.　　　　　210
Good cousin, give me audience for a while.

  Hotspur. I cry you mercy.

  Worcester.　　　　　Those same noble Scots
That are your prisoners,—

  Hotspur.　　　　　I'll keep them all;
By God, he shall not have a Scot of them.
No, if a Scot would save his soul, he shall not.

I'll keep them, by this hand.

Worcester.   You start away,
And lend no ear unto my purposes...
Those prisoners you shall keep.

Hotspur.   Nay, I will: that's flat:
He said he would not ransom Mortimer,
220 Forbad my tongue to speak of Mortimer,
But I will find him when he lies asleep,
And in his ear I'll holla 'Mortimer!'
Nay,
I'll have a starling shall be taught to speak
Nothing but 'Mortimer', and give it him
To keep his anger still in motion.

Worcester. Hear you, cousin, a word.

Hotspur. All studies here I solemnly defy,
Save how to gall and pinch this Bolingbroke.
230 And that same sword-and-buckler Prince of Wales,
But that I think his father loves him not
And would be glad he met with some mischance,
I would have him poisoned with a pot of ale.

Worcester. Farewell, kinsman! I'll talk to you
When you are better tempered to attend.

Northumberland. Why, what a wasp-stung and
          impatient fool
Art thou, to break into this woman's mood,
Tying thine ear to no tongue but thine own!

Hotspur. Why, look you, I am whipped and scourged
          with rods,
240 Nettled, and stung with pismires, when I hear
Of this vile politician, Bolingbroke.
In Richard's time—what de'ye call the place?—
A plague upon't, it is in Gloucestershire;
'Twas where the madcap duke his uncle kept,
His uncle York—where I first bowed my knee

Unto this king of smiles, this Bolingbroke—
'Sblood! When you and he came back from
      Ravenspurgh—
  Northumberland. At Berkeley castle.
  Hotspur. You say true.
Why, what a candy deal of courtesy   250
This fawning greyhound then did proffer me!
'Look when his infant fortune came to age',
And, 'gentle Harry Percy', and 'kind cousin':
O, the devil take such cozeners! God forgive me!
Good uncle, tell your tale—I have done.
  Worcester. Nay, if you have not, to it again,
We will stay your leisure.
  Hotspur.   I have done, i'faith.
  Worcester. Then once more to your Scottish prisoners.
Deliver them up without their ransom straight,
And make the Douglas' son your only mean   260
For powers in Scotland, which, for divers reasons
Which I shall send you written, be assured
Will easily be granted. You, my lord,
              [to Northumberland
Your son in Scotland being thus employed,
Shall secretly into the bosom creep
Of that same noble prelate, well beloved,
The archbishop.
  Hotspur.   Of York, is't not?
  Worcester.   True; who bears hard
His brother's death at Bristow, the Lord Scroop.
I speak not this in estimation,
As what I think might be, but what I know   270
Is ruminated, plotted, and set down,
And only stays but to behold the face
Of that occasion that shall bring it on.
  Hotspur. I smell it. Upon my life, it will do well.

Northumberland. Before the game's afoot thou still
    let'st slip.

Hotspur. Why, it cannot choose but be a noble plot.
And then the power of Scotland and of York,
To join with Mortimer, ha?

Worcester.   And so they shall.

Hotspur. In faith, it is exceedingly well aimed.

280 *Worcester.* And 'tis no little reason bids us speed,
To save our heads by raising of a head,
For, bear ourselves as even as we can,
The king will always think him in our debt,
And think we think ourselves unsatisfied,
Till he hath found a time to pay us home.
And see already how he doth begin
To make us strangers to his looks of love.

Hotspur. He does, he does, we'll be revenged on him.

Worcester. Cousin, farewell. No further go in this

290 Than I by letters shall direct your course.
When time is ripe, which will be suddenly,
I'll steal to Glendower and Lord Mortimer,
Where you and Douglas and our powers at once,
As I will fashion it, shall happily meet,
To bear our fortunes in our own strong arms,
Which now we hold at much uncertainty.

Northumberland. Farewell, good brother, we shall
    thrive, I trust.

Hotspur. Uncle, adieu: O, let the hours be short,
Till fields, and blows, and groans applaud our sport!

                                        [*they go*

[2. 1.]   *An inn yard at Rochester*

'*Enter a Carrier with a lantern in his hand*'

1 *Carrier*. Heigh-ho! An't be not four by the day, I'll be hanged. Charles' wain is over the new chimney, and yet our horse not packed. What, ostler!

Ostler [*sleepily, within*]. Anon, anon.

1 *Carrier*. I prithee, Tom, beat Cut's saddle, put a few flocks in the point, poor jade is wrung in the withers, out of all cess.

'*Enter another Carrier*'

2 *Carrier*. Peas and beans are as dank here as a dog, and that is the next way to give poor jades the bots: this house is turned upside down since Robin Ostler 10 died.

1 *Carrier*. Poor fellow never joyed since the price of oats rose, it was the death of him.

2 *Carrier*. I think this be the most villainous house in all London road for fleas, I am stung like a tench.

1 *Carrier*. Like a tench! by the mass, there is ne'er a king christen could be better bit than I have been since the first cock.

2 *Carrier*. Why, they will allow us ne'er a jordan, and then we leak in your chimney, and your chamber-lye 20 breeds fleas like a loach.

1 *Carrier*. What, ostler! come away, and be hanged, come away.

2 *Carrier*. I have a gammon of bacon, and two razes of ginger, to be delivered as far as Charing-cross.

1 *Carrier*. God's body! the turkeys in my pannier are quite starved....What, ostler! a plague on thee! hast thou never an eye in thy head? canst not hear? An 'twere not as good deed as drink, to break the pate on thee, I am a very villain. Come, and be hanged! hast no faith in thee? 30

Enter GADSHILL

Gadshill. Good morrow, carriers, what's o'clock?

1 *Carrier.* I think it be two o'clock.

Gadshill. I prithee, lend me thy lantern to see my gelding in the stable.

1 *Carrier.* Nay, by God, soft, I know a trick worth two of that, ay, faith!

Gadshill. I pray thee, lend me thine.

2 *Carrier.* Ay, when? canst tell? Lend me thy lantern, quoth-a? marry, I'll see thee hanged first.

40 *Gadshill.* Sirrah carrier, what time do you mean to come to London?

2 *Carrier.* Time enough to go to bed with a candle, I warrant thee. [*aside*] Come, neighbour Mugs, we'll call up the gentlemen. They will along with company, for they have great charge. 　　　　[*the carriers go within*

Gadshill. What, ho! chamberlain!

Voice from within. At hand, quoth pick-purse.

Gadshill. That's even as fair as—at hand, quoth the chamberlain: for thou variest no more from picking of 50 purses than giving direction doth from labouring; thou layest the plot how.

A Chamberlain comes from the inn

Chamberlain. Good morrow, Master Gadshill. It holds current that I told you yesternight. There's a franklin in the wild of Kent, hath brought three hundred marks with him in gold, I heard him tell it to one of his company last night at supper, a kind of auditor, one that hath abundance of charge too, God knows what. They are up already, and call for eggs and butter. They will away presently.

60 *Gadshill.* Sirrah, if they meet not with Saint Nicholas' clerks, I'll give thee this neck.

Chamberlain. No, I'll none of it. I pray thee, keep that for the hangman, for I know thou worshippest Saint Nicholas, as truly as a man of falsehood may.

Gadshill. What talkest thou to me of the hangman? if I hang, I'll make a fat pair of gallows: for, if I hang, old Sir John hangs with me, and thou knowest he's no starveling. Tut! there are other Trojans that thou dream'st not of, the which for sport sake are content to do the profession some grace, that would, if matters 70 should be looked into, for their own credit sake make all whole. I am joined with no foot-land-rakers, no long-staff sixpenny strikers, none of these mad mustachio purple-hued malt-worms, but with nobility and tranquillity, burgomasters and great onyers, such as can hold in, such as will strike sooner than speak, and speak sooner than drink, and drink sooner than pray. And yet, 'zounds, I lie, for they pray continually to their saint, the commonwealth, or rather not pray to her, but prey on her, for they ride up and down on her, and make her 80 their boots.

Chamberlain. What, the commonwealth their boots? will she hold out water in foul way?

Gadshill. She will, she will—Justice hath liquored her: we steal as in a castle, cock-sure: we have the receipt of fern-seed, we walk invisible.

Chamberlain. Nay, by my faith, I think you are more beholding to the night than to fern-seed for your walking invisible.

Gadshill. Give me thy hand, thou shalt have a share 90 in our purchase, as I am a true man.

Chamberlain. Nay, rather let me have it, as you are a false thief.

Gadshill. Go to, 'homo' is a common name to all men: bid the ostler bring my gelding out of the stable. Farewell, you muddy knave.　　　　　*[they go their ways*

[2. 2.] *A narrow lane, near the top of Gad's Hill, some two miles from Rochester; bushes and trees. A dark night*

The PRINCE, PETO *and* BARDOLPH *come up the hill;*
POINS *hurrying after*

Poins. Come, shelter, shelter! I have removed Falstaff's horse, and he frets like a gummed velvet.

Prince. Stand close.   [*Poins hides behind a bush*

FALSTAFF *comes up, breathless*

Falstaff. Poins! Poins, and be hanged! Poins!

Prince. Peace, ye fat-kidneyed rascal! what a brawling dost thou keep!

Falstaff. Where's Poins, Hal?

Prince. He is walked up to the top of the hill, I'll go seek him.   [*he joins Poins*

10   *Falstaff.* I am accursed to rob in that thief's company. The rascal hath removed my horse, and tied him I know not where. If I travel but four foot by the squier further afoot, I shall break my wind....Well, I doubt not but to die a fair death for all this, if I 'scape hanging for killing that rogue. I have forsworn his company hourly any time this two and twenty years, and yet I am bewitched with the rogue's company. If the rascal have not given me medicines to make me love him, I'll be hanged. It could not be else—I have drunk medicines. Poins! Hal!
20   a plague upon you both! Bardolph! Peto! I'll starve ere I'll rob a foot further. An 'twere not as good a deed as drink, to turn true man and to leave these rogues, I am the veriest varlet that ever chewed with a tooth...Eight yards of uneven ground is threescore and ten miles afoot with me, and the stony-hearted villains know it well enough. A plague upon't, when thieves cannot be

true one to another! ['*they whistle*'.] Whew! A plague
upon you all! Give me my horse, you rogues, give me
my horse and be hanged.

Prince [*coming forward*]. Peace, ye fat-guts! lie down, 30
lay thine ear close to the ground and list if thou canst hear
the tread of travellers.

Falstaff. Have you any levers to lift me up again, being
down? 'Sblood, I'll not bear mine own flesh so far
afoot again for all the coin in thy father's exchequer.
What a plague mean ye to colt me thus?

Prince. Thou liest, thou art not colted, thou art un-
colted.

Falstaff. I prithee, good Prince Hal, help me to my
horse, good king's son.   40

Prince. Out, ye rogue! shall I be your ostler?

Falstaff. Go hang thyself in thine own heir-apparent
garters! If I be ta'en, I'll peach for this...An I have not
ballads made on you all and sung to filthy tunes, let a
cup of sack be my poison—when a jest is so forward, and
afoot too! I hate it.

GADSHILL approaches, coming down the hill

Gadshill. Stand!

Falstaff. So I do, against my will.

POINS, BARDOLPH, and PETO come forward

Poins. O, 'tis our setter. I know his voice.

Bardolph. What news?   50

Gadshill. Case ye, case ye, on with your vizards,
there's money of the king's coming down the hill, 'tis
going to the king's exchequer.

Falstaff. You lie, ye rogue, 'tis going to the king's
tavern.

Gadshill. There's enough to make us all.

Falstaff. —To be hanged.

Prince. Sirs, you four shall front them in the narrow
lane: Ned Poins and I will walk lower. If they 'scape
60 from your encounter, then they light on us.

Peto. How many be there of them?

Gadshill. Some eight, or ten.

Falstaff. 'Zounds, will they not rob us?

Prince. What, a coward, Sir John Paunch?

Falstaff. Indeed, I am not John of Gaunt, your grandfather, but yet no coward, Hal.

Prince. Well, we leave that to the proof.

Poins. Sirrah Jack, thy horse stands behind the hedge,
when thou need'st him, there thou shalt find him...Fare-
70 well, and stand fast.

Falstaff. Now cannot I strike him, if I should be
hanged.

(*Prince.* Ned, where are our disguises?

(*Poins.* Here, hard by, stand close.

[*The Prince and Poins slip away*

Falstaff. Now, my masters, happy man be his dole!
say I; every man to his business.

The Travellers are heard coming down the hill

1 *Traveller.* Come, neighbour, the boy shall lead our
horses down the hill, we'll walk afoot awhile and ease
our legs.

80 *Thieves.* Stand!

Travellers. Jesus bless us!

Falstaff. Strike, down with them, cut the villains'
throats! Ah, whoreson caterpillars! bacon-fed knaves!
they hate us youth. Down with them, fleece them.

1 *Traveller.* O, we are undone, both we and ours for
ever.

Falstaff. Hang ye, gorbellied knaves, are ye undone?
No, ye fat chuffs. I would your store were here! On,

bacons, on! What, ye knaves? young men must live.
You are grandjurors, are ye? We'll jure ye, faith.   90

['*Here they rob them and bind them*' *and
then drive them down the hill*

The PRINCE *and* POINS *steal from the bushes
disguised in buckram*

Prince. The thieves have bound the true men. Now
could thou and I rob the thieves, and go merrily to
London, it would be argument for a week, laughter for
a month, and a good jest for ever.

Poins. Stand close, I hear them coming.

The Thieves return

Falstaff. Come, my masters, let us share, and then to
horse before day. An the Prince and Poins be not two
arrant cowards, there's no equity stirring. There's no
more valour in that Poins than in a wild-duck.

['*As they are sharing, the Prince and
Poins set upon them*'

Prince. Your money!   100
Poins. Villains!

['*They all run away, leaving the booty behind them,
and Falstaff, after a blow or two, runs away too*',
*roaring for mercy as the Prince and Poins prick
him from behind with their swords*

Prince. Got with much ease. Now merrily to horse:
the thieves are all scattered, and possessed with fear
so strongly that they dare not meet each other. Each
takes his fellow for an officer. Away, good Ned.
Falstaff sweats to death, and lards the lean earth as he
walks along. Were't not for laughing, I should pity
him.

Poins. How the fat rogue roared!   [*they go*

'*Enter* HOTSPUR, *solus, reading a letter*'
and striding to and fro

Hotspur. 'But, for mine own part, my lord, I could
be well contented to be there, in respect of the love I
bear your house.'
He could be contented: why is he not then? In
respect of the love he bears our house: he shows in this,
he loves his own barn better than he loves our house.
Let me see some more.
    'The purpose you undertake is dangerous.'
Why, that's certain. 'Tis dangerous to take a cold, to
10 sleep, to drink, but I tell you, my lord fool, out of this
nettle, danger, we pluck this flower, safety.
    'The purpose you undertake is dangerous, the
friends you have named uncertain, the time itself
unsorted, and your whole plot too light for the counter-
poise of so great an opposition.'
Say you so, say you so? I say unto you again, you are
a shallow cowardly hind, and you lie...What a lack-
brain is this! By the Lord, our plot is a good plot as ever
was laid, our friends true and constant: a good plot, good
20 friends, and full of expectation: an excellent plot, very
good friends...What a frosty-spirited rogue is this! Why,
my lord of York commends the plot and the general
course of the action. 'Zounds, an I were now by this
rascal, I could brain him with his lady's fan. Is there
not my father, my uncle, and myself? Lord Edmund
Mortimer, my lord of York, and Owen Glendower?
is there not besides the Douglas? have I not all their
letters to meet me in arms by the ninth of the next month?
and are they not some of them set forward already?
30 What a pagan rascal is this! an infidel! Ha! you shall
see now, in very sincerity of fear and cold heart, will he

to the king, and lay open all our proceedings! O, I
could divide myself and go to buffets, for moving such
a dish of skim milk with so honourable an action! Hang
him! let him tell the king, we are prepared: I will set
forward to-night.

'Enter his Lady'

How now, Kate? I must leave you within these two
hours.

   Lady Percy. O my good lord, why are you thus alone?
For what offence have I this fortnight been   40
A banished woman from my Harry's bed?
Tell me, sweet lord, what is't that takes from thee
Thy stomach, pleasure, and thy golden sleep?
Why dost thou bend thine eyes upon the earth,
And start so often when thou sit'st alone?
Why hast thou lost the fresh blood in thy cheeks,
And given my treasures and my rights of thee
To thick-eyed musing and curst melancholy?
In thy faint slumbers I by thee have watched,
And heard thee murmur tales of iron wars,   50
Speak terms of manage to thy bounding steed,
Cry 'Courage! to the field!' And thou hast talked
Of sallies and retires, of trenches, tents,
Of palisadoes, frontiers, parapets,
Of basilisks, of cannon, culverin,
Of prisoners' ransom, and of soldiers slain,
And all the currents of a heady fight.
Thy spirit within thee hath been so at war,
And thus hath so bestirred thee in thy sleep,
That beads of sweat have stood upon thy brow,   60
Like bubbles in a late-disturbéd stream,
And in thy face strange motions have appeared,
Such as we see when men restrain their breath

On some great sudden hest. O, what portents are these?
Some heavy business hath my lord in hand,
And I must know it, else he loves me not.
  Hotspur. What, ho!

               A servant enters

              Is Gilliams with the packet gone?
  Servant. He is, my lord, an hour ago.
  Hotspur Hath Butler brought those horses from
    the sheriff?
70 *Servant.* One horse, my lord, he brought even now.
  Hotspur. What horse? a roan, a crop-ear, is it not?
  Servant. It is, my lord.
  Hotspur. [*rapt*]   That roan shall be my throne.
Well, I will back him straight: O esperance !
Bid Butler lead him forth into the park.
                     [*the servant goes*
  Lady Percy. But hear you, my lord.
  Hotspur. What say'st thou, my lady?
  Lady Percy. What is it carries you away?
  Hotspur. Why, my horse, my love, my horse.
  Lady Percy. Out, you mad-headed ape!
80 A weasel hath not such a deal of spleen
  As you are tossed with. In faith,
  I'll know your business, Harry, that I will.
  I fear my brother Mortimer doth stir
  About his title, and hath sent for you
  To line his enterprize. But if you go—
    Hotspur. So far afoot, I shall be weary, love.
    Lady Percy. Come, come, you paraquito, answer me
Directly unto this question that I ask.
In faith, I'll break thy little finger, Harry,
90 An if thou wilt not tell me all things true.
  Hotspur. Away,

Away, you trifler! Love! I love thee not,
I care not for thee, Kate. This is no world
To play with mammets and to tilt with lips.
We must have bloody noses and cracked crowns,
And pass them current too....God's me, my horse!
What say'st thou, Kate? what wouldst thou have
          with me?
  Lady Percy. Do you not love me? do you not, indeed?
Well, do not then, for since you love me not
I will not love myself. Do you not love me?   100
Nay, tell me if you speak in jest or no.
  Hotspur. Come, wilt thou see me ride?
And when I am a-horseback, I will swear
I love thee infinitely. But hark you, Kate,
I must not have you henceforth question me
Whither I go, nor reason whereabout.
Whither I must, I must. And, to conclude,
This evening must I leave you, gentle Kate.
I know you wise, but yet no farther wise
Than Harry Percy's wife; constant you are,   110
But yet a woman, and for secrecy,
No lady closer, for I well believe
Thou wilt not utter what thou dost not know.
And so far will I trust thee, gentle Kate!
  Lady Percy. How! so far?
  Hotspur. Not an inch further. But hark you, Kate,
Whither I go, thither shall you go too:
To-day will I set forth, to-morrow you—
Will this content you, Kate?
  Lady Percy.   It must, of force.
                    [*he hurries forth; she follows, musing*

*[2. 4.] A room at the Boar's Head Tavern in Eastcheap;
at the back a great fireplace with a settle. Midnight*

The PRINCE *enters at one door, crosses the room,
opens a door opposite, and calls*

Prince. Ned, prithee, come out of that fat room, and
lend me thy hand to laugh a little.

Poins. Where hast been, Hal?   *[comes forth*

Prince. With three or four loggerheads, amongst three
or four score hogsheads. I have sounded the very base-
string of humility. Sirrah, I am sworn brother to a leash
of drawers, and can call them all by their christen names,
as Tom, Dick, and Francis. They take it already upon
their salvation, that though I be but Prince of Wales, yet
10 I am the king of Courtesy, and tell me flatly I am no
proud Jack like Falstaff, but a Corinthian, a lad of
mettle, a good boy (by the Lord, so they call me!) and
when I am king of England, I shall command all the
good lads in Eastcheap. They call drinking deep 'dyeing
scarlet', and when you breathe in your watering, they
cry 'hem!' and bid you 'play it off'. To conclude, I am
so good a proficient in one quarter of an hour, that I can
drink with any tinker in his own language during my
life. I tell thee, Ned, thou hast lost much honour, that
20 thou wert not with me in this action...But, sweet Ned—
to sweeten which name of Ned, I give thee this pennyworth of sugar, clapped even now into my hand by an
underskinker, one that never spake other English in his
life than 'Eight shillings and sixpence', and 'You are
welcome', with this shrill addition, 'Anon, anon, sir!
Score a pint of bastard in the Half-moon', or so. But,
Ned, to drive away the time till Falstaff come, I prithee,
do thou stand in some by-room, while I question my
puny drawer to what end he gave me the sugar, and do

thou never leave calling 'Francis', that his tale to me 30
may be nothing but 'Anon'. Step aside, and I'll show
thee a precedent.

POINS *returns to the room whence he came, leaving
the door open behind him*

Poins [*calls*]. Francis!
Prince. Thou art perfect.
Poins. Francis!

FRANCIS *bustles in through the other door*

Francis. Anon, anon, sir.   [*turns back*
Look down into the Pomgarnet, Ralph.
  Prince. Come hither, Francis.
  Francis. My lord?
  Prince. How long hast thou to serve, Francis?   40
  Francis. Forsooth, five years, and as much as to—
  Poins [*within*]. Francis!
  Francis. Anon, anon, sir.
  Prince. Five year! by'r lady, a long lease for the clink-
ing of pewter...But, Francis, darest thou be so valiant
as to play the coward with thy indenture and show it a
fair pair of heels and run from it?
  Francis. O Lord, sir! I'll be sworn upon all the books
in England, I could find in my heart—
  Poins [*within*]. Francis!   50
  Francis. Anon, sir.
  Prince. How old art thou, Francis?
  Francis. Let me see—about Michaelmas next I shall
be—
  Poins [*within*]. Francis!
  Francis. Anon, sir. Pray stay a little, my lord.
                              [*he makes toward the by-room*

Prince [*checks him*]. Nay, but hark you, Francis. For the sugar thou gavest me—'twas a pennyworth, was't not?

Francis. O Lord, I would it had been two!

60 *Prince.* I will give thee for it a thousand pound. Ask me when thou wilt, and thou shalt have it—

Poins [*within*]. Francis!

Francis. Anon, anon.

Prince. Anon, Francis? No, Francis, but to-morrow, Francis; or, Francis, a-Thursday; or, indeed, Francis, when thou wilt. But, Francis!

Francis. My lord?

Prince. Wilt thou rob this leathern jerkin, crystal-button, not-pated, agate-ring, puke-stocking, caddis-

70 garter, smooth-tongue, Spanish-pouch,—

Francis. O Lord, sir, who do you mean?

Prince. Why then, your brown bastard is your only drink! for, look you, Francis, your white canvas doublet will sully. In Barbary, sir, it cannot come to so much.

Francis. What, sir?

Poins [*within*]. Francis!

Prince. Away, you rogue, dost thou not hear them call?

['*Here they both call him; the drawer stands amazed, not knowing which way to go*'

The VINTNER *comes in*

Vintner. What! stand'st thou still, and hear'st such a calling? Look to the guests within. [*Francis goes.*] My

80 lord, old Sir John, with half-a-dozen more, are at the door. Shall I let them in?

Prince. Let them alone awhile, and then open the door. [*Vintner goes.*] Poins!

Poins [*returning*]. Anon, anon, sir.

Prince. Sirrah, Falstaff and the rest of the thieves are at the door. Shall we be merry?

Poins. As merry as crickets, my lad. But hark ye, what cunning match have you made with this jest of the drawer? come, what's the issue?

Prince. I am now of all humours that have showed 90 themselves humours since the old days of goodman Adam to the pupil age of this present twelve o'clock at midnight. [*Francis hurries past carrying drink.*] What's o'clock, Francis?

Francis. Anon, anon, sir.　　　　　　　　[*he goes out*

Prince. That ever this fellow should have fewer words than a parrot, and yet the son of a woman! His industry is up-stairs and down-stairs, his eloquence the parcel of a reckoning.... I am not yet of Percy's mind, the Hotspur of the north, he that kills me some six or seven dozen of 100 Scots at a breakfast, washes his hands, and says to his wife, 'Fie upon this quiet life! I want work.' 'O my sweet Harry,' says she, 'how many hast thou killed to-day?' 'Give my roan horse a drench', says he, and answers, 'Some fourteen', an hour after; 'a trifle, a trifle.' I prithee, call in Falstaff. I'll play Percy, and that damned brawn shall play Dame Mortimer his wife. 'Rivo!' says the drunkard: call in Ribs, call in Tallow.

FALSTAFF enters with GADSHILL, BARDOLPH and PETO; FRANCIS follows with cups of sack FALSTAFF, taking no heed of PRINCE and POINS, sits wearily at a table

Poins. Welcome, Jack. Where hast thou been?

Falstaff [*to himself*]. A plague of all cowards, I say, 110 and a vengeance too! marry, and amen! Give me a cup of sack, boy. Ere I lead this life long, I'll sew netherstocks, and mend them, and foot them too. A plague of all cowards! Give me a cup of sack, rogue. Is there no virtue extant?   ['*he drinketh*'

Prince [*points*]. Didst thou never see Titan kiss a dish of butter (pitiful-hearted Titan!) that melted at the sweet tale of the sun's? If thou didst, then behold that compound.

120 *Falstaff* [*giving Francis the empty cup*]. You rogue, here's lime in this sack too...There is nothing but roguery to be found in villainous man, yet a coward is worse than a cup of sack with lime in it. A villainous coward! Go thy ways, old Jack, die when thou wilt. If manhood, good manhood, be not forgot upon the face of the earth, then am I a shotten herring...There lives not three good men unhanged in England, and one of them is fat, and grows old. God help the while! a bad world, I say. I would I were a weaver—I could sing psalms or any thing. A 130 plague of all cowards, I say still.

Prince. How now, wool-sack! what mutter you?

Falstaff [*rounds upon him*]. A king's son! If I do not beat thee out of thy kingdom with a dagger of lath, and drive all thy subjects afore thee like a flock of wild-geese, I'll never wear hair on my face more. You, Prince of Wales!

Prince. Why, you whoreson round man! what's the matter?

Falstaff. Are not you a coward? answer me to that— 140 and Poins there?

Poins. 'Zounds, ye fat paunch, an ye call me coward, by the Lord I'll stab thee.   [*he draws his dagger*

Falstaff. I call thee coward! I'll see thee damned ere I call thee coward—but I would give a thousand pound I could run as fast as thou canst. You are straight enough in the shoulders, you care not who sees your back: call you that backing of your friends? A plague upon such

backing! give me them that will face me. [*to Francis*]
Give me a cup of sack—I am a rogue, if I drunk to-day.

Prince. O villain! thy lips are scarce wiped since thou 150
drunk'st last.

Falstaff. All's one for that. ['*he drinketh*'] A plague
of all cowards, still say I.

Prince. What's the matter?

Falstaff. What's the matter? there be four of us here
have ta'en a thousand pound this day morning.

Prince. Where is it, Jack? where is it?

Falstaff. Where is it? taken from us it is: a hundred
upon poor four of us.

Prince. What, a hundred, man? 160

Falstaff. I am a rogue, if I were not at half-sword with
a dozen of them two hours together. I have 'scaped by
miracle. I am eight times thrust through the doublet,
four through the hose, my buckler cut through and
through, my sword hacked like a handsaw, ecce signum!
[*he draws it*] I never dealt better since I was a man: all
would not do. A plague of all cowards! Let them speak.
If they speak more or less than truth, they are villains
and the sons of darkness.

Prince. Speak, sirs, how was it? 170

Gadshill. We four set upon some dozen—

Falstaff. Sixteen at least, my lord.

Gadshill. And bound them.

Peto. No, no, they were not bound.

Falstaff. You rogue, they were bound, every man of
them, or I am a Jew else, an Ebrew Jew.

Gadshill. As we were sharing, some six or seven fresh
men set upon us—

Falstaff. And unbound the rest, and then come in the
other. 180

Prince. What, fought you with them all?

Falstaff. All! I know not what you call all, but if I fought not with fifty of them I am a bunch of radish: if there were not two or three and fifty upon poor old Jack, then am I no two-legged creature.

Prince. Pray God you have not murdered some of them.

Falstaff. Nay, that's past praying for. I have peppered two of them. Two I am sure I have paid, two rogues in 190 buckram suits...I tell thee what, Hal, if I tell thee a lie, spit in my face, call me horse. Thou knowest my old ward: here I lay, and thus I bore my point. Four rogues in buckram let drive at me—

Prince. What, four? thou said'st but two even now.

Falstaff. Four, Hal, I told thee four.

Poins. Ay, ay, he said four.

Falstaff. These four came all afront, and mainly thrust at me. I made me no more ado, but took all their seven points in my target, thus.

200 *Prince.* Seven? why, there were but four even now.

Falstaff. In buckram?

Poins. Ay, four, in buckram suits.

Falstaff. Seven, by these hilts, or I am a villain else.

(*Prince.* Prithee, let him alone, we shall have more anon.

Falstaff. Dost thou hear me, Hal?

Prince. Ay, and mark thee too, Jack.

Falstaff. Do so, for it is worth the listening to. These nine in buckram that I told thee of—

210 (*Prince.* So, two more already.

Falstaff. Their points being broken—

Poins. Down fell their hose.

Falstaff. Began to give me ground: but I followed me close, came in foot and hand, and with a thought, seven of the eleven I paid.

(*Prince*. O monstrous! eleven buckram men grown out of two!

Falstaff. But, as the devil would have it, three mis-begotten knaves in Kendal green came at my back, and let drive at me, for it was so dark, Hal, that thou couldest 220 not see thy hand.

Prince. These lies are like their father that begets them, gross as a mountain, open, palpable. Why, thou clay-brained guts, thou knotty-pated fool, thou whoreson, obscene, greasy tallow-catch—

Falstaff. What, art thou mad? art thou mad? is not the truth the truth?

Prince. Why, how couldst thou know these men in Kendal green, when it was so dark thou couldst not see thy hand? come tell us your reason. What sayest thou 230 to this?

Poins. Come, your reason, Jack, your reason.

Falstaff. What, upon compulsion? 'Zounds, an I were at the strappado, or all the racks in the world, I would not tell you on compulsion. Give you a reason on compulsion! if reasons were as plentiful as black-berries, I would give no man a reason upon com-pulsion, I.

Prince. I'll be no longer guilty of this sin. [*points*] This sanguine coward, this bed-presser, this horseback- 240 breaker, this huge hill of flesh—

Falstaff. 'Sblood, you starveling, you†eel-skin, you dried neat's-tongue, you bull's-pizzle, you stock-fish! O, for breath to utter what is like thee! you tailor's-yard, you sheath, you bow-case, you vile standing tuck—

Prince. Well, breathe awhile, and then to it again, and when thou hast tired thyself in base comparisons, hear me speak but this.

Poins. Mark, Jack.

250 *Prince.* We two saw you four set on four, and bound
them and were masters of their wealth: mark now, how
a plain tale shall put you down. Then did we two set on
you four, and with a word, out-faced you from your
prize, and have it, yea, and can show it you here in the
house: and, Falstaff, you carried your guts away as
nimbly, with as quick dexterity, and roared for mercy,
and still run and roared, as ever I heard bull-calf. What
a slave art thou, to hack thy sword as thou hast done,
and then say it was in fight! What trick, what device,
260 what starting-hole, canst thou now find out, to hide thee
from this open and apparent shame?

Poins. Come, let's hear, Jack—what trick hast thou
now?

Falstaff. [*solemnly*] By the Lord, I knew ye as well as
he that made ye....Why, hear you, my masters—was it
for me to kill the heir-apparent? should I turn upon the
true prince? why, thou knowest I am as valiant as Her-
cules: but beware instinct—the lion will not touch the true
prince. Instinct is a great matter—I was now a coward
270 on instinct. I shall think the better of myself and thee
during my life; I for a valiant lion, and thou for a true
prince...But, by the Lord, lads, I am glad you have the
money. [*he dances*] Hostess, clap to the doors. Watch
to-night, pray to-morrow. Gallants, lads, boys, hearts of
gold, all the titles of good fellowship come to you! What,
shall we be merry? shall we have a play extempore?

Prince. Content—and the argument shall be thy running away.

Falstaff. Ah! no more of that, Hal, an thou lovest me.

HOSTESS enters

280 *Hostess.* O Jesu, my lord the prince,—
Prince. How now, my lady the hostess! what say'st
thou to me?

Hostess. Marry, my lord, there is a nobleman of the court at door would speak with you: he says he comes from your father.

Prince. Give him as much as will make him a royal man, and send him back again to my mother.

Falstaff. What manner of man is he?

Hostess. An old man.

Falstaff. What doth gravity out of his bed at midnight? 290 Shall I give him his answer?

Prince. Prithee, do, Jack.

Falstaff. Faith, and I'll send him packing. [*he goes out*

Prince. Now, sirs! By'r lady, you fought fair, so did you, Peto, so did you, Bardolph. You are lions too, you ran away upon instinct, you will not touch the true prince, no, fie!

Bardolph. Faith, I ran when I saw others run.

Prince. Faith, tell me now in earnest, how came Falstaff's sword so hacked?   300

Peto. Why, he hacked it with his dagger, and said he would swear truth out of England but he would make you believe it was done in fight, and persuaded us to do the like.

Bardolph. Yea, and to tickle our noses with spear-grass to make them bleed, and then to beslubber our garments with it, and swear it was the blood of true men. I did that I did not this seven year before, I blushed to hear his monstrous devices.

Prince. O villain, thou stolest a cup of sack eighteen 310 years ago, and wert taken with the manner, and ever since thou hast blushed extempore. Thou hadst fire and sword on thy side, and yet thou ran'st away. What instinct hadst thou for it?

Bardolph [*thrusts forward his face*]. My lord, do you see these meteors? do you behold these exhalations?

Prince. I do.

Bardolph. What think you they portend?

Prince. Hot livers, and cold purses.

320 *Bardolph.* Choler, my lord, if rightly taken.

Prince. No, if rightly taken, halter.

FALSTAFF *returns*

Here comes lean Jack, here comes bare-bone: how now, my sweet creature of bombast? how long is't ago, Jack, since thou sawest thine own knee?

Falstaff. My own knee! when I was about thy years, Hal, I was not an eagle's talon in the waist, I could have crept into any alderman's thumb-ring: a plague of sighing and grief! it blows a man up like a bladder. There's villainous news abroad. Here was Sir John Bracy from

330 your father: you must to the court in the morning. That same mad fellow of the north, Percy, and he of Wales, that gave Amaimon the bastinado, and made Lucifer cuckold, and swore the devil his true liegeman upon the cross of a Welsh hook...what a plague call you him?

Poins. Owen Glendower.

Falstaff. Owen, Owen, the same—and his son-in-law, Mortimer, and old Northumberland, and that sprightly Scot of Scots, Douglas, that runs a-horseback up a hill perpendicular—

340 *Prince.* He that rides at high speed, and with his pistol kills a sparrow flying.

Falstaff. You have hit it.

Prince. So did he never the sparrow.

Falstaff. Well, that rascal hath good mettle in him, he will not run.

Prince. Why, what a rascal art thou then, to praise him so for running.

Falstaff. A-horseback, ye cuckoo, but afoot he will not budge a foot.

Prince. Yes, Jack, upon instinct.   350

Falstaff. I grant ye, upon instinct...Well, he is there too, and one Mordake, and a thousand blue-caps more. Worcester is stolen away to-night, thy father's beard is turned white with the news, you may buy land now as cheap as stinking mackerel.

Prince. Why then, it is like, if there come a hot June, and this civil buffeting hold, we shall buy maidenheads as they buy hob-nails, by the hundreds.

Falstaff. By the mass, lad, thou sayest true, it is like we shall have good trading that way...But, tell me, Hal, 360 art not thou horrible afeard? thou being heir-apparent, could the world pick thee out three such enemies again, as that fiend Douglas, that spirit Percy, and that devil Glendower? art thou not horribly afraid? doth not thy blood thrill at it?

Prince. Not a whit, i'faith, I lack some of thy instinct.

Falstaff. Well, thou wilt be horribly chid to-morrow when thou comest to thy father. If thou love me, practise an answer.

Prince. Do thou stand for my father, and examine me 370 upon the particulars of my life.

Falstaff. Shall I? content. This chair shall be my state, this dagger my sceptre, and this cushion my crown.

Prince. Thy state is taken for a joined-stool, thy golden sceptre for a leaden dagger, and thy precious rich crown for a pitiful bald crown!

Falstaff. Well, an the fire of grace be not quite out of thee, now shalt thou be moved. Give me a cup of sack to make my eyes look red, that it may be thought I have wept—for I must speak in passion, and I will do it in 380 King Cambyses' vein.

Prince [*bows*]. Well, here is my leg.

Falstaff. And here is my speech....Stand aside, nobility.

Hostess. O Jesu, this is excellent sport, i'faith.

Falstaff. Weep not, sweet queen, for trickling tears
are vain.

Hostess. O, the father, how he holds his countenance!

Falstaff. For God's sake, lords, convey my tristful
queen,

For tears do stop the flood-gates of her eyes.

Hostess. O Jesu, he doth it as like one of these harlotry
390 players as ever I see!

Falstaff. Peace, good pint-pot, peace, good tickle-
brain.

Harry, I do not only marvel where thou spendest thy
time, but also how thou art accompanied: for though the
camomile, the more it is trodden on the faster it grows,
yet youth, the more it is wasted the sooner it wears...That
thou art my son, I have partly thy mother's word, partly
my own opinion, but chiefly a villainous trick of thine
eye, and a foolish hanging of thy nether lip, that doth
400 warrant me. If then thou be son to me, here lies the
point—why, being son to me, art thou so pointed at?
Shall the blessed sun of heaven prove a micher and eat
blackberries? a question not to be asked. Shall the son
of England prove a thief and take purses? a question to
be asked. There is a thing, Harry, which thou hast often
heard of, and it is known to many in our land by the
name of pitch: this pitch (as ancient writers do report)
doth defile, so doth the company thou keepest: for,
Harry, now I do not speak to thee in drink, but in tears;
410 not in pleasure, but in passion; not in words only, but in
woes also: and yet there is a virtuous man whom I have
often noted in thy company, but I know not his name

Prince. What manner of man, an it like your majesty?

Falstaff. A goodly portly man, i'faith, and a corpulent,
of a cheerful look, a pleasing eye, and a most noble

carriage, and as I think his age some fifty, or by'r lady
inclining to threescore. And now I remember me, his
name is Falstaff. If that man should be lewdly given,
he deceiveth me; for, Harry, I see virtue in his looks...If
then the tree may be known by the fruit, as the fruit by 420
the tree, then, peremptorily I speak it, there is virtue in
that Falstaff—him keep with, the rest banish. And tell
me now, thou naughty varlet, tell me, where hast thou
been this month?

Prince. Dost thou speak like a king? Do thou stand
for me, and I'll play my father.

Falstaff. Depose me? if thou dost it half so gravely,
so majestically, both in word and matter, hang me up by
the heels for a rabbit-sucker, or a poulter's hare.

[*they change places*

Prince. Well, here I am set.   430

Falstaff. And here I stand—judge, my masters.

Prince. Now, Harry, whence come you?

Falstaff. My noble lord, from Eastcheap.

Prince. The complaints I hear of thee are grievous.

Falstaff. 'Sblood, my lord, they are false: [*aside*]
nay, I'll tickle ye for a young prince, i'faith.

Prince. Swearest thou, ungracious boy? henceforth
ne'er look on me. Thou art violently carried away from
grace, there is a devil haunts thee in the likeness of an
old fat man, a tun of man is thy companion: why dost 440
thou converse with that trunk of humours, that bolting-
hutch of beastliness, that swollen parcel of dropsies, that
huge bombard of sack, that stuffed cloak-bag of guts,
that roasted Manningtree ox with the pudding in his
belly, that reverend vice, that grey iniquity, that father
ruffian, that vanity in years? Wherein is he good, but to
taste sack and drink it? wherein neat and cleanly, but to
carve a capon and eat it? wherein cunning, but in craft?

wherein crafty, but in villainy? wherein villainous, but
450 in all things? wherein worthy, but in nothing?

Falstaff. I would your grace would take me with you.
Whom means your grace?

Prince. That villainous abominable misleader of
youth, Falstaff, that old white-bearded Satan.

Falstaff. My lord, the man I know.

Prince. I know thou dost.

Falstaff. But to say I know more harm in him than in
myself, were to say more than I know: that he is old,
the more the pity, his white hairs do witness it, but that
460 he is, saving your reverence, a whoremaster, that I
utterly deny: if sack and sugar be a fault, God help the
wicked! if to be old and merry be a sin, then many an
old host that I know is damned: if to be fat be to be
hated, then Pharaoh's lean kine are to be loved. No,
my good lord—banish Peto, banish Bardolph, banish
Poins, but for sweet Jack Falstaff, kind Jack Falstaff,
true Jack Falstaff, valiant Jack Falstaff, and therefore
more valiant being as he is old Jack Falstaff, banish not
him thy Harry's company, banish not him thy Harry's
470 company, banish plump Jack, and banish all the world.

Prince. I do, I will.

'Enter BARDOLPH, running'

Bardolph. O, my lord, my lord, the sheriff with a most
monstrous watch is at the door!

Falstaff. Out, ye rogue! play out the play. I have
much to say in the behalf of that Falstaff.

'Enter the Hostess'

Hostess. O Jesu, my lord, my lord!—

Prince. Heigh, heigh! the devil rides upon a fiddle-
stick. What's the matter?

Hostess. The sheriff and all the watch are at the door, they are come to search the house, shall I let them in? 480

Falstaff. Dost thou hear, Hal? never call a true piece of gold a counterfeit. Thou art essentially made, without seeming so.

Prince. And thou a natural coward, without instinct.

Falstaff. I deny your major, if you will deny the sheriff, so, if not, let him enter. If I become not a cart as well as another man, a plague on my bringing up! I hope I shall as soon be strangled with a halter as another.

Prince. Go, hide thee behind the arras, the rest walk 490 up above. Now, my masters, for a true face and good conscience.

Falstaff. Both which I have had, but their date is out, and therefore I'll hide me.

> [*he does so; all but the Prince and Poins*
> *go out*

Prince. Call in the sheriff.—

'Enter Sheriff and the Carrier'

Now, master sheriff, what is your will with me?

Sheriff. First, pardon me, my lord. A hue and cry Hath followed certain men unto this house.

Prince. What men?

Sheriff. One of them is well known, my gracious lord, 500 A gross fat man.

Carrier. As fat as butter.

Prince. The man, I do assure you, is not here,
For I myself at this time have employed him:
And, sheriff, I will engage my word to thee
That I will by to-morrow dinner-time
Send him to answer thee, or any man,

For any thing he shall be charged withal.
And so let me entreat you leave the house.

510 *Sheriff.* I will, my lord...There are two gentlemen
Have in this robbery lost three hundred marks.

Prince. It may be so: if he have robbed these men,
He shall be answerable—and so, farewell.

Sheriff. Good night, my noble lord.

Prince. I think it is good morrow, is it not?

Sheriff. Indeed, my lord, I think it be two o'clock.

                    [Sheriff and Carrier depart

Prince. This oily rascal is known as well as Paul's...
Go, call him forth.

Poins. [*lifts the arras*] Falstaff! fast asleep behind the
520 arras, and snorting like a horse.

Prince. Hark, how hard he fetches breath. Search
his pockets. ['*He searcheth his pocket, and findeth
certain papers*'] What hast thou found?

Poins. Nothing but papers, my lord.

Prince. Let's see what they be—read them.

Poins. Item, A capon   .   .   .   .   2*s.* 2*d.*
Item, Sauce   .   .   .   .   .   .   4*d.*
Item, Sack, two gallons   .   .   .   5*s.* 8*d.*
Item, Anchovies and sack after supper . 2*s.* 6*d.*
530 Item, Bread   .   .   .   .   .   .   ob.

Prince. O monstrous! but one half-pennyworth of
bread to this intolerable deal of sack! What there is else
keep close, we'll read it at more advantage; there let him
sleep till day. I'll to the court in the morning. We must
all to the wars, and thy place shall be honourable. I'll
procure this fat rogue a charge of foot, and I know his
death will be a march of twelve-score. The money shall
be paid back again with advantage.... Be with me betimes
in the morning, and so good morrow, Poins.

540 *Poins.* Good morrow, good my lord.   *[they go*

[3. 1.]   *Wales. A room in Glendower's house*

'*Enter* HOTSPUR, WORCESTER, LORD MORTIMER,
and OWEN GLENDOWER', *carrying papers*

Mortimer. These promises are fair, the parties sure,
And our induction full of prosperous hope.
Hotspur. Lord Mortimer, and cousin Glendower, will
you sit down? and uncle Worcester: a plague upon it,
I have forgot the map!
Glendower. No, here it is...Sit cousin Percy, sit good
cousin Hotspur, for by that name as oft as Lancaster doth
speak of you, his cheek looks pale, and with a rising sigh
he wisheth you in heaven.   [*they sit*
Hotspur. And you in hell, as oft as he hears Owen 10
Glendower spoke of.
Glendower. I cannot blame him: at my nativity
The front of heaven was full of fiery shapes,
Of burning cressets, and at my birth
The frame and huge foundation of the earth
Shaked like a coward.
Hotspur. Why, so it would have done at the same
season, if your mother's cat had but kittened, though
yourself had never been born.
Glendower. I say the earth did shake, when I was born. 20
Hotspur. And I say the earth was not of my mind,
If you suppose as fearing you it shook.
Glendower. The heavens were all on fire, the earth
         did tremble.
Hotspur. O, then the earth shook to see the heavens
         on fire,
And not in fear of your nativity.
Diseaséd nature oftentimes breaks forth
In strange eruptions; oft the teeming earth

Is with a kind of colic pinched and vexed
By the imprisoning of unruly wind
30 Within her womb, which for enlargement striving
Shakes the old beldam earth, and topples down
Steeples and moss-grown towers. At your birth
Our grandam earth, having this distemperature,
In passion shook.

   Glendower.   Cousin, of many men
I do not bear these crossings. Give me leave
To tell you once again that at my birth
The front of heaven was full of fiery shapes,
The goats ran from the mountains, and the herds
Were strangely clamorous to the frighted fields.
40 These signs have marked me extraordinary,
And all the courses of my life do show
I am not in the roll of common men...
Where is he living, clipped in with the sea
That chides the banks of England, Scotland, Wales,
Which calls me pupil or hath read to me?
And bring him out that is but woman's son
Can trace me in the tedious ways of art,
And hold me pace in deep experiments.

   Hotspur. I think there's no man speaks better Welsh:
50 I'll to dinner.   [*he rises*

   (*Mortimer.* Peace, cousin Percy, you will make
      him mad.

   Glendower. I can call spirits from the vasty deep.

   Hotspur. Why, so can I, or so can any man,
But will they come when you do call for them?

   Glendower. Why, I can teach you, cousin, to
      command the devil.

   Hotspur. And I can teach thee, coz, to shame the devil,
By telling truth. Tell truth and shame the devil...
If thou have power to raise him, bring him hither,

And I'll be sworn I have power to shame him hence:
O, while you live, tell truth and shame the devil.　　60

Mortimer. Come, come, no more of this unprofitable
　　chat.

Glendower. Three times hath Henry Bolingbroke
　　made head
Against my power—thrice from the banks of Wye
And sandy-bottomed Severn have I sent him
Bootless home and weather-beaten back.

Hotspur. Home without boots, and in foul weather too!
How 'scapes he agues, in the devil's name?

Glendower. Come, here's the map, shall we divide
　　our right,
According to our threefold order ta'en?

　　　　　　　　　　[*the map is spread upon the table*

Mortimer. The archdeacon hath divided it　　70
Into three limits, very equally:
England, from Trent to Severn hitherto,
By south and east is to my part assigned:
All westward, Wales beyond the Severn shore,
And all the fertile land within that bound,
To Owen Glendower: and, dear coz, to you
The remnant northward, lying off from Trent.
And our indentures tripartite are drawn,
Which being sealéd interchangeably,
(A business that this night may execute)　　80
To-morrow, cousin Percy, you and I
And my good Lord of Worcester will set forth
To meet your father and the Scottish power,
As is appointed us, at Shrewsbury.
My father Glendower is not ready yet,
Nor shall we need his help these fourteen days.
[*to Glendower*] Within that space you may have
　　drawn together

Your tenants, friends, and neighbouring gentlemen.

Glendower. A shorter time shall send me to you, lords,
90 And in my conduct shall your ladies come,
From whom you now must steal and take no leave,
For there will be a world of water shed
Upon the parting of your wives and you.

Hotspur [*studying the map*]. Methinks, my moiety, north from Burton here,
In quantity equals not one of yours.
See how this river comes me cranking in,
And cuts me from the best of all my land
A huge half-moon, a monstrous cantle out.
I'll have the current in this place dammed up,
100 And here the smug and silver Trent shall run
In a new channel, fair and evenly.
It shall not wind with such a deep indent,
To rob me of so rich a bottom here.

Glendower. Not wind? it shall, it must—you see, it doth.

Mortimer. Yea, but
Mark how he bears his course, and runs me up
With like advantage on the other side,
Gelding the opposéd continent as much
As on the other side it takes from you.

110 *Worcester.* Yea, but a little charge will trench him here,
And on this north side win this cape of land,
And then he runs straight and even.

Hotspur. I'll have it so, a little charge will do it.

Glendower. I'll not have it altered.

Hotspur.   Will not you?

Glendower. No, nor you shall not.

Hotspur.   Who shall say me nay?

Glendower. Why, that will I.

Hotspur. Let me not understand you then, speak it in Welsh.

Glendower. I can speak English, lord, as well as you,
For I was trained up in the English court,   120
Where being but young I framéd to the harp
Many an English ditty, lovely well,
And gave the tongue a helpful ornament,
A virtue that was never seen in you.
  Hotspur. Marry,
And I am glad of it with all my heart!
I had rather be a kitten and cry mew
Than one of these same metre ballad-mongers—
I had rather hear a brazen canstick turned,
Or a dry wheel grate on the axle-tree,   130
And that would set my teeth nothing on edge,
Nothing so much as mincing poetry—
'Tis like the forced gait of a shuffling nag.
  Glendower. Come, you shall have Trent turned.
  Hotspur. I do not care, I'll give thrice so much land
To any well-deserving friend:
But in the way of bargain, mark ye me,
I'll cavil on the ninth part of a hair.
Are the indentures drawn? shall we be gone?
  Glendower. The moon shines fair, you may away   140
      by night:
I'll haste the writer, and withal
Break with your wives of your departure hence.
I am afraid my daughter will run mad,
So much she doteth on her Mortimer.   [*he goes out*
  Mortimer. Fie, cousin Percy! how you cross
      my father!
  Hotspur. I cannot choose. Sometime he angers me
With telling me of the moldwarp and the ant,
Of the dreamer Merlin and his prophecies,
And of a dragon and a finless fish,
A clip-winged griffin and a moulten raven,   150

A couching lion and a ramping cat,
And such a deal of skimble-skamble stuff
As puts me from my faith. I tell you what—
He held me last night at least nine hours
In reckoning up the several devils' names
That were his lackeys. I cried, 'hum', and 'well,
　　go to',
But marked him not a word. O, he is as tedious
As a tired horse, a railing wife,
Worse than a smoky house—I had rather live
160 With cheese and garlic in a windmill, far,
Than feed on cates and have him talk to me
In any summer house in Christendom.
　　Mortimer. In faith, he is a worthy gentleman,
Exceedingly well read, and profited
In strange concealments, valiant as a lion,
And wondrous affable, and as bountiful
As mines of India...Shall I tell you, cousin?
He holds your temper in a high respect,
And curbs himself even of his natural scope,
170 When you come 'cross his humour, faith, he does.
I warrant you, that man is not alive
Might so have tempted him as you have done,
Without the taste of danger and reproof—
But do not use it oft, let me entreat you.
　　Worcester. In faith, my lord, you are too wilful blame,
And since your coming hither have done enough
To put him quite beside his patience.
You must needs learn, lord, to amend this fault.
Though sometimes it show greatness, courage, blood—
180 And that's the dearest grace it renders you—
Yet oftentimes it doth present harsh rage,
Defect of manners, want of government,
Pride, haughtiness, opinion, and disdain,

The least of which haunting a nobleman
Loseth men's hearts, and leaves behind a stain
Upon the beauty of all parts besides,
Beguiling them of commendation.

Hotspur. Well, I am schooled—good manners be
    your speed!
Here come our wives, and let us take our leave.

    '*Enter* GLENDOWER *with the* LADIES'

Mortimer. This is the deadly spite that angers me—   **190**
My wife can speak no English, I no Welsh.

Glendower. My daughter weeps, she'll not part
    with you,
She'll be a soldier too, she'll to the wars.

Mortimer. Good father, tell her that she and my
    aunt Percy
Shall follow in your conduct speedily.

    '*Glendower speaks to her in Welsh, and she*
        answers him in the same'

Glendower. She is desperate here, a peevish self-willed
harlotry, one that no persuasion can do good upon.

    She turns to Mortimer and '*speaks in Welsh*'

Mortimer. I understand thy looks. That pretty Welsh
Which thou pourest down from these swelling heavens
I am too perfect in, and but for shame   **200**
In such a parley should I answer thee.

    '*The lady*' *speaks* '*again in Welsh*'

I understand thy kisses and thou mine,
And that's a feeling disputation,
But I will never be a truant, love,
Till I have learned thy language, for thy tongue
Makes Welsh as sweet as ditties highly penned,
Sung by a fair queen in a summer's bower,
With ravishing division, to her lute.

Glendower. Nay, if you melt, then will she run mad.

'*The lady speaks again in Welsh*'

210   *Mortimer.* O, I am ignorance itself in this!

Glendower. She bids you on the wanton rushes lay
    you down,
And rest your gentle head upon her lap,
And she will sing the song that pleaseth you,
And on your eyelids crown the god of sleep,
Charming your blood with pleasing heaviness,
Making such difference 'twixt wake and sleep
As is the difference betwixt day and night,
The hour before the heavenly-harnessed team
Begins his golden progress in the east.

220   *Mortimer.* With all my heart I'll sit and hear her sing,
By that time will our book, I think, be drawn.

Glendower. Do so,   [*Mortimer sits, and she with him*
And those musicians that shall play to you
Hang in the air a thousand leagues from hence,
And straight they shall be here. Sit and attend.

Hotspur. Come, Kate, thou art perfect in lying down.
Come, quick, quick, that I may lay my head in thy lap.

Lady Percy. Go, ye giddy goose.

[*he catches her by the wrist; she struggles; they
sit upon the rushes, he with his head in her lap;*
'*the music plays*'

Hotspur. Now I perceive the devil understands Welsh,
230 And 'tis no marvel, he is so humorous.
By'r lady, he is a good musician.

Lady Percy. Then should you be nothing but musical,
for you are altogether governed by humours. Lie still,
ye thief, and hear the lady sing in Welsh.

Hotspur. I had rather hear Lady, my brach, howl in
Irish.

Lady Percy. Wouldst thou have thy head broken?

Hotspur. No.

Lady Percy. Then be still.

Hotspur. Neither—'tis a woman's fault.   240

Lady Percy. Now God help thee!

Hotspur. To the Welsh lady's bed.

Lady Percy. What's that?

Hotspur. Peace! she sings.

['*Here the lady sings a Welsh song*'

Hotspur. Come, Kate, I'll have your song too.

Lady Percy. Not mine, in good sooth.

Hotspur. Not yours, in good sooth! Heart! you swear
like a comfit-maker's wife—'not you, in good sooth',
and 'as true as I live', and 'as God shall mend me', and
'as sure as day'—   250
And givest such sarcenet surety for thy oaths,
As if thou never walk'st further than Finsbury.
Swear me, Kate, like a lady as thou art,
A good mouth-filling oath, and leave 'in sooth',
And such protest of pepper-gingerbread,
To velvet-guards and Sunday citizens.
Come, sing.

Lady Percy. I will not sing.

Hotspur. 'Tis the next way to turn tailor, or be red-
breast teacher. An the indentures be drawn, I'll away 260
within these two hours—and so come in when ye will.

[*he goes*

Glendower. Come, come, Lord Mortimer, you are
      as slow
As hot Lord Percy is on fire to go.
By this our book is drawn. We'll but seal,
And then to horse immediately.

Mortimer.   With all my heart.

[*they go*

[3. 2.]   *London. A room in the palace*

'*The* KING, PRINCE *of* WALES, *and others*'

King. Lords, give us leave. The Prince of Wales and I
Must have some private conference. But be near
    at hand,
For we shall presently have need of you....
                                        [*Lords withdraw*
I know not whether God will have it so
For some displeasing service I have done,
That, in his secret doom, out of my blood
He'll breed revengement and a scourge for me;
But thou dost in thy passages of life
Make me believe that thou art only marked
10 For the hot vengeance and the rod of heaven,
To punish my mistreadings. Tell me else,
Could such inordinate and low desires,
Such poor, such bare, such lewd, such mean attempts,
Such barren pleasures, rude society,
As thou art matched withal, and grafted to,
Accompany the greatness of thy blood,
And hold their level with thy princely heart?
    Prince. So please your majesty, I would I could
Quit all offences with as clear excuse
20 As well as I am doubtless I can purge
Myself of many I am charged withal.
Yet such extenuation let me beg,
As, in reproof of many tales devised,
Which oft the ear of greatness needs must hear,
By smiling pickthanks and base newsmongers,
I may for some things true, wherein my youth
Hath faulty wand'red and irregular,
Find pardon on my true submission.

King. God pardon thee! yet let me wonder, Harry,
At thy affections, which do hold a wing   30
Quite from the flight of all thy ancestors.
Thy place in council thou hast rudely lost,
Which by thy younger brother is supplied,
And art almost an alien to the hearts
Of all the court and princes of my blood.
The hope and expectation of thy time
Is ruined, and the soul of every man
Prophetically do forethink thy fall...
Had I so lavish of my presence been,
So common-hackneyed in the eyes of men,   40
So stale and cheap to vulgar company,
Opinion, that did help me to the crown,
Had still kept loyal to possession,
And left me in reputeless banishment,
A fellow of no mark nor likelihood.
By being seldom seen, I could not stir
But like a comet I was wond'red at;
That men would tell their children 'This is he!'
Others would say 'Where? which is Bolingbroke?'
And then I stole all courtesy from heaven,   50
And dressed myself in such humility
That I did pluck allegiance from men's hearts,
Loud shouts and salutations from their mouths,
Even in the presence of the crownéd king....
Thus did I keep my person fresh and new,
My presence like a robe pontifical,
Ne'er seen but wond'red at, and so my state,
Seldom but sumptuous, showéd like a feast,
And wan by rareness such solemnity....
The skipping king, he ambled up and down   60
With shallow jesters and rash bavin wits,
Soon kindled and soon burnt, carded his state.

Mingled his royalty with cap'ring fools,
Had his great name profanéd with their scorns,
And gave his countenance, against his name,
To laugh at gibing boys, and stand the push
Of every beardless vain comparative,
Grew a companion to the common streets,
Enfeoffed himself to popularity,
70 That, being daily swallowed by men's eyes,
They surfeited with honey and began
To loathe the taste of sweetness, whereof a little
More than a little is by much too much.
So when he had occasion to be seen,
He was but as the cuckoo is in June,
Heard, not regarded; seen, but with such eyes
As, sick and blunted with community,
Afford no extraordinary gaze,
Such as is bent on sun-like majesty,
80 When it shines seldom in admiring eyes;
But rather drowzed and hung their eyelids down,
Slept in his face, and rend'red such aspect
As cloudy men use to their adversaries,
Being with his presence glutted, gorged, and full.
And in that very line, Harry, standest thou,
For thou hast lost thy princely privilege
With vile participation. Not an eye
But is a-weary of thy common sight,
Save mine, which hath desired to see thee more,
90 Which now doth that I would not have it do,
Make blind itself with foolish tenderness.
    Prince. I shall hereafter, my thrice gracious lord,
Be more myself.
    King.   For all the world
As thou art to this hour was Richard then,
When I from France set foot at Ravenspurgh,

And even as I was then is Percy now.
Now by my sceptre and my soul to boot,
He hath more worthy interest to the state
Than thou the shadow of succession.
For of no right, nor colour like to right,   100
He doth fill fields with harness in the realm,
Turns head against the lion's arméd jaws,
And, being no more in debt to years than thou,
Leads ancient lords and reverend bishops on
To bloody battles and to bruising arms.
What never-dying honour hath he got
Against renownéd Douglas! whose high deeds,
Whose hot incursions and great name in arms
Holds from all soldiers chief majority,
And military title capital,   110
Through all the kingdoms that acknowledge Christ.
Thrice hath this Hotspur, Mars in swathling clothes,
This infant warrior, in his enterprizes
Discomfited great Douglas, ta'en him once,
Enlargéd him and made a friend of him,
To fill the mouth of deep defiance up,
And shake the peace and safety of our throne.
And what say you to this? Percy, Northumberland,
The Archbishop's grace of York, Douglas, Mortimer,
Capitulate against us and are up....   120
But wherefore do I tell these news to thee?
Why, Harry, do I tell thee of my foes,
Which art my nearest and dearest enemy?
Thou that art like enough, through vassal fear,
Base inclination and the start of spleen,
To fight against me under Percy's pay,
To dog his heels and curtsy at his frowns,
To show how much thou art degenerate.

   Prince. Do not think so, you shall not find it so;

130 And God forgive them that so much have swayed
Your majesty's good thoughts away from me!
I will redeem all this on Percy's head,
And in the closing of some glorious day
Be bold to tell you that I am your son,
When I will wear a garment all of blood,
And stain my favours in a bloody mask,
Which washed away shall scour my shame with it.
And that shall be the day, whene'er it lights,
That this same child of honour and renown,
140 This gallant Hotspur, this all-praiséd knight,
And your unthought-of Harry chance to meet.
For every honour sitting on his helm
Would they were multitudes, and on my head
My shames redoubled! for the time will come,
That I shall make this northern youth exchange
His glorious deeds for my indignities.
Percy is but my factor, good my lord,
To engross up glorious deeds on my behalf,
And I will call him to so strict account
150 That he shall render every glory up,
151 Yea, even the slightest worship of his time,
Or I will tear the reckoning from his heart....
This, in the name of God, I promise here,
The which if He be pleased I shall perform,
I do beseech your majesty may salve
The long-grown wounds of my intemperature:
If not, the end of life cancels all bands,
And I will die a hundred thousand deaths.158
Ere break the smallest parcel of this vow.
160   *King.* A hundred thousand rebels die in this—
Thou shalt have charge and sovereign trust herein.
               Enter BLUNT
How now, good Blunt? thy looks are full of speed.

Blunt. So hath the business that I come to speak of.
Lord Mortimer of Scotland hath sent word
That Douglas and the English rebels met
The eleventh of this month at Shrewsbury.
A mighty and a fearful head they are,
If promises be kept on every hand,
As ever off'red foul play in a state.

King. The Earl of Westmoreland set forth to-day,   170
With him my son, Lord John of Lancaster,
For this advertisement is five days old.
On Wednesday next, Harry, you shall set forward,
On Thursday, we ourselves will march: our meeting
Is Bridgenorth, and, Harry, you shall march
Through Gloucestershire; by which account,
Our business valuéd, some twelve days hence
Our general forces at Bridgenorth shall meet.
Our hands are full of business, let's away,
Advantage feeds him fat while men delay.   [*they go* 180

[3. 3.]   *A room at the Boar's Head Tavern
in Eastcheap; early morning*

Enter FALSTAFF (*a truncheon hanging at his girdle*)
and BARDOLPH

Falstaff. Bardolph, am I not fallen away vilely since
this last action? do I not bate? do I not dwindle? Why,
my skin hangs about me like an old lady's loose gown, I
am withered like an old apple-John. Well, I'll repent,
and that suddenly, while I am in some liking. I shall be
out of heart shortly, and then I shall have no strength
to repent. An I have not forgotten what the inside of a
church is made of, I am a peppercorn, a brewer's horse.
The inside of a church! Company, villainous company,
hath been the spoil of me.   10

Bardolph. Sir John, you are so fretful you cannot live long.

Falstaff. Why, there is it: come, sing me a bawdy song, make me merry....I was as virtuously given as a gentleman need to be; virtuous enough, swore little, diced not above seven times a week, went to a bawdy-house not above once in a quarter of an hour, paid money that I borrowed three or four times, lived well, and in good compass: and now I live out of all order, out of all
20 compass.

Bardolph. Why, you are so fat, Sir John, that you must needs be out of all compass; out of all reasonable compass, Sir John.

Falstaff. Do thou amend thy face, and I'll amend my life: thou art our admiral, thou bearest the lantern in the poop, but 'tis in the nose of thee: thou art the Knight of the Burning Lamp.

Bardolph. Why, Sir John, my face does you no harm.

Falstaff. No, I'll be sworn—I make as good use of it
30 as many a man doth of a death's-head or a memento mori. I never see thy face but I think upon hell-fire, and Dives that lived in purple; for there he is in his robes, burning, burning. If thou wert any way given to virtue, I would swear by thy face; my oath should be, 'by this fire, that's God's angel'. But thou art altogether given over; and wert indeed, but for the light in thy face, the son of utter darkness. When thou ran'st up Gad's Hill in the night to catch my horse, if I did not think thou hadst been an ignis fatuus or a ball of wildfire, there's no
40 purchase in money. O, thou art a perpetual triumph, an everlasting bonfire-light! Thou hast saved me a thousand marks in links and torches, walking with thee in the night betwixt tavern and tavern: but the sack that thou hast drunk me would have bought me lights as good

cheap at the dearest chandler's in Europe. I have maintained that salamander of yours with fire any time this
two and thirty years, God reward me for it!

Bardolph. 'Sblood, I would my face were in your
belly!

Falstaff. God-a-mercy! so should I be sure to be heart- 50
burned.

HOSTESS *enters*

How now, Dame Partlet the hen! have you inquired yet
who picked my pocket?

Hostess. Why, Sir John, what do you think, Sir
John? do you think I keep thieves in my house? I have
searched, I have inquired, so has my husband, man by
man, boy by boy, servant by servant. The tithe of a hair
was never lost in my house before.

Falstaff. Ye lie, hostess—Bardolph was shaved, and
lost many a hair, and I'll be sworn my pocket was 60
picked: go to, you are a woman, go.

Hostess. Who, I? no, I defy thee: God's light, I was
never called so in mine own house before.

Falstaff. Go to, I know you well enough.

Hostess. No, Sir John, you do not know me, Sir John.
I know you, Sir John. You owe me money, Sir John,
and now you pick a quarrel to beguile me of it. I bought
you a dozen of shirts to your back.

Falstaff. Dowlas, filthy dowlas. I have given them
away to bakers' wives. They have made bolters of 70
them.

Hostess. Now, as I am a true woman, holland of eight
shillings an ell! You owe money here besides, Sir John,
for your diet and by-drinkings, and money lent you,
four and twenty pound.

Falstaff. He had his part of it, let him pay.

Hostess. He? alas, he is poor, he hath nothing.

Falstaff. How! poor? look upon his face. What call you rich? let them coin his nose, let them coin his cheeks.
80 I'll not pay a denier! What, will you make a younker of me? shall I not take mine ease in mine inn but I shall have my pocket picked? I have lost a seal-ring of my grandfather's worth forty mark.

Hostess. O Jesu! I have heard the prince tell him, I know not how oft, that that ring was copper.

Falstaff. How! the prince is a Jack, a sneak-up. 'Sblood, an he were here, I would cudgel him like a dog, if he would say so.

'*Enter the* PRINCE' *and* POINS, '*marching*', *single file;* '*FALSTAFF meets*' *them* '*playing upon his truncheon like a fife.*' *They march together round the room;* BARDOLPH *falling in beside* POINS.

Falstaff. How now, lad! is the wind in that door, 90 i'faith? must we all march?

Bardolph. Yea, two and two, Newgate fashion.

Hostess. My lord, I pray you, hear me.

Prince. What say'st thou, Mistress Quickly? How doth thy husband? I love him well, he is an honest man.

Hostess. Good my lord, hear me.

Falstaff. Prithee, let her alone, and list to me.

Prince. What say'st thou, Jack?

Falstaff. The other night I fell asleep here, behind the arras, and had my pocket picked. This house is turned 100 bawdy-house, they pick pockets.

Prince. What didst thou lose, Jack?

Falstaff. Wilt thou believe me, Hal? three or four bonds of forty pound a-piece, and a seal-ring of my grandfather's.

Prince. A trifle, some eight-penny matter.

Hostess. So I told him, my lord, and I said I heard your grace say so: and, my lord, he speaks most vilely of you, like a foul-mouthed man as he is, and said he would cudgel you.

Prince. What! he did not?   110

Hostess. There's neither faith, truth, nor womanhood in me else.

Falstaff. There's no more faith in thee than in a stewed prune, nor no more truth in thee than in a drawn fox—and for womanhood, Maid Marian may be the deputy's wife of the ward to thee. Go, you thing, go.

Hostess. Say, what thing? what thing?

Falstaff. What thing? why, a thing to thank God on.

Hostess. I am nothing to thank God on, I would thou shouldst know it. I am an honest man's wife, and setting 120 thy knighthood aside, thou art a knave to call me so.

Falstaff. Setting thy womanhood aside, thou art a beast to say otherwise.

Hostess. Say, what beast, thou knave, thou?

Falstaff. What beast? why, an otter.

Prince. An otter, Sir John! why an otter?

Falstaff. Why? she's neither fish nor flesh, a man knows not where to have her.

Hostess. Thou art an unjust man in saying so, thou or any man knows where to have me, thou knave, thou! 130

Prince. Thou say'st true, hostess, and he slanders thee most grossly.

Hostess. So he doth you, my lord, and said this other day you ought him a thousand pound.

Prince. Sirrah, do I owe you a thousand pound?

Falstaff. A thousand pound, Hal? a million. Thy love is worth a million, thou owest me thy love.

Hostess. Nay, my lord, he called you Jack, and said he would cudgel you.

140 *Falstaff.* Did I, Bardolph?

Bardolph. Indeed, Sir John, you said so.

Falstaff. Yea, if he said my ring was copper.

Prince. I say 'tis copper. Darest thou be as good as thy word now?

Falstaff. Why, Hal, thou knowest, as thou art but man I dare, but as thou art prince I fear thee as I fear the roaring of the lion's whelp.

Prince. And why not as the lion?

Falstaff. The king himself is to be feared as the lion.
150 Dost thou think I'll fear thee as I fear thy father? nay, an I do, I pray God my girdle break.

Prince. O, if it should, how would thy guts fall about thy knees! But, sirrah, there's no room for faith, truth, nor honesty, in this bosom of thine—it is all filled up with guts and midriff. Charge an honest woman with picking thy pocket! why, thou whoreson, impudent, embossed rascal, if there were anything in thy pocket but tavern-reckonings, memorandums of bawdy-houses, and one poor pennyworth of sugar-candy to make thee long-
160 winded—if thy pocket were enriched with any other injuries but these, I am a villain. And yet you will stand to it, you will not pocket up wrong! Art thou not ashamed?

Falstaff. Dost thou hear, Hal? thou knowest in the state of innocency Adam fell, and what should poor Jack Falstaff do in the days of villainy? Thou seest I have more flesh than another man, and therefore more frailty...You confess then, you picked my pocket?

Prince. It appears so by the story.
170 *Falstaff.* Hostess, I forgive thee. Go, make ready breakfast, love thy husband, look to thy servants, cherish thy guests. Thou shalt find me tractable to any honest reason, thou seest I am pacified still. Nay, prithee, be

gone. [*Hostess goes*] Now Hal, to the news at court: for
the robbery, lad, how is that answered?

Prince. O, my sweet beef, I must still be good angel
to thee. The money is paid back again.

Falstaff. O, I do not like that paying back, 'tis a
double labour.

Prince. I am good friends with my father, and may 180
do any thing.

Falstaff. Rob me the exchequer the first thing thou
doest, and do it with unwashed hands too.

Bardolph. Do, my lord.

Prince. I have procured thee, Jack, a charge of foot.

Falstaff. I would it had been of horse. Where shall I
find one that can steal well? O for a fine thief, of the age
of two and twenty or thereabouts! I am heinously unprovided. Well, God be thanked for these rebels, they
offend none but the virtuous; I laud them, I praise them. 190

Prince. Bardolph—

Bardolph. My lord.

Prince. Go bear this letter to Lord John of Lancaster,
to my brother John, this to my Lord of Westmoreland.
Go, Poins, to horse, to horse, for thou and I
Have thirty miles to ride yet ere dinner time.
Jack, meet me to-morrow in the Temple hall
at two o'clock in the afternoon.
There shalt thou know thy charge, and there receive
Money and order for their furniture.   200
The land is burning, Percy stands on high,
And either we or they must lower lie.

                [*he follows Bardolph and Poins*

Falstaff. Rare words! brave world! Hostess, my
      breakfast, come!
O, I could wish this tavern were my drum.   [*he goes*

[4. 1.] *A tent in the rebel camp near Shrewsbury*

Hotspur, Worcester, and Douglas

Hotspur. Well said, my noble Scot! If speaking truth
In this fine age were not thought flattery,
Such attribution should the Douglas have,
As not a soldier of this season's stamp
Should go so general current through the world.
By God, I cannot flatter, I do defy
The tongues of soothers, but a braver place
In my heart's love hath no man than yourself.
Nay, task me to my word, approve me, lord.
10 *Douglas.* Thou art the king of honour.
No man so potent breathes upon the ground
But I will beard him.
    Hotspur.   Do so, and 'tis well.

         '*Enter one with letters*'

What letters hast thou there?—I can but thank you.
  Messenger. These letters come from your father—
  Hotspur. Letters from him! why comes he not himself?
  Messenger. He cannot come, my lord, he is
      grievous sick.
  Hotspur. 'Zounds! how has he the leisure to be sick
In such a justling time? Who leads his power?
Under whose government come they along?
20 *Messenger.* His letters bear his mind, not I, my lord.
  Worcester. I prithee, tell me, doth he keep his bed?
  Messenger. He did, my lord, four days ere I set forth,
And at the time of my departure thence
He was much feared by his physicians.
  Worcester. I would the state of time had first
      been whole,
Ere he by sickness had been visited.
His health was never better worth than now.

Hotspur. Sick now! droop now! this sickness doth infect
The very life-blood of our enterprise,
'Tis catching hither, even to our camp.   30
He writes me here that inward sickness—
And that his friends by deputation could not
So soon be drawn, nor did he think it meet
To lay so dangerous and dear a trust
On any soul removed but on his own.
Yet doth he give us bold advertisement
That with our small conjunction we should on,
To see how fortune is disposed to us.
For as he writes there is no quailing now,
Because the king is certainly possessed   40
Of all our purposes. What say you to it?
Worcester. Your father's sickness is a maim to us.
Hotspur. A perilous gash, a very limb lopped off—
And yet, in faith, it is not. His present want
Seems more than we shall find it: were it good
To set the exact wealth of all our states
All at one cast? to set so rich a main
On the nice hazard of one doubtful hour?
It were not good, for therein should we read
The very bottom and the soul of hope,   50
The very list, the very utmost bound
Of all our fortunes.
   Douglas.   Faith, and so we should.
Where now remains a sweet reversion,
We may boldly spend upon the hope of what
Is to come in.
A comfort of retirement lives in this.
Hotspur. A rendezvous, a home to fly unto,
If that the devil and mischance look big
Upon the maidenhead of our affairs.
Worcester. But yet I would your father had been here... 60

The quality and hair of our attempt
Brooks no division. It will be thought,
By some that know not why he is away,
That wisdom, loyalty, and mere dislike
Of our proceedings kept the earl from hence.
And think how such an apprehension
May turn the tide of fearful faction,
And breed a kind of question in our cause:
For well you know we of the off'ring side
70 Must keep aloof from strict arbitrement,
And stop all sight-holes, every loop from whence
The eye of reason may pry in upon us.
This absence of your father's draws a curtain
That shows the ignorant a kind of fear
Before not dreamt of.
   Hotspur.   You strain too far.
I rather of his absence make this use—
It lends a lustre and more great opinion,
A larger dare to our great enterprise,
Than if the earl were here; for men must think,
80 If we without his help can make a head
To push against a kingdom, with his help
We shall o'erturn it topsy-turvy down.
Yet all goes well, yet all our joints are whole.
   Douglas. As heart can think. There is not such a word
Spoke of in Scotland as this term of fear.

    Sir Richard Vernon *enters the tent*

   Hotspur. My cousin Vernon! welcome, by my soul.
   Vernon. Pray God, my news be worth a welcome, lord.
The Earl of Westmoreland, seven thousand strong,
Is marching hitherwards, with him Prince John.
90 *Hotspur.* No harm—what more?
   Vernon.   And further, I have learned,

The king himself in person is set forth,
Or hitherwards intended speedily,
With strong and mighty preparation.

Hotspur. He shall be welcome too: where is his son,
The nimble-footed madcap Prince of Wales,
And his comrades, that daffed the world aside,
And bid it pass?

Vernon.   All furnished, all in arms;
†All plumed like estridges that wing the wind,
Baited like eagles having lately bathed,
Glittering in golden coats like images,   100
As full of spirit as the month of May,
And gorgeous as the sun at midsummer,
Wanton as youthful goats, wild as young bulls.
I saw young Harry with his beaver on,
His cushes on his thighs, gallantly armed,
Rise from the ground like feathered Mercury,
And vaulted with such ease into his seat,
As if an angel dropped down from the clouds,
To turn and wind a fiery Pegasus,
And witch the world with noble horsemanship.   110

Hotspur. No more, no more! worse than the sun
          in March,
This praise doth nourish agues. Let them come,
They come like sacrifices in their trim,
And to the fire-eyed maid of smoky war
All hot and bleeding will we offer them.
The mailéd Mars shall on his altar sit,
Up to the ears in blood. I am on fire
To hear this rich reprisal is so nigh,
And yet not ours...Come, let me taste my horse,
Who is to bear me like a thunderbolt   120
Against the bosom of the Prince of Wales.
Harry to Harry shall, hot horse to horse,

Meet and ne'er part till one drop down a corse.
O, that Glendower were come!

Vernon.   There is more news.
I learned in Worcester, as I rode along,
He cannot draw his power this fourteen days.

Douglas. That's the worst tidings that I hear of yet.

Worcester. Ay, by my faith, that bears a frosty sound.

Hotspur. What may the king's whole battle reach unto?

130 *Vernon.* To thirty thousand.

Hotspur.   Forty let it be!
My father and Glendower being both away,
The powers of us may serve so great a day.
Come, let us take a muster speedily—
Doomsday is near—die all, die merrily.

Douglas. Talk not of dying, I am out of fear
Of death or death's hand for this one half year.

                    [*they hurry from the tent*

[4. 2.]   *A highway near Coventry*

Enter FALSTAFF, *in quilted leather jack-coat and with
a pistol-case slung at his belt, talking with* BARDOLPH

Falstaff. Bardolph, get thee before to Coventry, fill
me a bottle of sack, our soldiers shall march through.
We'll to Sutton Co'fil' to-night. [*he gives him a bottle*

Bardolph. Will you give me money, captain?

Falstaff. Lay out, lay out.

Bardolph. This bottle makes an angel.

Falstaff. An if it do, take it for thy labour—and if it
make twenty, take them all, I'll answer the coinage.
Bid my lieutenant Peto meet me at town's end.

10 *Bardolph.* I will, captain. Farewell.   [*he goes*

Falstaff. If I be not ashamed of my soldiers, I am a
soused gurnet. I have misused the king's press damnably.

I have got in exchange of a hundred and fifty soldiers
three hundred and odd pounds. I press me none but
good householders, yeomen's sons, inquire me out contracted bachelors, such as had been asked twice on the
banns, such a commodity of warm slaves, as had as lieve
hear the devil as a drum, such as fear the report of a
caliver worse than a struck fowl or a hurt wild-duck: I
pressed me none but such toasts-and-butter, with hearts 20
in their bellies no bigger than pins' heads, and they
have bought out their services, and now my whole
charge consists of ancients, corporals, lieutenants,
gentlemen of companies—slaves as ragged as Lazarus
in the painted cloth, where the Glutton's dogs licked his
sores, and such as indeed were never soldiers, but discarded unjust serving-men, younger sons to younger
brothers, revolted tapsters, and ostlers trade-fallen, the
cankers of a calm world and a long peace, ten times more
dishonourable ragged than an old feazed ancient; and 30
such have I to fill up the rooms of them as have
bought out their services, that you would think that I
had a hundred and fifty tattered prodigals, lately come
from swine-keeping, from eating draff and husks. A
mad fellow met me on the way, and told me I had un-
loaded all the gibbets and pressed the dead bodies. No
eye hath seen such scarecrows. I'll not march through
Coventry with them, that's flat: nay, and the villains
march wide betwixt the legs as if they had gyves on,
for indeed I had the most of them out of prison. There's 40
not a shirt and a half in all my company, and the half
shirt is two napkins tacked together and thrown over
the shoulders like a herald's coat without sleeves, and
the shirt, to say the truth, stolen from my host at Saint
Alban's or the red-nose innkeeper of Daventry. But
that's all one; they'll find linen enough on every hedge.

Prince HENRY and WESTMORELAND come up from behind

Prince. How now, blown Jack? how now, quilt?

Falstaff. What, Hal? how now, mad wag? what a devil dost thou in Warwickshire?—My good Lord of 50 Westmoreland, I cry you mercy. I thought your honour had already been at Shrewsbury.

Westmoreland. Faith, Sir John, 'tis more than time that I were there, and you too; but my powers are there already. The king, I can tell you, looks for us all, we must away all night.

Falstaff. Tut, never fear me, I am as vigilant as a cat to steal cream.

Prince. I think, to steal cream indeed, for thy theft hath already made thee butter. But tell me, Jack, whose 60 fellows are these that come after?

Falstaff. Mine, Hal, mine.

Prince. I did never see such pitiful rascals.

Falstaff. Tut, tut, good enough to toss, food for powder, food for powder—they'll fill a pit as well as better; tush, man, mortal men, mortal men.

Westmoreland. Ay, but, Sir John, methinks they are exceeding poor and bare, too beggarly.

Falstaff. Faith, for their poverty, I know not where they had that, and for their bareness I am sure they 70 never learned that of me.

Prince. No, I'll be sworn, unless you call three fingers in the ribs, bare. But, sirrah, make haste. Percy is already in the field.   [*he goes*

Falstaff. What, is the king encamped?

Westmoreland. He is, Sir John. I fear we shall stay too long.   [*he hurries forward*

Falstaff. Well,

To the latter end of a fray and the beginning of a feast
Fits a dull fighter and a keen guest.   [*he follows*

[4. 3.]   *The rebel camp near Shrewsbury*

Enter HOTSPUR, WORCESTER, DOUGLAS, *and*
VERNON

Hotspur. We'll fight with him to-night.

Worcester.   It may not be.

Douglas. You give him then advantage.

Vernon.   Not a whit.

Hotspur. Why say you so? looks he not for supply?

Vernon. So do we.

Hotspur.   His is certain, ours is doubtful.

Worcester. Good cousin, be advised, stir not to-night.

Vernon. Do not, my lord.

Douglas.   You do not counsel well;

You speak it out of fear and cold heart.

Vernon. Do me no slander, Douglas. By my life,

And I dare well maintain it with my life,

If well-respected honour bid me on,   10

I hold as little counsel with weak fear

As you, my lord, or any Scot that this day lives.

Let it be seen to-morrow in the battle,

Which of us fears.

Douglas.   Yea, or to-night.

Vernon.   Content.

Hotspur. To-night, say I.

Vernon. Come, come, it may not be. I wonder much,

Being men of such great leading as you are,

That you foresee not what impediments

Drag back our expedition. Certain horse

Of my cousin Vernon's are not yet come up,   20

Your uncle Worcester's horse came but to-day,

And now their pride and mettle is asleep,

Their courage with hard labour tame and dull,

That not a horse is half the half himself.

Hotspur. So are the horses of the enemy
In general, journey-bated and brought low.
The better part of ours are full of rest.
   Worcester. The number of the king exceedeth ours.
For God's sake, cousin, stay till all come in.
['the trumpet sounds a parley'

SIR WALTER BLUNT comes up

30 *Blunt.* I come with gracious offers from the king,
If you vouchsafe me hearing and respect.
   Hotspur. Welcome, Sir Walter Blunt; and would
       to God,
You were of our determination!
Some of us love you well, and even those some
Envy your great deservings and good name,
Because you are not of our quality,
But stand against us like an enemy.
   Blunt. And God defend but still I should stand so,
So long as out of limit and true rule
40 You stand against anointed majesty.
But to my charge. The king hath sent to know
The nature of your griefs, and whereupon
You conjure from the breast of civil peace
Such bold hostility, teaching his duteous land
Audacious cruelty. If that the king
Have any way your good deserts forgot,
Which he confesseth to be manifold,
He bids you name your griefs, and with all speed
You shall have your desires with interest,
50 And pardon absolute for yourself and these
Herein misled by your suggestion.
   Hotspur. The king is kind, and well we know the king
Knows at what time to promise, when to pay:
My father and my uncle and myself

Did give him that same royalty he wears:
And when he was not six and twenty strong,
Sick in the world's regard, wretched and low,
A poor unminded outlaw sneaking home,
My father gave him welcome to the shore;
And when he heard him swear and vow to God   60
He came but to be Duke of Lancaster,
To sue his livery and beg his peace
With tears of innocency and terms of zeal,
My father, in kind heart and pity moved,
Swore him assistance and performed it too.
Now when the lords and barons of the realm
Perceived Northumberland did lean to him,
The more and less came in with cap and knee;
Met him in boroughs, cities, villages,
Attended him on bridges, stood in lanes,   70
Laid gifts before him, proffered him their oaths,
Gave him their heirs as pages, followed him
Even at the heels in golden multitudes.
He presently, as greatness knows itself,
Steps me a little higher than his vow
Made to my father while his blood was poor
Upon the naked shore at Ravenspurgh;
And now, forsooth, takes on him to reform
Some certain edicts and some strait decrees
That lie too heavy on the commonwealth,   80
Cries out upon abuses, seems to weep
Over his country's wrongs, and by this face,
This seeming brow of justice, did he win
The hearts of all that he did angle for;
Proceeded further—cut me off the heads
Of all the favourites that the absent king
In deputation left behind him here,
When he was personal in the Irish war.

Blunt. Tut, I came not to hear this.
Hotspur.   Then to the point.
90 In short time after he deposed the king,
Soon after that deprived him of his life,
And in the neck of that tasked the whole state;
To make that worse, suffered his kinsman March
(Who is, if every owner were well placed,
Indeed his king) to be engaged in Wales,
There without ransom to lie forfeited;
Disgraced me in my happy victories,
Sought to entrap me by intelligence,
Rated mine uncle from the council-board,
100 In rage dismissed my father from the court,
Broke oath on oath, committed wrong on wrong,
And in conclusion drove us to seek out
This head of safety, and withal to pry
Into his title, the which we find
Too indirect for long continuance.
    Blunt. Shall I return this answer to the king?
    Hotspur. Not so, Sir Walter. We'll withdraw awhile;
Go to the king, and let there be impawned
Some surety for a safe return again,
110 And in the morning early shall mine uncle
Bring him our purposes—and so farewell.
    Blunt. I would you would accept of grace and love.
    Hotspur. And may be so we shall.
    Blunt.   Pray God you do.
                                    [*they withdraw*

[4. 4.] *York. A room in the Archbishop's palace*

    The ARCHBISHOP *of* YORK, *and* SIR MICHAEL

Archbishop. Hie, good Sir Michael, bear this
     sealéd brief
With wingéd haste to the lord marshal,
This to my cousin Scroop, and all the rest
To whom they are directed. If you knew
How much they do import, you would make haste.
   Sir Michael. My good lord,
I guess their tenour.
   Archbishop.   Like enough you do.
To-morrow, good Sir Michael, is a day
Wherein the fortune of ten thousand men
Must bide the touch; for, sir, at Shrewsbury,   10
As I am truly given to understand,
The king with mighty and quick-raiséd power
Meets with Lord Harry: and I fear, Sir Michael,
What with the sickness of Northumberland,
Whose power was in the first proportion,
And what with Owen Glendower's absence thence,
Who with them was a rated sinew too,
And comes not in, o'er-ruled by prophecies,
I fear the power of Percy is too weak
To wage an instant trial with the king.   20
   Sir Michael. Why, my good lord, you need not fear,
There is Douglas and Lord Mortimer.
   Archbishop. No, Mortimer is not there.
   Sir Michael. But there is Mordake, Vernon, Lord
     Harry Percy,
And there is my Lord of Worcester, and a head
Of gallant warriors, noble gentlemen.
   Archbishop. And so there is: but yet the king hath drawn

The special head of all the land together—
The Prince of Wales, Lord John of Lancaster,
30 The noble Westmoreland and warlike Blunt,
And many moe corrivals and dear men
Of estimation and command in arms.
  Sir Michael. Doubt not, my lord, they shall be
      well opposed.
  Archbishop. I hope no less, yet needful 'tis to fear.
And, to prevent the worst, Sir Michael, speed:
For if Lord Percy thrive not, ere the king
Dismiss his power, he means to visit us,
For he hath heard of our confederacy,
And 'tis but wisdom to make strong against him.
40 Therefore, make haste. I must go write again
To other friends, and so farewell, Sir Michael.
                        [they go

[5. 1.]   *The King's camp near Shrewsbury*

Enter the KING, *Prince* HENRY (*his helm fluttering
with ostrich-feathers*), LORD JOHN *of* LANCASTER,
SIR WALTER BLUNT, *and* FALSTAFF

  King. How bloodily the sun begins to peer
Above yon busky hill! the day looks pale
At his distemp'rature.
  Prince.   The southern wind
Doth play the trumpet to his purposes,
And by his hollow whistling in the leaves
Foretells a tempest and a blust'ring day.
  King. Then with the losers let it sympathize,
For nothing can seem foul to those that win.
                ['the trumpet sounds'
      Enter WORCESTER *and* VERNON

How now, my Lord of Worcester? 'tis not well

That you and I should meet upon such terms   10
As now we meet. You have deceived our trust,
And made us doff our easy robes of peace,
To crush our old limbs in ungentle steel.
This is not well, my lord, this is not well.
What say you to it? will you again unknit
This churlish knot of all-abhorréd war?
And move in that obedient orb again
Where you did give a fair and natural light,
And be no more an exhaled meteor,
A prodigy of fear, and a portent   20
Of broachéd mischief to the unborn times?

  Worcester. Hear me, my liege:
For mine own part, I could be well content
To entertain the lag-end of my life
With quiet hours; for I do protest
I have not sought the day of this dislike.

  King. You have not sought it! how comes it then?

  Falstaff. Rebellion lay in his way and he found it.

  Prince. Peace, chewet, peace!

  Worcester. It pleased your majesty to turn your looks 30
Of favour from myself and all our house,
And yet I must remember you, my lord,
We were the first and dearest of your friends.
For you my staff of office did I break
In Richard's time, and posted day and night
To meet you on the way, and kiss your hand,
When yet you were in place and in account
Nothing so strong and fortunate as I.
It was myself, my brother, and his son,
That brought you home, and boldly did outdare   40
The dangers of the time. You swore to us,
And you did swear that oath at Doncaster,
That you did nothing purpose 'gainst the state,

Nor claim no further than your new-fall'n right,
The seat of Gaunt, dukedom of Lancaster:
To this we swore our aid...But in short space
It rained down fortune show'ring on your head,
And such a flood of greatness fell on you,
What with our help, what with the absent king,
50 What with the injuries of a wanton time,
The seeming sufferances that you had borne,
And the contrarious winds that held the king
So long in his unlucky Irish wars
That all in England did repute him dead:
And from this swarm of fair advantages
You took occasion to be quickly wooed
To gripe the general sway into your hand,
Forgot your oath to us at Doncaster,
And being fed by us you used us so
60 As that ungentle gull, the cuckoo's bird,
Useth the sparrow—did oppress our nest,
Grew by our feeding to so great a bulk
That even our love durst not come near your sight
For fear of swallowing; but with nimble wing
We were enforced for safety sake to fly
Out of your sight and raise this present head,
Whereby we stand opposéd by such means
As you yourself have forged against yourself,
By unkind usage, dangerous countenance,
70 And violation of all faith and troth
Sworn to us in your younger enterprise.
   King. These things indeed you have articulate,
Proclaimed at market-crosses, read in churches,
To face the garment of rebellion
With some fine colour that may please the eye
Of fickle changelings and poor discontents,
Which gape and rub the elbow at the news

Of hurlyburly innovation.
And never yet did insurrection want
Such water-colours to impaint his cause,   80
Nor moody beggars starving for a time
Of pellmell havoc and confusion.

Prince. In both our armies there is many a soul
Shall pay full dearly for this encounter,
If once they join in trial. Tell your nephew,
The Prince of Wales doth join with all the world
In praise of Henry Percy. By my hopes,
This present enterprise set off his head,
I do not think a braver gentleman,
More active-valiant or more valiant-young,   90
More daring or more bold, is now alive
To grace this latter age with noble deeds.
For my part, I may speak it to my shame,
I have a truant been to chivalry,
And so I hear he doth account me too;
Yet this before my father's majesty—
I am content that he shall take the odds
Of his great name and estimation,
And will, to save the blood on either side,
Try fortune with him in a single fight.   100

King. And, Prince of Wales, so dare we venture thee,
Albeit considerations infinite
Do make against it...No, good Worcester, no,
We love our people well—even those we love
That are misled upon your cousin's part—
And will they take the offer of our grace,
Both he, and they, and you, yea, every man
Shall be my friend again and I'll be his.
So tell your cousin, and bring me word
What he will do. But if he will not yield,   110
Rebuke and dread correction wait on us,

And they shall do their office. So, be gone;
We will not now be troubled with reply.
We offer fair, take it advisedly.

                [Worcester and Vernon go

   Prince. It will not be accepted, on my life.
The Douglas and the Hotspur both together
Are confident against the world in arms.

   King. Hence, therefore, every leader to his charge,
For on their answer will we set on them,
120 And God befriend us, as our cause is just!

       *[they disperse to their commands; Falstaff plucks
        the Prince by the sleeve as he turns away*

   Falstaff. Hal, if thou see me down in the battle and
bestride me, so, 'tis a point of friendship.

   Prince. Nothing but a colossus can do thee that
friendship. Say thy prayers, and farewell.

   Falstaff. I would 'twere bed-time, Hal, and all well.

   Prince. Why, thou owest God a death.

                  [he hurries off

   Falstaff. 'Tis not due yet, I would be loath to pay him
before his day. What need I be so forward with him
that calls not on me? Well, 'tis no matter, honour pricks
130 me on. Yea, but how if honour prick me off when I
come on? how then? can honour set to a leg? no—or an
arm? no—or take away the grief of a wound? no.
Honour hath no skill in surgery then? no. What is
honour? a word. What is in that word honour? what is
that honour? air. A trim reckoning! Who hath it?
he that died a-Wednesday. Doth he feel it? no. Doth
he hear it? no. 'Tis insensible then? yea, to the dead.
But will it not live with the living? no. Why? Detraction
will not suffer it. Therefore I'll none of it. Honour is
140 a mere scutcheon—and so ends my catechism. *[he goes*

[5. 2.]   *A plain near the rebel camp*

WORCESTER and VERNON approach, returning from the King

Worcester. O, no, my nephew must not know,
    Sir Richard,
The liberal and kind offer of the king.
    Vernon. 'Twere best he did.
      Worcester.   Then are we all undone.
It is not possible, it cannot be,
The king should keep his word in loving us.
He will suspect us still, and find a time
To punish this offence in other faults.
Supposition all our lives shall be stuck full
Of eyes,
For treason is but trusted like the fox,   10
Who, ne'er so tame, so cherished and locked up,
Will have a wild trick of his ancestors.
Look how we can, or sad or merrily,
Interpretation will misquote our looks,
And we shall feed like oxen at a stall,
The better cherished still the nearer death.
My nephew's trespass may be well forgot,
It hath the excuse of youth and heat of blood,
And an adopted name of privilege—
A hare-brained Hotspur, governed by a spleen.   20
All his offences live upon my head
And on his father's. We did train him on,
And his corruption being ta'en from us,
We as the spring of all shall pay for all...
Therefore, good cousin, let not Harry know,
In any case, the offer of the king.
    Vernon. Deliver what you will, I'll say 'tis so.
Here comes your cousin.

*HOTSPUR and DOUGLAS, with officers
and soldiers come to meet them*

Hotspur. My uncle is returned.
30 Deliver up my Lord of Westmoreland.
Uncle, what news?
  Worcester. The king will bid you battle presently.
  Douglas. Defy him by the Lord of Westmoreland.
  Hotspur. Lord Douglas, go you and tell him so.
  Douglas. Marry, and shall, and very willingly.
                                        [*he goes*

  Worcester. There is no seeming mercy in the king.
  Hotspur. Did you beg any? God forbid!
  Worcester. I told him gently of our grievances,
Of his oath-breaking—which he mended thus,
40 By now forswearing that he is forsworn.
He calls us rebels, traitors, and will scourge
With haughty arms this hateful name in us.

DOUGLAS returns

  Douglas. Arm, gentlemen, to arms! for I have thrown
A brave defiance in King Henry's teeth,
And Westmoreland that was engaged did bear it,
Which cannot choose but bring him quickly on.
  Worcester. The Prince of Wales stepped forth before
      the king,
And, nephew, challenged you to single fight.
  Hotspur. O, would the quarrel lay upon our heads,
50 And that no man might draw short breath to-day
But I and Harry Monmouth! Tell me, tell me,
How showed his tasking? seemed it in contempt?
  Vernon. No, by my soul. I never in my life
Did hear a challenge urged more modestly,
Unless a brother should a brother dare

To gentle exercise and proof of arms.
He gave you all the duties of a man,
Trimmed up your praises with a princely tongue,
Spoke your deservings like a chronicle,
Making you ever better than his praise   60
By still dispraising praise valued with you,
And, which became him like a prince indeed,
He made a blushing cital of himself,
And chid his truant youth with such a grace,
As if he mast'red there a double spirit
Of teaching and of learning instantly.
There did he pause. But let me tell the world,
If he outlive the envy of this day,
England did never owe so sweet a hope,
So much misconstrued in his wantonness.   70

  Hotspur. Cousin, I think thou art enamouréd
Upon his follies. Never did I hear
Of any prince so wild a liberty.
But be he as he will, yet once ere night
I will embrace him with a soldier's arm,
That he shall shrink under my courtesy.
Arm, arm, with speed—and, fellows, soldiers, friends,
Better consider what you have to do
Than I, that have not well the gift of tongue,
Can lift your blood up with persuasion.   80

A messenger comes up

  Messenger. My lord, here are letters for you.
  Hotspur. I cannot read them now.
O gentlemen, the time of life is short!
To spend that shortness basely were too long,
If life did ride upon a dial's point,
Still ending at the arrival of an hour.
An if we live, we live to tread on kings,

If die, brave death, when princes die with us!
Now, for our consciences, the arms are fair,
90 When the intent of bearing them is just.

Another messenger hurries up

Messenger. My lord, prepare, the king comes
   on apace.
Hotspur. I thank him that he cuts me from my tale,
For I profess not talking—only this,
Let each man do his best. And here draw I
A sword, whose temper I intend to stain
With the best blood that I can meet withal
In the adventure of this perilous day.
Now, Esperance! Percy! and set on.
Sound all the lofty instruments of war,
100 And by that music let us all embrace,
For, heaven to earth, some of us never shall
A second time do such a courtesy.

   ['*The trumpets sound.*' '*They embrace,*'
      and depart in haste to arm

[5. 3.] '*The king enters with his power*' *and marches
past.* '*Alarum to battle. Then enter* DOUGLAS *and* SIR
WALTER BLUNT' (*disguised as the king*) *fighting; they
pause*

Blunt. What is thy name, that in the battle thus
Thou crossest me? what honour dost thou seek
Upon my head?
Douglas.   Know then, my name is Douglas,
And I do haunt thee in the battle thus
Because some tell me that thou art a king.
Blunt. They tell thee true.
Douglas. The Lord of Stafford dear to-day hath bought
Thy likeness, for instead of thee, King Harry,

This sword hath ended him. So shall it thee,
Unless thou yield thee as my prisoner.   10
  Blunt. I was not born a yielder, thou proud Scot,
And thou shalt find a king that will revenge
Lord Stafford's death.

         ['*They fight, Douglas kills Blunt*'

         HOTSPUR *comes up*

  Hotspur. O Douglas, hadst thou fought at
       Holmedon thus,
I never had triumphed upon a Scot.
  Douglas. All's done, all's won! here breathless lies
       the king.
  Hotspur. Where?
  Douglas. Here.
  Hotspur. This, Douglas? no, I know this face full well.
A gallant knight he was, his name was Blunt,   20
Semblably furnished like the king himself.
  Douglas. A fool go with thy soul, whither it goes!
A borrowed title hast thou bought too dear.
Why didst thou tell me that thou wert a king?
  Hotspur. The king hath many marching in his coats.
  Douglas. Now, by my sword, I will kill all his coats,
I'll murder all his wardrobe, piece by piece,
Until I meet the king.
  Hotspur.   Up, and away!
Our soldiers stand full fairly for the day.

         [*they rejoin the forces*

     '*Alarum. Enter* FALSTAFF, *solus*'

  Falstaff. Though I could 'scape shot-free at London, 30
I fear the shot here, here's no scoring but upon the pate.
Soft! who are you? Sir Walter Blunt—there's honour
for you! here's no vanity! I am as hot as molten lead,

W.H. IV–9

and as heavy too: God keep lead out of me! I need no more weight than mine own bowels. I have led my ragamuffins where they are peppered, there's not three of my hundred and fifty left alive, and they are for the town's end, to beg during life...But who comes here?

Prince HENRY approaches

Prince. What, stand'st thou idle here? lend me
    thy sword.
40 Many a nobleman lies stark and stiff
Under the hoofs of vaunting enemies,
whose deaths are yet unrevenged. I prithee, lend me
thy sword.
    Falstaff. O Hal, I prithee, give me leave to breathe
awhile. Turk Gregory never did such deeds in arms
as I have done this day.
I have paid Percy, I have made him sure.
    Prince. He is, indeed, and living to kill thee....
I prithee, lend me thy sword.
50 *Falstaff.* Nay, before God, Hal, if Percy be alive,
thou get'st not my sword, but take my pistol if thou wilt.
    Prince. Give it me. What, is it in the case?
    Falstaff. Ay, Hal, 'tis hot, 'tis hot. There's that will
sack a city.
            ['*The Prince draws it out and finds
                it to be a bottle of sack*'
    Prince. What, is it a time to jest and dally now?
            ['*he throws the bottle at him*', *and goes*
    Falstaff. Well, if Percy be alive, I'll pierce him...
[*aside*] If he do come in my way, so. If he do not, if I
come in his willingly, let him make a carbonado of me.
I like not such grinning honour as Sir Walter hath. Give
60 me life, which if I can save, so; if not, honour comes
unlooked for, and there's an end.   [*he goes*

[5. 4.] 'Alarum, excursions. Enter the KING, the PRINCE', wounded in the cheek, 'LORD JOHN of LANCASTER, and EARL of WESTMORELAND'

King. I prithee,
Harry, withdraw thyself, thou bleedest too much.
Lord John of Lancaster, go you with him.

Lancaster. Not I, my lord, unless I did bleed too.

Prince. I beseech your majesty, make up,
Lest your retirement do amaze your friends.

King. I will do so. My Lord of Westmoreland,
lead him to his tent.

Westmoreland. Come, my lord, I'll lead you to your tent.

Prince. Lead me, my lord? I do not need your help, 10
And God forbid a shallow scratch should drive
The Prince of Wales from such a field as this,
Where stained nobility lies trodden on,
And rebels' arms triumph in massacres!

Lancaster. We breathe too long. Come, cousin
       Westmoreland,
Our duty this way lies; for God's sake, come.
         [*Lancaster and Westmoreland hurry forward*

Prince. By God, thou hast deceived me, Lancaster,
I did not think thee lord of such a spirit.
Before, I loved thee as a brother, John,
But now, I do respect thee as my soul.   20

King. I saw him hold Lord Percy at the point,
With lustier maintenance than I did look for
Of such an ungrown warrior.

Prince.   O, this boy
Lends mettle to us all!   [*he follows*

    DOUGLAS *appears from another part of the field*

Douglas. Another king! they grow like Hydra's heads.
I am the Douglas, fatal to all those

That wear those colours on them. What art thou,
That counterfeit'st the person of a king?
  King. The king himself, who, Douglas, grieves
      at heart
30 So many of his shadows thou hast met,
And not the very king. I have two boys
Seek Percy and thyself about the field,
But seeing thou fall'st on me so luckily
I will assay thee: so, defend thyself.
  Douglas. I fear thou art another counterfeit,
And yet in faith thou bear'st thee like a king,
But mine I am sure thou art, whoe'er thou be,
And thus I win thee.
        ['*They fight. The King being in danger,
            enter Prince of Wales*'
  Prince. Hold up thy head, vile Scot, or thou art like
40 Never to hold it up again! the spirits
Of valiant Shirley, Stafford, Blunt, are in my arms.
It is the Prince of Wales that threatens thee,
Who never promiseth but he means to pay....
        ['*they fight, Douglas flieth*'
Cheerly, my lord, how fares your grace?
Sir Nicholas Gawsey hath for succour sent,
And so hath Clifton—I'll to Clifton straight.
  King. Stay, and breathe awhile.
Thou hast redeemed thy lost opinion,
And showed thou mak'st some tender of my life,
50 In this fair rescue thou hast brought to me.
  Prince. O God! they did me too much injury
That ever said I heark'ned for your death.
If it were so, I might have let alone
The insulting hand of Douglas over you,
Which would have been as speedy in your end
As all the poisonous potions in the world,

And saved the treacherous labour of your son.

 King. Make up to Clifton, I'll to Sir Nicholas Gawsey.

            [*he goes*

    HOTSPUR *comes up*

 Hotspur. If I mistake not, thou art Harry Monmouth.

 Prince. Thou speak'st as if I would deny my name. 60

 Hotspur. My name is Harry Percy.

 Prince.   Why, then I see

A very valiant rebel of the name.

I am the Prince of Wales, and think not, Percy,

To share with me in glory any more:

Two stars keep not their motion in one sphere,

Nor can one England brook a double reign,

Of Harry Percy and the Prince of Wales.

 Hotspur. Nor shall it, Harry, for the hour is come

To end the one of us, and would to God

Thy name in arms were now as great as mine! 70

 Prince. I'll make it greater ere I part from thee,

And all the budding honours on thy crest

I'll crop, to make a garland for my head.

 Hotspur. I can no longer brook thy vanities.

          ['*they fight*'

    FALSTAFF *draws near*

 Falstaff. Well said, Hal! to it, Hal! Nay, you shall find no boy's play here, I can tell you.

DOUGLAS *returns;* '*he fighteth with* FALSTAFF', *who* '*falls down as if he were dead*'; *he passes on.* HOTSPUR *is wounded, and falls.*

 Hotspur. O, Harry, thou hast robbed me of my youth!

I better brook the loss of brittle life

Than those proud titles thou hast won of me.

They wound my thoughts worse than thy sword my flesh. 80

But thought's the slave of life, and life time's fool,
And time that takes survey of all the world
Must have a stop. O, I could prophesy,
But that the earthy and cold hand of death
Lies on my tongue: no, Percy, thou art dust,
And food for—   [*he dies*
   Prince. For worms, brave Percy. Fare thee well,
      great heart!
Ill-weaved ambition, how much art thou shrunk!
When that this body did contain a spirit,
90 A kingdom for it was too small a bound,
But now two paces of the vilest earth
Is room enough. This earth, that bears thee dead,
Bears not alive so stout a gentleman.
If thou wert sensible of courtesy,
I should not make so dear a show of zeal—
But let my favours hide thy mangled face!
   [*he covers Hotspur's eyes with a plume from his helm*
And even in thy behalf I'll thank myself
For doing these fair rites of tenderness.
Adieu, and take thy praise with thee to heaven!
100 Thy ignominy sleep with thee in the grave,
But not remembered in thy epitaph!
        [*'he spieth Falstaff on the ground'*
What! old acquaintance! could not all this flesh
Keep in a little life? poor Jack, farewell!
I could have better spared a better man:
O, I should have a heavy miss of thee,
If I were much in love with vanity:
Death hath not struck so fat a deer to-day,
Though many dearer, in this bloody fray.
Embowelled will I see thee by and by,
110 Till then in blood by noble Percy lie.   [*he goes*
   Falstaff [*'riseth up'*]. Embowelled! if thou embowel
me to-day, I'll give you leave to powder me and eat me

too to-morrow. 'Sblood, 'twas time to counterfeit, or
that hot termagant Scot had paid me, scot and lot too.
Counterfeit? I lie, I am no counterfeit. To die is to be
a counterfeit, for he is but the counterfeit of a man, who
hath not the life of a man: but to counterfeit dying, when
a man thereby liveth, is to be no counterfeit, but the
true and perfect image of life indeed. The better part
of valour is discretion, in the which better part I have 120
saved my life. 'Zounds, I am afraid of this gunpowder
Percy, though he be dead. How, if he should counterfeit too, and rise? by my faith, I am afraid he would
prove the better counterfeit. Therefore I'll make him
sure, yea, and I'll swear I killed him. Why may not he
rise as well as I? Nothing confutes me but eyes, and
nobody sees me: therefore, sirrah, [*stabs him*] with a
new wound in your thigh, come you along with me.

[' *he takes up Hotspur on his back*'

The PRINCE *and* LORD JOHN *of* LANCASTER *return*

Prince. Come, brother John, full bravely hast
          thou fleshed
Thy maiden sword.
  Lancaster.   But, soft! whom have we here?   130
Did you not tell me this fat man was dead?
  Prince. I did, I saw him dead,
Breathless and bleeding on the ground. Art thou alive?
Or is it phantasy that plays upon our eyesight?
I prithee, speak. We will not trust our eyes,
Without our ears. Thou art not what thou seem'st.
  Falstaff. No, that's certain, I am not a double-man:
but if I be not Jack Falstaff, then am I a Jack: there is
Percy! [*throws the body down*] If your father will do me
any honour, so; if not, let him kill the next Percy him- 140
self...I look to be either earl or duke, I can assure you.

Prince. Why, Percy I killed myself, and saw thee
dead.

Falstaff. Didst thou? Lord, Lord, how this world is
given to lying! I grant you I was down and out of
breath, and so was he, but we rose both at an instant,
and fought a long hour by Shrewsbury clock. If I may
be believed, so: if not, let them that should reward
valour bear the sin upon their own heads. I'll take it
150 upon my death, I gave him this wound in the thigh. If
the man were alive, and would deny it, 'zounds, I
would make him eat a piece of my sword.

Lancaster. This is the strangest tale that ever I heard.

Prince. This is the strangest fellow, brother John.
Come, bring your luggage nobly on your back.

          [aside, to Falstaff
For my part, if a lie may do thee grace,
I'll gild it with the happiest terms I have.

        ['a retreat is sounded'
The trumpet sounds retreat, the day is ours.

Come, brother, let's to the highest of the field,
160 To see what friends are living, who are dead. *[they go*

Falstaff. I'll follow, as they say, for reward. He that
rewards me, God reward him! If I do grow great, I'll
grow less, for I'll purge, and leave sack, and live cleanly
as a nobleman should do.

      [he follows, dragging off the body

[5. 5.] *'The Trumpets sound. Enter the* KING, PRINCE
of WALES, LORD JOHN *of* LANCASTER, EARL *of* WEST-
MORELAND, *with* WORCESTER *and* VERNON *prisoners'*

King. Thus ever did rebellion find rebuke.
Ill-spirited Worcester! did not we send grace,
Pardon and terms of love to all of you?
And wouldst thou turn our offers contrary?

Misuse the tenour of thy kinsman's trust?
Three knights upon our party slain to-day,
A noble earl and many a creature else,
Had been alive this hour,
If like a Christian thou hadst truly borne
Betwixt our armies true intelligence.   10

  Worcester. What I have done my safety urged me to;
And I embrace this fortune patiently,
Since not to be avoided it falls on me.

  King. Bear Worcester to the death, and Vernon too:
Other offenders we will pause upon.

                [*Worcester and Vernon are led away*
How goes the field?

  Prince. The noble Scot, Lord Douglas, when he saw
The fortune of the day quite turned from him,
The noble Percy slain, and all his men
Upon the foot of fear, fled with the rest,   20
And falling from a hill, he was so bruised
That the pursuers took him. At my tent
The Douglas is; and I beseech your grace
I may dispose of him.

  King.   With all my heart.

  Prince. Then, brother John of Lancaster, to you
This honourable bounty shall belong.
Go to the Douglas, and deliver him
Up to his pleasure, ransomless and free.
His valours shown upon our crests to-day
Have taught us how to cherish such high deeds,   30
Even in the bosom of our adversaries.

  Lancaster. I thank your grace for this high courtesy,
Which I shall give away immediately.

  King. Then this remains, that we divide our power.
You, son John, and my cousin Westmoreland
Towards York shall bend, you with your dearest speed

To meet Northumberland and the prelate Scroop,
Who, as we hear, are busily in arms:
Myself and you, son Harry, will towards Wales,
40 To fight with Glendower and the Earl of March.
Rebellion in this land shall lose his sway,
Meeting the check of such another day,
And since this business so fair is done,
Let us not leave till all our own be won.   [*they go*

THE COPY FOR
1 HENRY IV, 1598 & 1623,
WITH A NOTE ON
THE DERING MS.

A. *The Q text*

The text of *1 Henry IV* presents few problems of a general character, and they may be briefly dealt with. Copy for the play was entered in the Stationers' Register on 25 February 1598 by the publisher Andrew Wise, and was printed by Peter Short, doubtless soon after. We can in fact trace two issues in 1598, the extant Q1 and an earlier quarto, of which all that is known is a single sheet, sig. C, that turned up in the binding of an Italian grammar found at Bristol in 1891. This sheet of an otherwise lost quarto, now labelled Q0, furnishes only one variant of any importance (2. 2. 109); but it demonstrates that in reprinting Q0 as Q1 the printer was trying to save paper, and for this purpose resorted to various devices, such as the dove-tailing of speeches. This, for instance, is how he saves a line at 3. 2. 92–4:

Prin. I shall hereafter my thrice gratious Lord,
Be more my selfe.   *King.* For all the world,
As thou art to this houre was Richard then.

And the economy, as is not surprising, has led to a misplacement of a speech-heading at 1. 1. 75–7, which lines Q1 (and F.) prints thus:

A gallant prize? Ha coosen, is it not? In faith it is.
    West. A conquest for a Prince to boast of.

And, seeing that *1 Henry IV* Q 1 is one of the cleanest and best printed of all Shakespearian quartos, we may suspect that there was tidying up as well as tightening up at the time of reprinting. I find it hard, for example, to believe that Shakespeare intended Falstaff to say 'all is one' and not 'all's one' (2. 4. 152) or 'rag of Muffins' and not 'ragamuffins' (5. 3. 36). Such sedate expansions, which are a special feature of Q 1, retarding the pace of the dialogue, muffling the voice of the speakers, and at times even impairing the metre, suggest the interference of a compositor or master-printer concerned rather with standards of orthography than with the reproduction of a highly colloquial play. On the other hand, Q 1 is full of little irregularities in stage-direction, speech-heading, and verse-lining, which would undoubtedly have been smoothed out in a prompt-book transcript, and are yet just what we should expect in an author's MS. or 'foul papers'. Even the spelling, though, thanks I take it to Short's tidying up, far more normal than that for example of *Hamlet* Q 2 or *Love's Labour's Lost* Q 1, preserves a Shakespearian flavour here and there. We have every encouragement to believe, in short, that the 'copy' used for Q o and entered on 25 February 1598 was Shakespeare's own manuscript. Nor need we doubt that it reached Wise's hands from those of the players themselves. Indeed, there is much to be said for the surmise, independently advanced by Sir Edmund Chambers and Professor J. Q. Adams[1], that the publication, which they put a few months later than the production of the play, was connected with the change from Oldcastle to Falstaff and promoted by the company 'to advertise the purging of the offence'.

[1] Chambers, *William Shakespeare*, i. 382; Adams, *Life of Shakespeare*, p. 513.

B. *Relation between Q1 and F*

The play was such good business from the publisher's standpoint that Qo had to be reprinted no fewer than six times before it appeared in the First Folio of 1623. And when, as Malone first noted, the F. compositors came to set it up in type, they made use of Q5 (1613) as 'copy'; in this following their usual practice with plays that had already appeared in good quarto form. In other cases, however, the quarto they reprinted had first been collated with the prompt-book at the theatre, so that the text thus produced generally possessed an authority, inferior indeed to that of Q1, but to some extent independent of it. The main textual problem of *1 Henry IV* is whether its F. text is an exception to this rule. Sir Edmund Chambers and Dr Greg think it is. They point out that the clearest evidence of collation of a quarto with the prompt-book is usually a marked difference between Q. and F. in stage-directions and speech-headings, about which an author may be careless, but which must be adequate, clear, and consistent in the 'book' on which performances are based; and that those in the F. *1 Henry IV* are virtually identical with their parallels in Q1, i.e. display all the inadequacy, inequality, and inconsistency that we associate with author's 'foul papers'. In a word they show no influence of the prompt-book whatever, and a reference to note 5. 2. 102 should suffice of itself to prove that the F. text could not be played as it stands. True, the F. compositors cannot have reprinted Q5 exactly, since before the copy reached them act and scene divisions had been inserted, and the text had been purged of profanity in accordance with the Act of 1606 to prevent players from 'the great abuse of the Holy Name of God' on the stage; but these changes Chambers and Greg ascribe to a F. editor.

The foregoing diagnosis would leave us with the
comforting assurance that Q 1 is the only text an editor
need consider, did it not overlook a reading in the F.
dialogue which is indubitably Shakespearian, cannot
have been arrived at without access to the true text,
and must therefore be accepted, as it always has been
by editors, in preference to its Q. variant, which is not
only nonsense but proves, upon examination, to be a
palpable misprint of the reading F. gives us. The
reading in question occurs at 2. 4. 32. After coaching
Poins for his part in the interlude with Francis the
drawer, Hal remarks according to the two texts:

> Q. step aside and ile shew thee a present.
> F. step aside, and Ile shew thee a President.

Here 'President', the ordinary Elizabethan spelling of
'precedent', suits the context perfectly and is most
unlikely to have occurred to the unaided intelligence
of a printer or scrivener. 'An example...worthy to
be followed or copied; a pattern, model, exemplar' is
one of its sixteenth-century meanings according to the
O.E.D., and it carries with it, I think, the further
sense of 'something quite original'. Anyhow, the word
seems patently Shakespearian, while the spelling 'president' offers a satisfactory explanation of the Q. misprint, 'present', which is the same word with the
letters 'id' accidentally omitted at the press. The
reading in short may be claimed as impregnable; and,
being so, forges a firm link between the F. *1 Henry IV*
and the Globe prompt-book. And if Q 5 was certainly
corrected by the prompt-book in this instance, the
simplest way of accounting for it is to attribute it to
a scribe instructed to collate the texts with a view to
ridding the Q 5 copy of its oaths before printing it
in F. Presumably the acting version at the Globe had
been purged soon after the passing of the Act of 1606;
and that being so the easiest way to do the like with

the F. text was to read through a specimen of Q5 with
the expurgated prompt-book and make the necessary
adjustments. As he proceeded with his task, such a
scribe would occasionally and inevitably notice other
differences in the dialogue and transfer readings to his
Q5 copy when he saw fit. That he left the stage-
directions alone would seem, on this theory, natural
enough; he was primarily concerned with removing
oaths from the dialogue and in no way with stage-
production. And after all, the condition of the F. stage-
directions in *1 Henry IV* is not very different from that
of the stage-directions in the F. *Much Ado* and *The
Merchant of Venice*, in which the influence of the
prompt-book is only slightly more evident.

However this may be, the duty of an editor of the
present text is plain: so far from being able to ignore
F., he must carefully weigh every variant therein
before rejecting it in favour of the more generally
authoritative Q1. Fortunately, the latter is so good on
the whole, and the significant variants so few, that the
burden of choice is lighter than might at first sight
appear. Beyond a number of readings in which F.
corrects obvious Q. misprints, a handful of adjustments
in punctuation (v. p. 112), and the restoration of certain
colloquialisms which, as explained above, I believe to
have been 'improved' away by the compositors responsible for Q1, there are in point of fact only four
readings apart from 'precedent' that I have felt obliged
to adopt from the F. (v. notes 1. 3. 242; 2. 2. 42;
3. 1. 98; 3. 2. 156).

C. *The Dering Manuscript*

Besides the early printed texts a MS. acting version
of *Henry IV*, combining the best scenes of Part 1 with
the conclusion of Part 2, and transcribed from copies
of *1 Henry IV* Q5 and *2 Henry IV* Q1, has come down

to us from the first quarter of the seventeenth century[1]
The MS. was discovered in the library of the Dering
family at Surrenden, Kent, and contains marginal cor-
rections and emendations in the hand of Sir Edward
Dering (1598–1644), who was evidently preparing it
for a private performance at his house about 1623.
But the transcript itself is older than this, perhaps
many years older, and Professor Hemingway believes
it may actually have been used for performance at
Court in May 1613, on the occasion of the marriage
of the Princess Elizabeth with the Elector Palatine.
For whatever purpose the MS. was first made, any
acting version belonging to the seventeenth century
must be of interest to an editor; and though, derived
as it is from the quartos, this one lacks all textual
authority, it may be cited as corroborative evidence on
occasions (cf. notes 2. 4. 335, 387, 519).

[1] The original, now at the Folger Library, Washington,
was printed by Halliwell-Phillipps in 1844 (Shakespeare
Soc. Pub. 27) and is described in detail by S. B. Hemingway
on pp. 495–501, *New Variorum 1 Henry IV.*

NOTES

All significant departures from Q 1 are recorded; the name of the critic or editor who first suggested or printed the accepted reading being placed in brackets. Line-numeration for references to plays not yet issued in this edition is that found in Bartlett's *Concordance* and the *Globe Shakespeare*.

Q., except where otherwise specified, stands for the First Quarto of *1 Henry IV* (1598), the extant fragment of an earlier edition of the same year being described as Q0; F. stands for the First Folio (1623); the five quartos published between 1598 and 1623 are numbered Q2 (1599), Q3 (1604), Q4 (1608), Q5 (1615), Q6 (1622), the last but one, after collation with the prompt-book, serving as copy for the F. text, as is noted above. For the Dering MS., v. p. 107.

Other abbreviations of a general character are: G.=Glossary; O.E.D.=*The Oxford Dictionary*; S.D. =stage-directions; Sh.=Shakespeare; other names and common words (e.g. Eliz.=Elizabethan, prob.= probably) are abbreviated where convenient.

The following is a list of the books cited, together with the abridged titles employed: Apperson=*English Proverbs and Proverbial Phrases* by G. L. Apperson, 1929; Arden=the ed. by R. P. Cowl and A. E. Morgan (Arden Sh.); *C.W.*=*The First Fowre Bookes of the Ciuile Wars* by Samuel Daniel, 1595; Camb.= *The Cambridge Shakespeare* ed. by W. A. Wright, 1891; Chambers, *Eliz. Stage*=*The Elizabethan Stage* by E. K. Chambers, 4 vols., 1923; Chambers, *Wm. Sh.*=*William Shakespeare: a Study of Facts and Problems* by E. K. Chambers, 2 vols., 1930; Cheyney= *A History of England, 1588–1603*, 2 vols., 1914; Clar.=the ed. by W. A. Wright (The Clarendon Sh.);

Cotgrave = Cotgrave's *French-English Dictionary*, 1611;
Elton = the ed. by Oliver Elton, 1889 (Falcon Sh.);
F.V. = *The Famous Victories of Henry the Fifth*, 1598,
ed. P. A. Daniel (Griggs-Praetorius facsimile, 1887);
Fortunes = *The Fortunes of Falstaff* by J. Dover Wilson,
1943; Franz = *Die Sprache Shakespeares* (4th ed.) by
W. Franz, 1939; Hall = *Hall's Chronicle*, 1548, rep.
1809; Hemingway = the ed. by S. B. Hemingway (New
Variorum Sh.), 1936; Hol. = *Holinshed's Chronicle of
England*, 1587; Jente = *Proverbs of Sh.* by R. Jente,
Washington Univ. Studies, vol. 13; Jonson = *Ben Jonson*
ed. C. H. Herford and Percy Simpson, 1925–;
Kittredge = the ed. by G. L. Kittredge (Ginn and Co.),
1940; Kyd = *Works of Thomas Kyd*, ed. F. S. Boas,
1901; *Library* = *The Library*, June 1945; Linthicum =
Costume in Elizabethan Drama by M. C. Linthicum,
1936; Lyly = *Works of John Lyly*, ed. R. W. Bond,
1902; M.L.R. = *Modern Language Review*; Madden =
Diary of Master William Silence by D. H. Madden,
1907; Marlowe = *Works of Marlowe*, gen. ed. R. H.
Case, 6 vols., 1930–3; Moore Smith (v. *Acknowledge-
ments* below); Moorman = the ed. by F. W. Moorman
(Warwick Sh.); Morgan = *Some Problems of Sh.'s
'Henry IV'* by A. E. Morgan (Sh. Assoc. 1924);
MSH = *The Manuscript of Sh.'s 'Hamlet'* by J. Dover
Wilson, 1934; Nashe = *Works of Thomas Nashe*, ed.
R. B. McKerrow, 5 vols., 1904–10; Noble = *Sh.'s
Biblical Knowledge* by Richmond Noble, 1935;
Onions = *Sh. Glossary* by C. T. Onions, 1919; R.E.S. =
Review of English Studies; Rye = *England as seen by
Foreigners in the days of Elizabeth and James* by W. B.
Rye, 1865; Schmidt = *Sh.-Lexicon* by A. Schmidt
(3rd ed. rev. by G. Sarrazin), 2 vols., 1902; *Sh. Eng.* =
Sh.'s England, Oxford, 1917; *Sh.'s Hand* = *Sh.'s Hand
in 'Sir Thomas More'*, by A. W. Pollard, etc., 1923;
Sprague = *Sh. and the Actors* by A. C. Sprague, 1944;
Stone = *Sh.'s Holinshed: the Chronicle and the Historical
Plays Compared* by W. G. Boswell-Stone, 1907; Stow =

Chronicles of England, 1580, reissued and enlarged as *Annals of England*, 1592 (cited from ed. of 1615); Sugden = *Topographical Dictionary to Sh.* by E. H. Sugden, 1925; Tilley = *Eliz. Proverb Lore* by M. P. Tilley, 1926; T.L.S. = *Times Literary Supplement*; Vaughan = *New Readings in Sh.* by H. H. Vaughan, 1886; Var. 1821 = Boswell's ed. of *Malone's Sh.*, 1821; Wylie = *Hist. of England under Henry IV* by J. H. Wylie, 4 vols., 1884–98.

Names of the Characters. List first given by Rowe. For *Sir John Falstaff* (orig. *Sir John Oldcastle*) v. Introd. pp. viii, ix, xv and Stage-history p. xxix; *Sir Michael* v. head-note 4. 4; *Gadshill* v. note 1. 2. 104; *Poins* v. note 1. 2. 105–7. *Bardolph* is spelt 'Bardoll' in Q., and the sp. occurs also in F. at 2. 4. 292, so that it may be the author's. In *2 Hen. IV*, however, the Q. sp. is 'Bardolfe'. Acc. to E. I. Fripp (*Richard Quyny*, 1924, pp. 29, 32, etc.) George Bardolf or Bardell was a well-known citizen of Stratford in Sh.'s time. Poss. Sh. adopted the name as a substitute for 'Russell' when that was cancelled with 'Oldcastle' and 'Harvey' (v. note 1. 2. 156). If so, 'Bardoll' may be a misprint for 'Bardell'. For the historical characters v. G. R. French, *Shakespeareana Genealogica*, 1869, and Stokes, *Shakespeare Dictionary of Characters and Proper Names*, 1924.

Acts and Scenes. No divisions in Q. Like other edd. I follow those of F. in my line-numeration, etc., except in act 5, where, since Pope, an additional scene has been introduced. Cf. note 5. 2. 102 S.D.

Punctuation. That in Q. is of the light type usually found in a 'good quarto' (cf. Pollard, *King Richard II: a new quarto*, 1916, pp. 64–73, and MSH, pp. 196–215); too light for a modern reader, so that I have sometimes substituted heavier stops for commas to clarify the sense. Yet I have been able to follow it pretty closely, since it is exceptionally good on the whole: there are, in fact, only eleven instances of what

I may call 'seriously misleading' pointing, i.e. they occur about once in every 300 lines, which is a low average, as Qq. go. My text has too, I think, benefited by the restoration of Q. points here and there, e.g. at 1. 3. 41; 4. 1. 53 (v. notes). Owing to lack of space, I have been obliged to desert the practice of previous volumes, and can record in my notes only such departures from the punctuation of Q. as call for special discussion. I may, however, quote here the eleven 'serious' differences just mentioned, giving the Q. reading first and that which I accept second: 1. 1. 69 'bloud. Did' (Q.), 'blood did' (Q5, F.); 1. 1. 96 'teaching. This' (Q., F.), 'teaching, this'; 1. 2. 33 'for proofe. Now a' (Q., F.), 'for proof now, a' (Rowe, etc., read 'for proof, now:'); 1. 3. 96 'Tongue: for' (Q.), 'tongue for' (Hanmer); 1. 3. 263 'granted you' (Q., F.), 'granted. You' (Hanmer); 2. 2. 39 'prince, Hal' (Q.), 'Prince Hal' (F.); 2. 4. 117 (v. note); 3. 3. 174 'court for' (Q., F.), 'Court: for' (Theobald); 4. 3. 72 'heires, as Pages followed' (Q., F.), 'heirs as pages, followed' (Malone); 5. 1. 131 'how then can' (Q.), 'how then? Can' (Q2); 5. 3. 22 'Ah foole, go' (Q.), 'A fool go' (Capell, v. note).

Stage-directions. Once again, only those in Q. and F. that call for special comment are quoted in the notes; for the rest readers are referred to facsimiles of the originals and to the interesting table of 'illustrative stage-directions' from Qq. and F. in an appendix to W. W. Greg's *Editorial Problem in Shakespeare*, 1942.

Lineation. This presents a major problem to an editor of *1 Henry IV*, and one that has never yet been properly faced. Something like 60 lines which modern editors print as verse appear as prose in Q. Yet, on the one hand, it is certain to my mind that some of these were not finally intended by Sh. to be spoken as verse at all (cf. notes 2. 2. 102–8; 3. 1. 3–5, 6–9), while, on the other, a very little ingenuity might have added a good many more to the total of 60 so far 'recovered' (cf. notes 2.2.77–88; 3.1.10–11; 3.3.193–8). Furthermore, we may legitimately assume Qo to have been printed from Sh.'s own MS., and the lineation of Q1, except for the dovetailing of speeches noted on p. 103, seems to follow Qo. In other words, we are here confronted, not as edd. have assumed with the aberrations of incompetent compositors, but with a lack of system, often even of decision, on the part of the author (cf. note 3.2.173–8). I discuss a possible explanation of this state of affairs elsewhere (v. *Library*, pp. 14–16). As an editor, my sole criterion has been the entirely arbitrary one of what I suppose might have been Sh.'s intention, though I feel sure that he must often have been quite indifferent whether the actor took his lines as verse or as prose (cf. notes 3.1.247–56; 3.3.193–8). Where Q. prints in prose a speech which can be re-arranged as verse without violence to the metre or the mood of the speaker, I see no harm in following Pope or some other 'improver of Shakespeare' (e.g. 2.3.79–90; 3.1.105–9). But in most instances I have thought it best to leave Q1's arrangement alone. For the general question of lineation in Sh., v. Greg, *Editorial Problem*, p. liii.

Acknowledgements. The preparation of the following notes has been facilitated by the recent publication of both parts of *Henry IV* in the *New Variorum Shakespeare*, edited by American scholars, 1 *Henry IV* by S. B. Hemingway, 1936, and 2 *Henry IV* by M. A. Shaaber, 1940. I have also profited from G. L. Kittredge's searching and brilliant little ed. of 1 *Henry IV*, 1940, and from the introductions and notes of R. P. Cowl in the Arden edition of both parts, the special feature of which is the wealth of parallels, at times irrelevant but often illuminating, drawn from contemporary literature. Certain notes and readings marked with his name are derived from pencilled jottings on the play given me by the late G. C. Moore Smith.

I. I.

S.D. Q., F. 'Enter the King, Lord Iohn of Lancaſter, Earle of Weſtmerland, with others.' Capell omits Lancaster and adds Blunt; mod. edd. follow.

1–28. *So shaken...twelve month old* The speech. (i) foreshadows the theme of the two Parts, viz. that peace is impossible to an England ruled by a usurper, that Carlisle's prophecy (*Ric. II*, 4. 1. 136–49) must be fulfilled to the letter, and that the only Jerusalem Henry IV will see is the 'Jerusalem Chamber' where he dies, and (ii) links the play with *Ric. II* on the one hand by its close relation to Carlisle's words, and with *Henry V* on the other by introducing the idea of foreign war as a unifying force. The guile that many detect in the speech is not intended; on the contrary, Henry is shown at the outset a man 'shaken', 'wan with care', and guilt-conscious.

1. *So shaken...care* The sick monarch identifies himself with his sick kingdom.

2–4. *Find we...remote* Let us now find time for harassed peace to take breath ('pant') and 'in broken accents to announce new wars' (Clar.).

2–3. *frighted peace...short-winded accents* 'The figure is probably that of a doe pursued by the hounds' (Herford).

3. *new broils* Cf. *C.W.* i. 1:

I sing the ciuil warrs, tumultuous broyles.

5–6. *No more...children's blood* Malone cites *The Troublesome Reign of K. John*, i, iv, 221–2:

Is all the bloud yspilt on either part,
Closing the crannies of the thirstie earth,

a close parallel; the origin being prob. *Gen.* iv. 11.

6. *daub* i.e. defile the lips, without satisfying the thirst.

9–16. *those opposèd eyes...and allies* Clar. notes:

Opposed eyes...after doing duty in their literal sense and being compared to flashing meteors, are changed to the opposed warriors who once met to conflict, but now march all one way.

10. *meteors...heaven* Alluding to the flashing hurly-burly of a thunder-storm; v. G. 'meteor'.

11. *of one nature...bred* v. G. 'exhaled meteor'.

21. *impressèd* 'The K. speaks...as if he were a conscript....His vow is the conscripting authority' (Kittredge).

28. *But this...twelve month old* This harks back to *Ric. II*, 5.6.49, where the 'purpose' is first expressed. Thus a year's interval is supposed between the two plays, though in history Richard was deposed in 1399 and the battle of Holmedon took place in 1402.

31. *Westmorland* Q., F. 'Weſtmerland'—and so throughout, as in Hall and Hol.

33. *dear expedience* all-important enterprise.

34–5. *hot in question...set down* West. stresses the forwardness of the preparations: the immediate dispatch was being actively discussed, and many of the commands had been actually assigned to their officers. Cf. *Ric. III*, 5.3.25 'Limit each leader to his several charge'.

38. *the noble Mortimer* v. note 1.3.80.

39. *Herefordshire* (F.) Q. 'Herdforſhire'.

40–6. *the irregular and wild...spoken of* This hardly accords with the Glendower, gentleman and scholar, we meet in 3.1.; cf. Hol. iii, 520 (Stone, p. 131).

43. *corpse* (F3) Q., F. 'corpes'. 'Corps' and 'corpes', used for both sing. and plur., are common spellings till the xixth cent.; cf. O.E.D. and *2 Hen. IV*, 1.1.192.

50. *uneven and unwelcome* Cf. l. 66, 'smooth and welcome'.

55. *Holmedon* So Hall; Hol. 'Homildon'; now Humbledon, near Wooler, Northumberland. Glen.'s defeat of Mort. was actually three months earlier than this battle.

55–6. *At Holmedon...hour* (Capell) Q., F. divide 'ſpend/A ſad'. v. G. 'sad'.

57. *artillery* Cf. 'these vile guns' (1. 3. 63). The battle was won by English archers; but Hol. (iii. 520; Stone, p. 131) writes of the 'violence of the English shot', and Sh. or his predecessor takes this for gun-shot.

58. *shape of likelihood* v. G. 'shape'.

62. *a dear* (Q3, F.) Q. 'deere'.
true industrious really zealous.

63. *Blunt* The news was actually brought by one Nicholas Merbury (Wylie, i, 293).

64. *with...each soil* with every kind of soil. Cf. *2 Henry IV*, 5. 5. 20 ff. 'To ride day and night, and... not to have patience to shift me', etc.

69. *balked...blood* v. G. 'balked'. The dead lay in ranks, as they fell, with the blood running between. A quibble also on 'balk'=thwart, check; v. M.L.R. xxxvii, 113 ff., esp. 118.

blood did (Q5, F.) Q. 'Bloud. Did.' If Sh. wrote 'did' with an oversized initial, the compositor might take it for a capital; cf. *Sh.'s Hand*, p. 106.

71–2. *Mordake...Douglas* A good example of the casual and haphazard correspondence between the drama and Hol. Sh.'s words are based on the following from Hol.'s list of the slain: 'Mordacke earle of Fife, son to the gouernour Archembald earle Dowglas' (iii. 520; Stone, p. 132, n. 1), in which a comma has been omitted; and the error is repeated at 1. 3. 260, although on the next page (iii. 521; Stone, p. 133) Hol. states that Murdach or Mordake was son to the Duke of Albany, governor or regent of Scotland. The fact that he was an 'eldest' son is mentioned in the *Chronicle of Scotland*, not in that of England, and prob. came from Stow.

71. *the Earl* (Pope) Q., F. 'Earle'.

73. *Menteith* This was another title of Mordake, but the mistake is Hol.'s (v. Stone, p. 132, n. 3).

75–7. *A gallant...boast of* (Steevens). Cf. Note on the Copy, p. 103.

78–90. *Yea, there...and he mine* In 1403, Hotspur was 39, K. Henry 36, and Hal only 16. Sh. takes from Daniel the idea of Hot. as a young man, and himself makes him the same age as Hal. Cf. 3. 2. 103, 112 and *Library*, pp. 4–6.

82. *Amongst...plant* Cf. Marlowe, Ep. to *Dr Faustus*, 'Cut is the branch that might have grown full straight'.

85. *riot* v. G. The traditional term for P. Hal's behaviour before his accession; cf. *Fortunes*, pp. 17–20.

92–5. *The prisoners...Fife* In fact, by the law of arms 'Percy had an exclusive right to these prisoners, except the Earl of Fife', the latter being of blood royal (Tollet, *ap*. Var. 1821). The chroniclers are silent on this point.

96–7. *This is his uncle's...aspects* Cf. Hol. iii. 521 (Stone, p. 133). 'Malevolent' and 'aspects' are astrol. terms.

98. *prune himself* preen himself, like a hawk.

98–9. *bristle up The crest* Cf. *K. John*, 4. 3. 149, 'Doth dogged war bristle his angry crest'.

100. *But I have...answer this* Hol. (iii. 521; Stone, p. 133) states that the Percies 'came to the king vnto Windsore, vpon a purpose to prooue him'. Sh. gives the K. the initiative; cf. ll. 103–4.

101–2. *We must neglect...Jerusalem* The crusade is postponed—for ever. Cf. *2 Hen. IV*, 3. 1. 108.

103–4. *we/Will hold at Windsor* (Pope) Q., F. 'we wil hold/At Windsore'.

I. 2.

For the significance of this scene, as determining
the relationship between Fal. and Hal, v. *Fortunes*,
pp. 36–43.

S.D. Theobald read 'London. An apartment of the
Prince's' (cf. Wylie, iii. 304, n. 3). For 'Sir John
Falstaff lies snoring', etc., cf. next note.

1. *Now, Hal, what...lad?* The point of this has
eluded the critics. A 'discovery' of Fal. asleep (behind
the curtains of the inner stage) would provide one and
is suggested by ll. 4–5. Stephen Kemble employed the
business in 1804 (Sprague, 83–4).

2–12. *Thou art...time of the day* This defines at
once Fal.'s way of life and Hal's attitude towards it.

3. *fat-witted* Cf. 'fat-brained' *Hen. V*, 3. 7. 143
and G.

3–4. *old sack* Cf. *2 Hen. IV*, 1. 2. 194. Sack=a
strong light-coloured wine, reckoned to be at its best
when 2 or 3 years old (Malone, citing Venner, *Via
Recta ad Vitam Longam*, 1622). The name derives
from *vin sec*, but was often used to cover sweet wines
from Spain or the Canaries, which were nevertheless
further sweetened with sugar (cf. Fynes Moryson,
Itinerary, 1617, iii. 152; Rye, p. 110). For the price v.
2. 4. 525. Fal.'s unlimited consumption of sack
might have a special point for Southampton and his
friends, since from 1590 to 1600 'the monopoly of
the collection of customs and licensing of dealers in
sweet wines, that is to say all wines but those of France
and Germany' constituted the Earl of Essex's 'principal source of free income' (Cheyney, ii. 517).

6–12. *What a devil..time of the day* For a parallel
in Nashe v. p. 191.

11. *flame-coloured taffeta* Arden cites Beaumont and
Fletcher's *Masque of the Inner Temple and Gray's Inn*:
'Enter four Cupids...attired in flame-coloured taffeta'.

Cf. *All's Well*, 2. 2. 21, 'your taffety punk', *2 Hen. IV*, 2. 2. 80 (note), and Linthicum, p. 38.

11–12. *thou...superfluous* you should indulge in the luxury. Fal. is a "superfluous (v. G.) and lust-dieted man" (*Lear*, 4. 1. 68).

13. *you come near me now* you have me there (a fencing metaphor). Fal., ignoring the talk of 'bawds', etc., catches up 'the time of the *day*', which he pretends is nothing to him, since his vocation (l. 102) makes him a night-worker.

14. *go by* (*a*) operate by, (*b*) walk by.

15–16. *Phoebus...knight so fair* Referring to chivalric romances: (i) *The Mirror of Knighthood* by Ortuñez de Calahorra (trans. 1578 by Margaret Tyler, and often reprinted) in which the Knight of the Sun is a leading character; (ii) *The Voyage of the Wandering Knight* by Jean de Cartigny (trans. by W. Goodyear, 1581). The sun was a planet in the old astronomy; hence the 'wandering' quibble on 'knight errant'.

16. *sweet wag* dear boy, v. G. 'wag'.

when thou art king Cf. *F.V.* i. 95, '*Hen. 5* [=P. Hal] I tell you, sirs, and the King my father were dead, we would all be kings'; and vi. 14–34.

king (Q2, F.) Q. 'a King'. Cf. ll. 23, 61; in l. 61 F. adds 'a'.

17. *grace* An obvious threefold quibble; 'grace' being at this date a courtesy title for princes.

24. *squires...body* A squire of the body='an officer charged with personal attendance upon a sovereign' etc. (O.E.D.). Cf. note ll. 105–7. H. Bradley (*Sh. Eng.* ii. 541) denies a pun upon 'knight' in 'night', since *k* before *n* was pronounced at this time; but one seems clearly intended at *2 Hen. IV*, 5. 4. 24. Cf. also the pun, 'nave-knave', in *2 Hen. IV*, 2. 4. 254.

25. *thieves...beauty* Obscure. Arden plausibly compares Ger. 'Tagesdieb' and explains: 'a euphemism

for a loafer' or wastrel, with a quibble on 'booty';
cf. 'burn daylight' (*M.W.W.* 2. 1. 48; *Rom*. 1. 4. 43).

let us...foresters i.e. let us be called, not thieves,
but rangers of Diana; cf. *Cymb*. 2. 3. 74.

26. *gentlemen of the shade* Cf. Gentlemen of the
Chamber, etc., members of the Royal Household. In
F.V. vi. 30 ff. Hal promises an annual pension to all
highwaymen.

27. *men of good government*=men of good conduct,
not wastrels (l. 25).

29. *countenance...steal* Both words used quibblingly. Arden quotes Wilkins, *Miseries of Inforst
Marriage*, 1607 (sig. F 2 v): 'The Moone, patroneſſe
of all purſe-takers'.

we steal Pope reads 'we—steal'.

30. *it holds well too* it's a good simile too.

too Q. 'to'—a common Eliz. sp., frequent in
this Q.

31–2. *the fortune...sea* Diana being a common
title for Elizabeth, this talk about 'minions of the
moon' seems pretty daring, esp. as it exactly describes
the condition of her favourites.

36. '*bring in*' The call to the drawer, for wine.

36–8. *now in...gallows* Refers back to the sea of
fortune.

37–8. *ladder...ridge* The condemned thief, rope
round neck, climbed by ladder to the ridge or cross-
beam of the gallows, whence the hangman 'turned
him off'. Cf. note 4. 2. 36.

39–40. *and is not...wench?* To change the subject, Fal. insinuates that a purse of gold might be put
to other uses; to which Hal replies with a reflection
on the 'wench' and a quid pro quo in 'old lad of the
castle'. In *F.V*. i. 89 the P., discussing where to
spend the £1000 taken at Gad's Hill, advises 'the olde
Tauerne in Eastcheape' because there is good wine
and 'a pretie wench that can talke well'.

41–2. *As the honey...the castle* i.e. to vary the words of a nineteenth-century music-hall song, 'She is the honey-suckle, but *you* are the bee!'

old lad of the castle i.e. old rip, v. G.; with a quibble on Oldcastle, Falstaff's original name. Cf. p. xxix.

42–3. *is not...durance?* Hal returns to his theme, punishment. 'A buff jerkin' = prison dress, and 'durance' = (*a*) stout material, (*b*) imprisonment, v. G.

49–50. *Well...time and oft* Fal. dares not maintain the innuendo of ll. 39–40.

56–7. *and so used...apparent* Implying 'that, but for his prospect of the throne' he 'would be credit-broken' (Hudson, ed. 1880). The pun 'hair—here—hair' recurs at *Err.* 3. 2. 124.

59. *resolution* courage, determination; cf. l. 33. Fal. makes the most of the valour of his vocation.

fubbed (Q.) F. 'fobb'd'; v. G.

60. *old father...law* i.e. the poor old Law, long since out of date with Corinthians and lads of mettle.

63–4. *I'll be...judge!* A relic of the L.C. Justice plot; cf. *Library*, p. 7 and *F.V.* vi. 23, 'Ile be the brauest Lord Chief Justice that euer was in England;' v. G. 'brave'.

65. *judgest false* (*a*) misunderstandest, (*b*) art a false judge.

69. *waiting* For preferment, or the 'obtaining of suits'.

71. *whereof...wardrobe* The criminal's clothes were the hangman's perquisite; cf. *Cor.* 1. 5. 7.

73. *melancholy* Because the talk kept returning to the hangman; cf. *Fortunes*, pp. 32–5.

gib cat...bear Tom-cats on the tiles and bears in pain both utter melancholy cries, v. G. 'gib', 'lugged'.

75. *drone* At once the bass-pipe and its single note.

76. *hare* Cf. Turbervile, *Book of Hunting*, 1576 (p. 160, ed. Tudor and Stuart Library): 'The Hare... is one of the moste melancholike beastes that is', and

Burton, *Anatomy of Melancholy*, 1621, I, ii, 2, 1:
'Hare, a black meat, melancholy and hard of digestion:
it breeds incubus, often eaten, and çauseth fearful
dreams'.

77. *Moor-ditch* v. G. Malone cites Taylor's *Pil-
grimage*, 1618, 'my mind attired in moody, muddy,
Moorditch, melancholy'.

78. *similes* (Q5) Q., F. 'ſmiles'—an independent
misprint.

79. *comparative* i.e. abusive, v. G. and 3. 2. 67.

81. *vanity* Fal. assumes sanctimony, and as usual
accuses Hal of leading him astray.

81–2. *I would...bought* v. G. 'commodity'. Reed
(ap. Var. 1821) cites *Discoverie of the knights of the
Poste*, 1597, sig. C: 'In troth they liue so so, and it
were well if they knew where a commoditie of names
were to be sould, and yet I thinke all the money in
their purses could not buy it.'

83–6. *an old lord of the council* etc. Perhaps another
relic of the L.C. Justice plot; cf. above, note, ll. 63–4,
2 Hen. IV, I. 2. 116–20, and *Library*, p. 7.

87–8. *wisdom cries...regards it* Cf. *Prov.* i. 20,
24.

89. *thou...damnable iteration* you can patter Scrip-
ture like the Devil. Cf. Apperson, 'Devil' 44, and
Chapman, *Bussy d'Ambois*, 5. 2. 5–6, 'men say Latin
prayers By rote of heart and daily iteration'. The
scribe responsible for the F. text found the P.'s iteration
so damnable that he cut it out. Cf. p. 105.

99. *baffle* v. G. and note 2. 4. 428–9. To call a
knight a villain (=serf) would 'baffle' him.

102–3. *'tis my vocation...vocation* Cf. Nashe, cited
p. 191.

104. *Poins!* (Q. 'Poynes') Q4, followed by Q5,
F., and edd. to Pope, take this as a speech-prefix.

Gadshill In *F.V.* the 'thief' is named Cuthbert
Cutter (sc. iv. 17 f.) but nicknamed 'Gadshill' by the

carrier robbed by him on Gad's Hill (ii. 67; x. 44). Sh. adopts the nickname from the old play, and omits the raison d'être. Cf. *Library*, pp. 2, 9.

set a match planned a robbery, v. G. 'match'. Cf. 'our setter' 2. 2. 49 and note 2. 1. 51.

105–7. *O, if men...true man* Poins is the P.'s body-squire or gentleman-in-waiting (cf. *Fortunes*, p. 39 and *2 Hen. IV*, 2. 2. 158, G.), not one of the Fal. gang; but of enmity between them, which some imagine, I can detect none, except in sport, as here.

105. *saved by merit* i.e. by works, not faith. Cf. *L.L.L.* 4. 1. 21; *Tw.Nt.* 1. 5. 128 note.

107. *omnipotent villain* almighty scoundrel. Cf. Nashe, cited p. 191.

a true man an honest man; cf. 2. 1. 91 note.

109–13. *What says...capon's leg?* A retort to Fal.'s 'what hole in hell', etc.

109. *Monsieur Remorse* Cf. *Fortunes*, pp. 32 f.

110. *Sir John...Sugar? Jack* (Rowe) Q. 'Sir Iohn Sacke, and Sugar Iacke?' v. note 1. 2. 3–4.

112. *Good Friday* The strictest of fast days. Cf. *K. John*, 1. 1. 235.

114–16. *Sir John...his due* i.e. as he is certain to go to hell anyway, the proverb will hold. 'His due'= the soul he owes to him. Cf. Apperson, p. 143, Jente, No. 103.

117–19. *Then art...the devil* It is an odd thing, says Poins, to be damned for keeping faith, even with the Devil; to which the P. replies that it matters little as he would be damned in any case.

121. *Gad's Hill* On the highway 27 miles from London and 2½ from Rochester, notorious for highway robberies. Cf. Rye, p. 49. My spelling distinguishes the place from the man.

121–2. *pilgrims...traders* Pilgrims travelled from London to the shrine of St Thomas, traders to London from the continent: an opulent two-way traffic.

123. *vizards* Not mentioned in *F.V.* though connected with the 'disguised array' of the orig. legend. Cf. *Library*, p. 7.

124. *you have horses* Cf. *F.V.* i. 28f., 61–2.

130. *I'll hang you* I'll have you hanged, by turning King's evidence. He threatens this again at 2. 2. 43.

131. *chops* i.e. fat chops. Cf. *Fortunes*, p. 29, G., and *2 Hen. IV*, 2. 4. 215.

135–6. *blood royal...ten shillings* Quibbles on 'royal'=10s. and 'stand for'=(*a*) represent, (*b*) be good for, (*c*) stand in ambush on the highway. Cf. 2. 4. 283 note; *Ric. II*, 5. 5. 68 note.

136. S.D. To explain the P.'s sudden compliance after the refusal at l. 133. Cf. *Fortunes*, p. 38.

137. *once in my days* for once. Cf. *Temp.* 3. 2. 21, 'once in thy life'.

146–50. *Well, God give...countenance* More mock sanctimony. Noble (p. 171) cites the Collect at the end of the Communion Service.

150. *the poor abuses...countenance* A double parody, (*a*) on 'the regular complaint that good causes are not properly encouraged by the nobility' (Kittredge), and (*b*) on puritans who attacked the 'abuses of the time', e.g. Philip Stubbes in *The Anatomy of Abuses*, 1583.

152. *thou latter* (Pope) Q., F. 'the latter'.

153. *All-hallown summer* i.e. the warm sunny weather that often comes about All Saints' Day (1 Nov.) or St Martin's Day (11 Nov.). Cf. *1 Hen. VI*, 1. 2. 131, 'St Martin's summer, halcyon days'.

156. *Bardolph, Peto* (Theobald) Q., F. 'Haruey, Rofsill'. Cf. 2. 4. 171, 173, 177 where Q. gives the prefix 'Rofs.', for which F. reads 'Gad', and the Q. entry S.D. at *2 Hen. IV*, 2. 2. 1 'Sir Iohn Ruffel' for which F. reads 'Bardolfe'. Harvey and Russell, names familiar at Eliz.'s court, were prob. altered when Oldcastle was changed to Falstaff. Cf. Chambers, *Wm. Sh.* i. 382, and *Library*, p. 15.

162–6. *Why, we...upon them* The action in 2. 1 does not tally with this, but Sh.'s ideas prob. shift as he passes from scene to scene.

163–4. *it is...fail* 'we can fail to keep our appointment if we please' (Clar.).

168. *habits* clothes.   171. *wood;* Q., F. 'wood,'

172. *sirrah* 'A term...usually employed in speaking to inferiors' (Clar.), thus indicating considerable familiarity on Poins's part.

cases of buckram canvas overalls. Eliz. buckram was not necessarily stiff; cf. G. 'case', and Linthicum, pp. 103–4.

173. *noted* well known.

174. *too hard* more than a match.

178. *incomprehensible* infinite. Cf. Nashe, cited p. 191, and the Athanasian creed.

182. *lives* (Q.) Q 2–5, F. 'lies'—which most edd. read. Cf. G.; *Ado*, 4. 1. 187; *K. John*, 4. 2. 72.

184. *meet me...Eastcheap* Cf. l. 151. This seems to overlook the earlier rendezvous on Gad's Hill; but Sh. wishes to fix the attention of the audience upon the coming disclosure at the Boar's Head, and knows they will notice nothing wrong.

187–209. *I know you all*, etc. For the relation of this speech to the problem of the P.'s character, v. *Fortunes*, pp. 41–3, and Kittredge, p. xi: 'This is, in effect, the author's explanation—a kind of chorus—and should be so understood.'

188. *unyoked humour* coltish pranks; cf. *2 Hen. IV*, 4. 2. 103.

189. *the sun* symbol of royalty; cf. *Ric. II*, pp. xii–xiii, and *Son.* 33.

190. *contagious* v. G. 'Pestilence was thought to be generated in fog, mist, and cloud' (Kittredge); cf. *M.N.D.* 2. 1. 90; *Ric. II*, 3. 3. 85–7; *K. John*, 5. 4. 33.

196–8. *If all...for come* Cf. *Son.* 52.

199. *accidents* events, phenomena.

203. *falsify...hopes* exceed men's expectations (in a neutral sense). Cf. *2 Hen. IV*, 5. 2. 126–9, 'mock the expectation of the world', etc.

204. *sullen ground* dark background. Cf. *Ric. II*, 1. 3. 265–7.

208. *make offence a skill* i.e. turn it to good purpose.

209. *redeeming time* making up for time misspent; cf. *Ephes.* v. 16.

1. 3.

S.D. Theobald, Camb. and most edd. read 'London, The Palace'; Halliwell 'Windsor. A Room in the Palace', while Arden notes that 1. 1. 103–4 and Hol. fix the scene at Windsor.

1–4. *My blood...patience* We begin in the middle of an altercation but catch glimpses at ll. 77–80, 140 ff. below of matters earlier touched upon. Perhaps an opening passage has been cut.

3. *found me* discovered this fact; cf. *Ham.* 3. 1. 188.

5–6. *rather...condition* rather play the strong king than yield to my native mildness; v. G. 'condition'. Cf. *Hen. V*, 1. Prol. 5, and *R.E.S.* Ap. 1940, p. 178.

8. *title of* claim to.   12. *too* (F.) Q. 'to'.

13. *portly* v. G.

15–16. *I do see...thine eye* Cf. *Ric. II*, 1. 3. 97–8.

17. *O, sir* Extrametrical; cf. l. 247.

19. *The moody frontier...brow* Wor.'s sullen looks are likened to fortifications erected on the boundaries of a vassal's domain; v. G. 'frontier'. The image prob. springs from 'front' = brow.

20. *good leave* full permission. Cf. *K. John*, 1. 1. 230–1.

21. *use and counsel* advice. Lit. 'to use you in counsel'.

25. *with...denied* so strenuously refused. Neither Stow nor Hol. give authority for North.'s moderation or Hot.'s later apology.

27. *Either envy, therefore* (Q.) F. 'Who either through enuy', v. G. 'envy'.

33. *neat...dressed* exquisitely turned out.

34. *his chin...reaped* his freshly clipped beard.

35. *at harvest-home* after the carting of the corn.

36. *perfuméd...milliner* v. G. 'milliner'.

38. *pouncet-box* v. G. The fop disinfects himself, on the battle-field, by snuffing up an aromatic powder. His modern equivalent would use a throat-spray.

40. *therewith* i.e. at being deprived of the pouncet-box.

41. *took it in snuff* = (*a*) took offence at it, (*b*) snuffed it up and sneezed. The first meaning is 'connected with the unpleasant smell' of a snuffed-out candle (O.E.D. 'snuff' sb¹). O.E.D. gives 1680 as the date at which tobacco snuff-taking became fashionable, but Capell notes that 'snuffs made of herbs, aromatic and other, were used medically long before Henry IV'.

talked: (Q., F.) Most edd. read a comma.

47. *questioned me* held me in talk ('much against my will' implied).

50. *To be...popinjay* That the line is difficult to place syntactically makes it the more suggestive of Hot.'s testiness. *popinjay* (Q7) Q, F. 'Popingay'.

51. *grief* pain of the wound.

58. *parmaceti...bruise* Moore Smith quotes B. Rich, *Riche his Farwell to the Military Profession*, 1581 (Sh. Soc. p. 154): 'But the Doctor took sparmaceti and suche like thinges that bee good for a bruse, and recouered hym self in a shorte space.' See Clar. for other parallels. The parmaceti goes with the valetudinarian's pouncet-box.

62. *tall* brave, stout.   65. *bald* trivial.

66. *I answered* (Q.) F. 'Made me to anſwer'.

68. *Come current* be accepted at its face value.

75–6. *impeach...he said* i.e. be laid to his charge for saying it. Sh. has tied himself up in a little knot, but the sense is clear.

80. *His brother-in-law* The following pedigree (p. 129), based on Malone, shows the historical relationships: Hol., Daniel and Sh. all confuse the two Edmund Mortimers, uncle and nephew; but Sh. also at times, as here, confuses Edmund, Earl of March, with Roger his father, who *was* Hot.'s 'brother-in-law'.

83–4. *the great...that Earl* Q. 'that great...that Earle', F. 'the great...the Earle'. Most edd. read 'that great...the Earl'; but unless we read 'that Earl' the audience will hardly grasp the fact that Mortimer and March are the same. For 'magician' v. note 3. 1. 223–5.

87–8. *indent...themselves* come to terms with a coward, like Mortimer, who has thrown up the sponge; [cf. *M.L.R.* XLII, 381]; v. G. 'indent'.

96. *Needs...wounds* Cf. *Ric. III*, 1. 2. 55–6; *Jul. Caes.* 3. 1. 259–61; *Cor.* 2. 3. 6–8.

98–107. *When on...combatants* These ornate lines, as many have noted, come oddly from Hot., who speaks the contemptuous words of poets and poetry at 3. 1. 127–33. Cf. *Library*, pp. 14–16.

101. *in changing hardiment* i.e. each excelling the other in turn, v. G.

106. *crisp head* Cf. *M.V.* 3. 2. 92 'crispéd locks'; *Temp.* 4. 1. 130 'crisp channels'. A quibble, 'head'= the pressure of water against a bank (O.E.D. sb. 17), and 'crisp'=rippled; v. G.

108. *bare* (Q.) F. 'baſe'. Many follow F. 'Bare policy'= patent cunning.

113. *dost belie him* dost not speak the truth about him.

118. *sirrah* v. note 1. 2. 172.

119. *speak* Emphatic (Kittredge).

124. *you'll* (F.) Q. 'you will'. Cf. p. 104.

125. *the devil...roar* i.e. the stage devil of the moralities; cf. *Hen. V*, 4. 4. 75, 'this roaring devil i' the old play'.

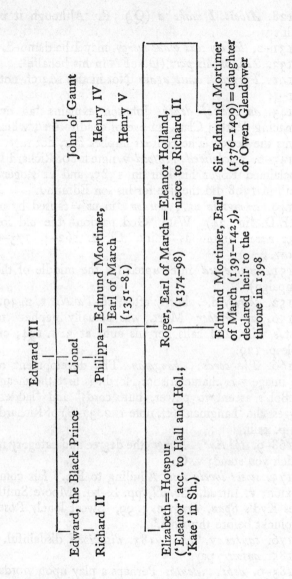

Edward III

— Edward, the Black Prince
　— Richard II

— Lionel
　— Philippa = Edmund Mortimer,
　　　　　　　　Earl of March
　　　　　　　　(1351–81)
　　— Roger, Earl of March = Eleanor Holland,
　　　　(1374–98)　　　　　niece to Richard II
　　　　— Edmund Mortimer, Earl
　　　　　of March (1391–1425),
　　　　　declared heir to the
　　　　　throne in 1398
　　　　— Elizabeth = Hotspur
　　　　　('Eleanor' acc. to Hall and Hol.;
　　　　　'Kate' in Sh.)

— John of Gaunt
　— Henry IV
　　— Henry V

— Sir Edmund Mortimer
　(1376–1409) = daughter
　　of Owen Glendower

128. *Albeit I make a* (Q.) F. 'Although it be with'.

131–2. *let my soul want mercy* may I be damned.

133. *Yea, on his part* (Q.) F. 'In his behalfe'.

141. *I urged...once again* Not in this sc.; cf. note ll. 1–4.

143. *an eye of death* Johnson explains 'an eye menacing death'; Clar. 'an eye of deadly fear', which seems the better. The context implies fear, not rage.

145–6. *proclaimed...blood* v. note l. 80. Richard II proclaimed Roger his heir in 1385, and at Roger's death in 1398 did the like for his son Edmund.

149. *wrongs in us...pardon* 'in us'=caused by us (O.E.D. 'in' 24). With 'God pardon' the old fox gives a sanctimonious smirk. Cl. ll. 162–4, 173–6 below.

151. *intercepted* interrupted (in the middle of the campaign).

152. *shortly* i.e. shortly after; cf. *Tw.Nt.* 1. 2. 39.

156. *my brother* Mort. was actually nephew to Hot.'s wife, and calls her his aunt at 3. 1. 194; cf. table p. 129.

166. *The cords...hangman* The development of the imagery is characteristic: North. is first the means of Bol.'s ascent to power, but 'cords' and 'ladder' suggest the 'hangman' (cf. note 1. 2. 37–8) of Richard. Cf. p. xxiii.

168–9. *the line...range* the degree and category in which you stand; v. G.

175. *sweet lovely rose* Alluding to Ric.'s fair complexion; v. Introd. *Ric. II*, pp. lx–lxi. Moore Smith cites Kyd's *Span. Trag.* 2. 5. 99, 'Sweet louely Rose, ill pluckt before thy time.'

176. *canker* v. G.   183. *disdained* disdainful.

185. *answer* pay.

185–6. *debt...deaths* Perhaps a play upon words; cf. note 5. 1. 126–7.

189. *Your...discontents* Your minds which discontent has made receptive.

191–3. *As full...spear* Worc. knows the language that appeals to Hot.

194. *good night* (Q2) Q. 'god-night', i.e. it's goodbye whether he sink or swim, in such a current. Cf. Apperson, 'sink or swim'.

201. *By heaven* etc. Q. omits 'Hot.' speech-prefix; Q5 supplies it.

201–7. *By heaven...dignities* The prentice Ralph recites these lines in the Induct. to Beaumont and Fletcher's *Knight of the Burning Pestle*.

208. *this half-faced fellowship* this wretched sharing of honours; cf. 'without corrival' (l. 207). A man to whom honour shared is not worth having is politically impossible. Cf. note 5. 4. 88, and *Fortunes*, p. 70.

209. *a world of figures* A universe of images; referring to 'pale-faced moon' and 'bottom of the deep'.

210. *form* the point in hand; v. G.

214–15. *Scot of them...save his soul* Double quibble: (*a*) 'scot'=a trifling amount (lit. a share in the payment of a tavern bill), (*b*) 'scot and lot'=a final settlement.

217. *purposes* meaning. Cf. ll. 209–10.

222. *holla 'Mortimer'* Malone cites a close parallel from Marlowe's *Ed. II*, 2. 2. 125–7:

Younger Mortimer. Cousin, an if he will not ransom him,
I'll thunder such a peal into his ears,
As never subject did unto his king.

228. *All studies...defy* i.e. I...renounce all pursuits.

230. *sword-and-buckler* swash-buckler. Sword and buckler were the weapons of the highwayman (cf. 2. 4. 164–5) or serving-man; gentlemen wore rapiers. Cf. *What Happens in 'Hamlet'*, pp. 272–80.

233. *poisoned...ale* Another allusion to the P.'s way of life. Actually only once does he 'remember the poor creature, small beer' (*2 Hen. IV*, 2. 2. 11); yet great men might drink small beer on occasions; the peers who tried Essex did so in court (v. Cheyney, ii. 539).

234. *Farewell...you* A line of prose, though edd. make various attempts to versify it.

238. *Tying thine ear...own* Kittredge cites Greene, *Ciceronis Amor*, 1589 (ed. Grosart, vii. 137–8): 'Tully tyed the peoples eares to his tongue by his eloquence.'

242. *de' ye* (F.) Q. 'do you'. F. gives the accent of impatience. Cf. p. 107.

243. *upon't* (F.) Q. 'vpon it'. Cf. p. 104.

244. *madcap duke* There is nothing 'madcap' about York in *Ric. II*, except in 5. 2, 5. 3, scenes I suspect by another hand; cf. Introd. *Ric. II*, pp. lxix–lxxiv.

245–8. *where I...castle* Cf. *Ric. II*, 2. 3. 41–50.

247. *'Sblood!* Extrametrical; cf. l. 17.

250. *a candy deal* a sweet quantity.

251. *fawning greyhound* The word 'candy' suggests the greyhound, since Sh. often associates dogs with sweetmeats. Cf. *Ham*. 3. 2. 58–60 (note), and Spurgeon, *Sh.'s Imagery*, pp. 195–9.

252–3. *Look...'kind cousin'* Cf. *Ric. II*, 2. 3. 45 'gentle Percy', 66 'till my infant fortune comes to years', and *C.W.* iii. 13, 'his tender raigne/And infant-young-beginning gouernment'.

254. *cozeners* v. G., with a quibble on 'cousin'.

257. *i'faith* seriously!

260. *the Douglas' son* v. note 1. 1. 71–2.

267. *is't* (F.) Q. 'is it'. Cf. p. 104.

268. *His brother's death* Cf. *Ric. II*, 3. 2. 142. William Scroop, Earl of Wiltshire, was cousin not brother to the Abp. (v. Wylie, ii. 197). The error is

Hol.'s (iii. 521; Stone, p. 135). A 'cousin Scroop' turns
up at 4. 4. 3 (v. note).

275. *Before...let'st slip* You always loose the hound
before the hare is afoot. Cf. Madden, p. 167; *Hen. V*,
3. 1. 31; *Jul. Caes.* 3. 1. 273. North. is annoyed that
Hot. interrupts Worc. just as he is about to say what
the plot is.

game's (Q5, F.) Q. 'game is'. Cf. p. 104.

278. *ha?* eh?

282–5. *For, bear...home* Cf. *Ric. II*, 5. 1. 59–68.

2. 1.

S.D. Theobald reads 'Rochester, an inn', citing
1. 2. 124.

The night sky, with Charles's wain 'over the new
chimney', the flickering gleam of the lanterns in the dirty
yard, the fresh air of the early dawn, the misty atmosphere,
the mingled odour of damp peas and beans, of bacon and
ginger, all comes straight home to our senses (Brandes,
Will. Sh., ed. in 1 vol. p. 198).

Sh.'s scenery is in his dialogue.

1. *An't* (F.) Q. 'an it'.

3. *horse* horses.　　*packed* loaded up on the pack-
saddle; a skilled operation.

4. *Anon* i.e. Coming! (lit. 'immediately').

5. *beat* So as to level out the lumps. The comic
carrier in *F.V.* (iv. 29) complains that the Thief 'hath
beaten and wounded my packe'.

6. *flocks* i.e. of wool.　　*poor jade is* Cf. 'poor
fellow never joyed' (l. 12). The omitted article implies rustic speech.　　*wrung in the withers* Cf. *Ham.*
3. 2. 241.

8. *dank...as a dog* Cf. 'dog-tired', 'dog-cheap',
'dog-drunk' (O.E.D. 'dog' 17d).　　*dank* i.e. 'not
like the "good dry oats" that Bottom wished for'
(Clar.).

9. *next way* quickest way.

15. *stung like a tench* Cf. l. 21; allusions to parasitic crustaceans found on fish; cf. O.E.D. 'fish-louse'.

17. *king christen* (Q.) Christian king. F. 'King in Christendome'. Cf. *Ham.* 5. 1. 28 'even-Christen'.

20. *leak...chimney* This unsavoury practice, expressly condemned by Dr Andrew Boorde (*Dyetary of Helth*, 1542, ed. Early Eng. Text Soc. pp. 236–7), was evidently common. Cf. G. 'chimney'.

21. *breeds...loach* Cf. note l. 15. Clearly 1 Carrier is a fisherman.　　　　22. *come away* v. G.

24. *razes of ginger* v. G. 'raze'. The carrier in *F.V.* (iv. 30) is robbed of a 'great rase of Ginger that bouncing Besse...should have had'.

25. *Charing-cross* i.e. the other side of London city.

26. *turkeys* First found in Mexico, 1518; brought to Europe soon after, v. O.E.D.

29. *as good...drink* Prov. Cf. 2. 2. 21.

32. *two o'clock* Cf. l. 1 above. 'The carrier... suspecting Gad., did not want him to think it was time to start' (Clar.).

35–6. *soft...ay, faith* not so fast! I'm not quite such a fool as all that. *ay, faith!* Q. 'I faith'.

38. *when? canst tell?* 'don't you wish you may get it!' (Deighton). Cf. *Err.* 3. 1. 52.

39. *quoth-a* (F.) Q. 'quoth he'. Cf. p. 104.

42. *Time enough...candle* sometime this evening. Gad. is trying to discover the carriers' timetable, so as to guess the hour they will be passing Gad's Hill; they see his purpose and put him off. Cf. note 1. 2. 121.

44. *They will...company* This implies that they would travel with the gentlemen; yet no carriers appear in 2. 2, though one comes as witness with the Sheriff who calls to arrest Fal. at 2. 4. 492, and a carrier is robbed on Gad's Hill in *F.V.* Cf. *Library*, pp. 7, 9.

45. *great charge* i.e. much money, as appears from ll. 54–7; cf. note l. 57.

46. *chamberlain* v. G. Inn-servants were notorious for complicity with highwaymen: 'Certes, I believe that not a chapman or traveller in England is robbed without the knowledge of some of them' (William Harrison, *Description of England*, 1587, quoted in my *Life in Sh.'s England*, p. 82).

47. *At hand, quoth pick-purse* Prov. = Here I am! (cf. Jente, No. 167). No one can be closer at hand than he who has his hand in your pocket.

48. *as fair* as apt.

50. *than giving...labouring* than the overseer does from the workman. But 'giving direction' also = the cant term for the Chamberlain's part in the robbery. Cf. Jonson, iii. 547 (*E.M.O.* 3. 6. 33–4).

51. *layest the plot how* Also equivocal: plot = (*a*) overseer's plan for the workmen, (*b*) highwayman's plot.

S.D. Q.F. give the entry at l. 46 when the Chamb. first speaks, correctly from the stage point of view.

54. *franklin...wild* freeholder from the weald; v. G.

three hundred marks £200; v. G. 'mark'. To judge from 2. 4. 508, this is all that is taken on Gad's Hill, though Fal. boasts of £1000 at 2. 4. 156 (v. note).

56. *auditor* An official of the Exchequer; cf. G. and *Library*, p. 7.

57. *too* Implies that the 300 marks is reckoned as 'charge'.

60. *Saint Nicholas' clerks* The special saint of clerics and travellers was also claimed as patron by highwaymen and cutpurses, partly no doubt because his name suggested at once 'nick' (= cut) and 'Old Nick' (= the Devil), and partly, I suspect, because he was usually represented with three purses in his hand (actually in celebration of a miracle by which he had

caused robbers to restore stolen goods, cf. Pollard, *Eng. Miracle Plays*, App. 11), and thus seemed to typify the cutpurse himself.

61. *neck* With a pun on 'Nick'.

65. *What* Why. Cf. *2 Hen. IV*, 1. 2. 111.

talkest...hangman Cf. notes 1. 2. 37–8, 42–3, 73; 4. 2. 36.

67. *he's* (F.). Q. 'he is'. Cf. p. 104.

·68. *Trojans* v. G.

72–4. *with no...malt-worms* with no vagabonds, footpads that will knock a man down for sixpence, or roistering purple-faced soakers with fierce moustaches. Cf. G. for separate terms.

72–3. *long-staff...strikers* v. G. 'striker'. Clar. cites Evelyn's *Diary*, 23 June 1652:

Two cut-throats started out, and striking with long staves at the horse and taking hold of the reins threw me down, took my sword, and hauled me into a deep thicket some quarter of a mile from the highway, where they might securely rob me, as they soon did.

74. *tranquillity* 'people who live at ease' (Onions).

75. *onyers* (Malone) Q. 'oneyres', F. 'Oneyers'. Much debated. Johnson takes it as plur. of 'great-one-yer' ('as we say privateer, auctioneer, etc.'). But Malone suggests '*onyers*, that is *public accountants*, men possessed of large sums of money belonging to the state'; and, quoting from Coke, *On Littleton*, 1628, iv. 116, notes that the vb. 'to ony' was still used in his day at the Exchequer, a word coined from *o.ni.* (=oneratur nisi habeat, etc.) which the sheriff set at the head of his statement in making up his accounts. Cf. O.E.D. 'O Ni', giving *oni*, a vb. trans. = 'to charge to the sheriff'—from which 'onier', a clerk to the Exchequer, is a short, if conjectural, step. The Chamb. claims franklins and auditors among the travellers, Gad. burgomasters and great Exchequer officials among

the highwaymen. Both 'auditor' and 'onyers' hark
back to the Receivers of the orig. legend; cf. *Library*,
p. 7.

75–6. *can hold in* will not blab.

76–7. *such as will*...*drink* the sort of fellows who
prefer blows to words and will rather cry 'lay by'
than 'bring in' (cf. note 1. 2. 36).

81. *boots* spoil. O.E.D. gives no other instance of
the plur. in this sense. The quibble is obvious.

83. *will she*...*way?* would she be any protection
in a tight corner? Lit. will she keep out the damp on
a muddy road?

84. *liquored* (*a*) greased (of boots), (*b*) made drunk
(of men).

85. *castle* A type of security. Also 'Gad. alludes
to the name of his leader—Sir John Oldcastle' (Kittredge).

86. *fern-seed* Being invisible itself, this was supposed, acc. to the primitive logic that governed the old
science, to confer invisibility upon those who carried
it. It could be found on Midsummer Eve (St John's
Eve), at which time alone it was visible.

91. *purchase* v. G.   *as I am a true man* in very
truth. But 'true man'=honest man, as distinguished
from criminal; hence the Chamb.'s retort. Cf. *F.V.*
ii. 75–8:

Iohn. My friend, what make you abroad now? It is too
late to walke now.
Theef [=Gad.]. It is not too late for true men to
walke.
Lawrence. We know thee not to be a true man.

94. '*homo*'...*all men* A sentence from Lyly's
Grammar, often quoted, e.g. by Nashe, v. p. 192:
'All men', i.e. honest and false alike.

2. 2.

S.D. Q. 'Enter Prince, Poines, and Peto, &c.' The
Q. '&c.' includes Bardolph (cf. l. 20), who is with
the party riding from London (1.2.124, 154, 167–70),
not with Gad. the 'setter', who comes from Rochester
and announces the victims' approach. Led astray by
a slight confusion of speech-prefixes in ll. 50–1 (v.
note), mod. edd. give Bard. his entry with Gad. at
l. 46. N.B. The carriers (cf. notes 2. 1. 44; 2. 4. 495)
do not appear.

Pope reads 'The Highway', and Capell 'Gadshill.
The road down to it'. Cf. note 1. 2. 121.

1–2. *Falstaff's horse* In *F.V.* i. 61 Oldcastle's horse
is a bay called Hobby; the only comic touch about him.

2. *frets...velvet* A common quibble. Stiffened
velvet was more liable to chafe, and so to grow shabby.

3. *stand close* hide yourself, v. G. 'close'.

11–35. *The rascal...afoot again* For a parallel in
Nashe v. p. 192: 'I'll not bear...afoot again' echo
his very words.

13–14. *Well, I doubt...all this* Yet I don't doubt
I shall make a fine death of it, in spite of all he can do;
i.e. Poins may be the death of me, but I mean to make
a godly end.　　18. *medicines* love-potions, v. G.

20. *starve* die.　　22. *true man* Cf. note 2. 1. 91.

26. *upon't* (F.) Q. 'vpon it'.

27. *Whew!* Fal. mocks at the whistling.

35. *all the coin...exchequer* The 'receivers' theme;
cf. *Library*, p. 7.

42. *Go hang* (F.) Q. 'Hang'. Cf. *Temp.* 2. 2. 53;
Troil. 4. 2. 26; *Ant.* 2. 7. 59.

43. *garters* 'Alluding to the Order of the Garter
in which he was enrolled as heir apparent' (Johnson).
Apperson ('Hang') and Jente cite Ray, *English Proverbs*,
1670, 'He may go hang himself in's own garters'.

44. *ballads...tunes* The Star Chamber frequently

punished the makers of libellous ballads, set to popular tunes, v. Cheyney, i. 92–3. Cf. p. 192 for parallel in Nashe.

46. *afoot* in action. Fal. quibbles.

S.D. Q., F. 'Enter Gadshill'. Pope and later edd. added 'Bardolph and Peto with him'. Cf. head-note and note ll. 49–51 below.

49–51. *O, 'tis our setter...Case ye, case ye*, etc. (Johnson) Q. prints:

> *Po.* O tis our setter, I know his voice, Bardoll, what newes.
> *Bar.* Cafe yee, cafe yee...Exchequer

F. and all mod. edd. follow. But Johnson notes that (i) it is absurd to recognize one man as the 'setter' and ask another for the 'news', and that (ii) Fal.'s cries at l. 20 show Bar. and Peto to have entered by then. We may add (iii) that ll. 51–3 must be spoken by the 'setter', whose function is to give notice of the prey's approach (1. 2. 104), while Peto's question at l. 61 and Gad.'s answer to him provide further evidence that Gad. enters alone. The Q. text is explained if we suppose that (*a*) Sh. wrote the two short speeches (ll. 49–50) in one line and their prefixes, as was his custom, in 'English' script like the rest, and (*b*) the printers, taking it as a query addressed to Bar., changed Gad. to Bar. accordingly at the beginning of l. 51. Cf. MSH. pp. 187–91.

51. *Case ye* mask yourselves; cf. note 1. 2. 123.

52–3. *money...exchequer* 'Receivers' theme again; cf. l. 35.

54–5. *the king's tavern* Why 'king's'? v. *Fortunes*, p. 132, n. 22.

62. *eight, or ten* Acc. to 2. 4. 250 only four appear on the stage.

65. *John of Gaunt* A retort to 'Sir John Paunch', i.e. 'I'm not one of *your* family'. Hal is himself 'gaunt'; cf. note 2. 4. 242.

75. *happy man...dole* v. G.

77–88. *Come, neighbour...here!* Morgan (p. 28) finds the following lines of verse in this passage:

> The boy shall lead our horses down the hill,
> We'll walk afoot awhile and ease our legs.
> O, we are undone, both we and ours for ever.
> Hang ye, gorbellied knaves, are ye undone?
> No, ye fat chuffs. I would your store were here!

77–9. *The boy...legs* With these words, and by the trick played on Fal., Sh. rids himself of horses, which could not be brought upon the stage.

82–90. *Strike...jure ye, faith* Fal.'s part in the attack is intimidation. The victims, he asserts, have fed on the fat of the land, while younger and better men (e.g. himself) are desperate for lack of means. Most of his terms of abuse (v. G.) are applicable to himself.

83. *bacon-fed knaves.*   89. *bacons* Both terms = fat country bumpkins.

87. *gorbellied* For Nashe parallel v. p. 192.

88. *chuffs* v. G. Another Nashe word, v. p. 192.

90. *grandjurors* Implies 'men of substance'. Cf. Nashe, *Lenten Stuffe*, 'Wealthy saide I? nay I'le be sworne hee was a grande iurie man in respect of me' (McKerrow, iii. 155, l. 20).

91. *true men* v. note 2. 1. 91.   93. *argument* v. G.

98. *equity stirring* C. E. Phelps, *Falstaff and Equity*, 1901, sees an allusion here to the contest between the courts of common law and of equity at this period, esp. to the judgment of the L. Chancellor in Throckmorton *v*. Finch, 15 Nov. 1597. Such an allusion would appeal to inns-of-court students in the audience.

99. *than in a wild-duck*—'which takes to flight at the first sight of danger' (Clar.).

99–101. S.Ds. Q. (with a brace, opposite ll. 100–1), 'As they are ſharing the Prince & Poins ſet vpon them,

they all runne away, and Falftaffe after a blow or two
runs away too, leauing the bootie behind them.' F.
omits the clause about Fal., which is clearly misplaced.
For my additions cf. l. 109, note 2.4.257, and *Fortunes*, pp. 43–8.

102–8. *Got with...pity him* Qo, Q1, F. print as
prose; Pope and all later edd. as verse. Cf. above,
pp.112–13, and *Library*, pp.14–16. Though the passage
was once verse, I revert to Q., since Sh. finally wrote
it as prose and intended it, I believe, to be spoken
as prose. N.B. Neither 'The thieves...with fear' nor
'Away, good Ned...death' are regular lines of verse.

104–5. *Each...officer* Cf. *3 Hen. VI*, 5.6.12, 'The
thief doth fear each bush an officer' and Nashe parallel,
p. 193.

105–6. *Away, good Ned...death* As Malone and
Ritson noted, if 'Oldcastle' be read for 'Falstaff', the
line becomes regular verse. Cf. *Library*, pp. 14–16.

106. *lards* Because sweat was supposed to be
melted fat. Cf. *Fortunes*, p. 28, and *2 Hen. IV*, 1.2.160.

109. *the fat rogue* (Qo) Q1, F. (and all edd.) 'the
rogue'. Cf. p. 103.

2.3.

S.D. Capell first read 'Warkworth. A room in the
Castle', and Clar. cites Hardyng, who was brought up
in Hot.'s household, and relates that he saw letters
from English lords, promising Hot. assistance, 'in the
castel of Werkeworth, when I was constable of it vnder
my lord, Sir Robert Vmfreuile' (cf. Hardyng's
Chronicle, ed. 1812, p. 361, notes 3. 1. 62–5, *2 Hen. IV*,
1. 1. 161–2 note, and Kingsford, *Eng. Hist. Lit. in the
Fifteenth Century*, p. 141), which statement may be
the origin of the present scene.

4–5. *In respect of* (F.) Q. 'In the refpect of'. Cf.
l. 2 above.

18–21. *our plot...good friends* Cf. *C.W.* iii. 88:

strong was their plot,
Their parties great, meanes good, th' occasion fit:
Their practise close, their faith suspected not.

22. *my lord of York* Cf. 1. 3. 268–70. 'Even an abp.', implies Hot., 'commends the plot'.

24. *brain...his lady's fan* i.e. knock him down with a feather (of which fans were made at this time).

31. *fear...heart* Cf. 4. 3. 7.

33. *divide...buffets* beat myself; v. G. 'buffets'.

34. *skim milk* (Q.) F. 'fkim'd Milk'. The least masculine drink he can name.

37. *Kate* Cf. table p. 129.

39–66. *O my...loves me not* Cf. Portia's speech, *Jul. Caes.* 2. 1. 237 ff.

39. *alone* A sign of melancholy.

43. *stomach, pleasure* Moore Smith suggests 'stomach-pleasure', i.e. relish for your food.

47. *my treasures...rights* my precious rights (in your time and attention).

50. *thee* (Q 2) Q. 'the'.   51. *manage* v. G.

52–7. *And thou...fight* Cf. *Rom.* 1. 4. 83–4.

54–5. *frontiers...basilisks...culverins* v. G. Names of reptiles were often applied to early cannon.

56. *ransom* Capell conj. 'ransomed' ('ransomd' read 'ransome'); attractive with 'slain' following.

64. *On some...hest* Meaning doubtful; poss. corrupt. Clar. 'when suddenly called upon to make a great effort'. Perhaps = on coming to a sudden great decision (v. O.E.D. 'hest' 3).

71. *a roan* (Q 3) Q. 'Roane'.

72–4. *That roan...the park* Q., F. print as prose. Pope rearranged, and I follow doubtfully. Cf. note ll. 79–90.

73. *O esperance!* The Percy motto; in full 'Esperance ma comforte' = 'Hope my reliance' (as Lord Eustace

Percy is good enough to translate it for me); the whole burden of 2. 3. 1–36. The mod. family motto is 'Esperance en Dieu'.

77. *carries you away* v. G.

79–90. *Out...things true* Q., F. print as prose, Pope and all later edd. as verse. Cf. above, pp. 112–13 and *Library*, pp. 14–16. I follow Pope with hesitation. L. Percy changes her tone at l. 79; and l. 88 is hardly a line of verse.

80–1. *A weasel...tossed with* v. G. 'spleen', 'tossed', and cf. *Cymb.* 3. 4. 162.

84. *his title* i.e. to the crown. Cf. note 1. 3. 80.

85–6. *go* = (*a*) depart, (*b*) walk.

88 *Directly* without evasion.

89–90 *In faith...things true* Prof. Peter Alexander brings to my notice an extract from the American *Nation*, 11 March 1875, reprinted p. 124, *Trans. New Sh. Soc.* 1875–6, which quotes the following passage about L. Percy:

> Saeva in familiares, petulans etiam erga maritum, cujus secreta se exquaesituram minitabat, vel *frangendo digitorum ossicula*, si veritatem pandere constantius recusaret.

This the writer claims to have found in Polydore Vergil, xxvi. 2, but unfortunately the reference is wrongly given, nor have I been able to trace the passage elsewhere. Yet it looks like Latin of the period; and, if genuine, might offer a clue to some hitherto undetected source of the play. See G. Fenton, *Tragicall Discourses*, 1567 (Tudor Trans. ii. 102): 'No sortes of kysses or follyes in love were forgotten, no kynde of crampe, no pynchyng by the little finger.'

92. *Love!* He replies to what she said at l. 66; cf. 2. 4. 105; 4. 1. 13 (notes).

94. *mammets* puppets. Cf. *Ham.* 3. 2. 246. Prob. 'play with mammets' = dally. Pinkerton, 1785, conj. 'mammels' = breasts, and some edd. agree.

95–6. *cracked crowns*...*current too* Quibble; 'cracked crowns' reminds Sh. of unsound coins; cf. Act Hen. VII, 1503, 'Half Groats...being Silver (howbeit they be cracked) shall be current'. Cf. G. 'current'.

113. *Thou wilt not...know* An ancient jest based on Seneca (cf. Jente, *Mod. Lang. Notes*, xli. 253 ff.); for Nashe parallel v. p. 193.

2.4.

S.D. Rowe reads 'The Tavern in Eastcheap' and Pope 'The Boar's-Head tavern in Eastcheap'. Eastcheap is often named in the text; the Boar's Head never. This silence, taken with allusions to Fal. as a boar, which seem to play upon the name of the tavern (*1 Hen. IV*, 2.4.107; *2 Hen. IV*, 1.1.19, 2.2.144, 2.4. 229) suggests (i) that it was too well-known to need naming, and (ii) that the name may have been kept off the stage to avoid complications with the contemporary proprietor. The Boar's Head, perhaps orig. a cook-shop, goes back to Ric. II's reign, and may have been the scene of Glutton's debauch in *Piers Plowman* (v. Skeat's note, Pass. v. 313 Clar. ed.). It was certainly a famous tavern in Sh.'s day. Cf. Sugden, and *Fortunes*, pp. 25–31.

1. *fat room* 'close, stuffy room' (Clar. Onions), v. G. Perhaps full of tobacco-smoke, and Poins may enter puffing a pipe to give effect to this. Some conj. 'vat-room' (cf. 'fats' *Ant.* 2.7.122), but that would be the cellar, from which the P. had just come.

4–5. *amongst...hogsheads* i.e. in the cellar. Dekker advises gallants (*Gull's Hornbook*, 1609, ch. vii) 'to accept of the courtesie of the Cellar when 'tis offered you by the drawers', which seems to imply that this was where the drawers themselves drank.

11–12. *lad of mettle* i.e. one who has the courage of his desires.

12. *a good boy* a good fellow. Familiar, like 'sweet wag', 'dear heart'—not usually addressed to a prince!

14–15. '*dyeing scarlet*' Topers' urine was supposed to make the best scarlet dye; hence 'dyeing scarlet' became a euphemism for drinking deep. H. C. Hart (*New Sh. Soc. Trans.* 1877–9, p. 464) cites

Parisiis quando purpura præparatur, tunc artifices invitant Germanos milites et studiosos, qui libenter bibunt; et eis præbent largiter optimum vinum, ea conditione, ut postea urinam reddant in illam lanam. (Note on bk II, ch. 22 in Ozell's trans. of le du Chat's ed. of *Rabelais*, Dublin, 1738.)

Prof. Daly of Edinburgh suggests to me that such notions derive from the common practice, still found among cloth-dyers of the Hebrides, of using urine as a mordant to fix the colours.

15. *breathe...watering* pause in the middle of a drink; v. G.

16. *cry 'hem'* i.e. to bid someone clear his throat. Thus 'Hem!'=clear your throat and down with it; cf. *2 Hen. IV*, 3. 2. 218. '*play it off*' v. G.

18. *drink...tinker* Tinkers were notorious drinkers; cf. Sly in *Shrew*.

20. *action* engagement; cf. 3. 3. 2.

21–2. *to sweeten...sugar* A vulgar action. Dekker (*Hornbook*, ch. vii) advises his gull:

Enquire what Gallants sup in the next room, and if they be any of your acquaintance, do not you (after the City fashion) send them in a pottle of wine and your name sweetened in two pittiful papers of sugar.

Sugar needed for sack (v. notes 1. 2. 3–4; 2. 4. 72–4) could be bought in small packets from the drawers.

25. *Anon, anon, sir!* Coming, sir, coming! For Nashe parallel cf. p. 193.

26. *Score...Half-moon* Spoken to the vintner at the buttery-bar. Cf. 'Pomgarnet' (l. 37) and Jonson, *Barth. Fair*, 5. 4. 205: 'Score a pint of sacke i'the Conney.' Such names for rooms are still found in inns to-day. For 'bastard' v. G.

32. *precedent* (F. 'Prefident') Q. 'prefent', i.e. something really original and worth copying. Cf. pp. 106–7.

33–99. *Francis...reckoning* The fun of this episode, hitherto overlooked, lies in the lad's agitation at the prospect, as he imagines, of an offer of a place in the P.'s household; an offer never made because constantly interrupted by Poins's calls, and his own conditioned reflexes thereto.

41. *five years* Apprenticeship began at 12 or 14, the normal term being 7 years. Francis is therefore 14 or 16.

45–7. *darest thou...run from it?* This is enough to make him think an offer impending. Cf. *M.V.* 2. 2. 1–29 (Lancelot Gobbo's debate with his conscience).

48–9. *sworn...England* Cf. note *M.V.* 2. 2. 157–8. One Bible was enough.

49. *I could...heart* I am ready. Cf. *A.Y.L.* 2. 4. 4.

68–70. *rob this...pouch* Alluding to the vintner, who would be robbed if Francis broke his indenture; and a comic inventory of the man's dress and appearance, as would be made clear at his entry in l. 77.

72–4. *Why then...so much* I paraphrase: 'If you haven't the courage to run away, you are doomed to serve (or to drink) "brown bastard" (v. G.) for the rest of your life, and to watch that nice white drawer's doublet of yours growing dirtier and dirtier. A thousand pounds for a penn'orth of sugar is a good offer, not to be had in Barbary itself.' Cf. Cheyney, i. ch. xviii for details of the extensive trade in sugar with Barbary.

78–9. *What! stand'st...within* Cf. Nashe parallel, p. 193.

87. *merry as crickets* Cf. Apperson, p. 413.

88–9. *what cunning...issue?* i.e. what's the pcint of it all?

90. i.e. he is not single-humoured like Francis or Hotspur. See Janet Spens, T.L.S. corr. 24. 8. 1946.

91–2. *since the...midnight* Cf. *L.L.L.* 4. 1. 118 ff. and *Edward III*, 2. 2. 117, 'Since letherne Adam till this youngest howre'.

96–9. *That ever...reckoning* A parenthetical remark due to Francis's re-entry.

98–9. *the parcel...reckoning* items on the bill.

99. *I am...mind* i.e. '"I am not yet of Percy's mind"—who thinks all the time lost that is not spent in bloodshed...and has nothing but the barren talk of a brutal soldier' (Johnson).

105. *an hour after* Cf. 2. 3. 92; 4. 1. 13.

106–7. *I'll play* etc. Plays extempore (cf. l. 273) were a feature of tavern life at this time. For 'brawn' cf. head-note and *2 Hen. IV*, 1. 1. 19.

107. *Dame Mortimer* v. table p. 129.

108. *'Rivo' says the drunkard* v. G. 'Rivo'. An admission that the speaker is not quite sober. Spoken, I suppose, with a slight hiccough.

Ribs...Tallow Sirloin and Gravy, v. G. 'tallow' and *Fortunes*, pp. 26–9.

S.D. Q., F. 'Enter Falſtaffe' Edd. add the rest.

112–13. *I'll sew...them too* A progressively worsening list of sweated occupations; 'sew'=stitch (part of the manufacturing process), 'mend'=darn, 'foot'= refoot when thoroughly worn out.

115. *virtue* manliness; cf. *2 Hen. IV*, 1. 2. 166.

117. *butter...melted* (Warburton) Q., F. 'butter, pittiful harted Titan that melted'. Theobald and other edd. read 'butter' for 'Titan' on the ground that Titan could not melt at his own sweet tale. Warburton's brackets avoid this difficulty, while 'pitiful-hearted'=

sentimental (Hemingway) is a natural epithet for
'common-kissing Titan' (*Cymb.* 3. 4. 166); cf. *Ham.*
2. 2. 182, Apperson 'sun', Tilley, No. 604, and *M.L.R.*
xi. pp. 462–4.   118. *tale* i.e. of love.

compound i.e. of Fal.'s face (red as the sun) and the
cup of sack (melting like butter before it).

121. *lime* 'To increase its dryness and to make it
sparkle' (Arden).

121–2. *There is...villainous man* These words
were already being quoted by Francis Meres in his
Palladis Tamia (§ xiv), pub. late summer, 1598.

124–5. *if manhood...earth* Cf. *Ado* 4. 1. 318.

126. *lives* (Q., F.) Mod. edd. 'live'.

128. *God help the while!* i.e. while things go on
like this.

129. *a weaver...sing psalms* i.e. could turn godly
weaver and retire from a bad world. Perhaps a relic
of Oldcastle's Lollardry (v. above, p. xxix; *Fortunes*,
pp. 16, 33; and *Library*, p. 8). Eliz. weavers, often
Calvinist Dutch refugees, were given to psalm-singing,
v. *Sh. Eng.* ii. 19–20; *Tw.Nt.* 2. 3. 61; *Wint.* 4. 3. 43.

I could...anything (Q.) The 'purged' F. reads 'I
could sing all manner of songs.' Cf. p. 105.

131. *wool-sack* Follows naturally on the talk about
weaving.

133. *dagger of lath* Used by the Vice (v. G.) to
beat the Devil with in the old interludes; cf. *Tw.Nt.*
4. 2. 136; *2 Hen. IV*, 3. 2. 318; and above, 1. 3. 125.

135. *I'll never wear hair* etc. A gibe at Hal's
hairless chin; cf. *2 Hen. IV*, 1. 2. 20–6.

152. *All's one* (F.) Q. 'all is one'. Cf. p. 104.

156. *a thousand pound* The sum named in *F.V.* i,
not in 2. 1. 54 above, v. note *ibid.*, and *Fortunes*,
p. 143, n. 25.

161. *at half-sword* i.e. at close quarters.

164–5. *buckler...sword* Cf. note 1. 3. 230.

170. *Speak*, etc.   171. *We four* etc.   173. *And*

bound etc. 177. *As we were* etc. (as in F.) Q. gives these speeches to *Gad.*, *Roff.*, *Roff.*, *Roff.* All edd. follow F. which is clearly right. I conj. that Sh.'s MS. orig. read 'Prin.', 'Roff.', 'Roff.', 'Roff.', that when 'Rossil' was cut out of the play (v. note 1. 2. 156) a single 'Gad.' was jotted in the margin as a note to the prompter to substitute that character, which he did in the 'book' from which F. was corrected (v. p. 105), and that when Sh.'s MS. reached the printer he altered the wrong prefix.

174. *No, no...not bound* The emphasis is on 'bound'. The binding of sixteen men by four is too much for Peto.

176. *an Ebrew Jew* i.e. 'a Jew of Jews' (Hemingway); cf. *Ado*, 2. 3. 256.   180. *other*=others.

183. *a bunch of radish* A symbol of leanness. Elyot, *Castle of Health*, 1539, p. 35, writes 'Radyshe rootes haue the vertu to extenuate or make thin'; cf. 'peppercorn' (3. 3. 8).

187–8. *peppered...paid* v. G.

188–9. *two rogues...suits* At this point, I think, Fal. winks at the audience; cf. *Fortunes*, p. 53.

191. *horse* As much a type of stupidity as the ass; cf. *Troil.* 3. 3. 126.

191–2. *my old ward* my usual fence.

192. *lay...bore* v. G. 'lie', 'bear'.

197. *all afront* all four abreast.

203. *by these hilts* Plur. because the hilt was of three parts. Being also often cruciform, an oath upon it was esp. sacred; cf. *Ham.* 1. 5. 147 (note, and add. note).

206. *Dost thou hear me* i.e. 'Listen!' The formula for attracting attention.

207. *mark*=(*a*) heed, (*b*) keep count.
too (Q2) Q. 'to'.

211–12. *Their points...hose* Cf. *Tw.Nt.* 1. 5. 22–5; v. G. 'point' and Linthicum, p. 282.

214. *came in...hand* i.e. not only thrust at them but advanced upon them.

218–19. *three...green* v. G. 'Kendal green' and cf. Linthicum, p. 79: 'Fal.'s imaginary "knaves" had dressed true to form either as robber woodmen, or as low-class thieves.'

220–1. *for it...thy hand* With this palpable lie Fal. deliberately gives the show away. Cf. *Fortunes*, p. 53.

222–5. *These lies...catch* Moore Smith and A. E. Morgan (p. 30) independently suggest that the speech is verse, the lines ending *them, palpable, fool, catch.* Cf. *Library*, pp. 14–16.

224. *clay-brained guts* clod-witted gormandizer.

225. *tallow-catch* Meaning much debated. I believe it to be nothing more recondite than the pan to catch the dripping from meat roasting on a spit; cf. G. 'tallow', note l. 108 above, and *Fortunes*, p. 28.

233. *upon compulsion?* 'Reasons' or opinions were in that age commonly extracted by the 'compulsion' of torture.

236–7. *reasons...blackberries* 'The Old French word for "grape" had the two dialectical forms *resin* and *raisin*, both of which came into English. Hence the word was often spelt and pronounced "reason"' (H. Bradley, *Sh. Eng.* ii. 544).

240. *sanguine coward* A kind of oxymoron (Arden); 'sanguine' = (*a*) red-faced, (*b*) courageous, whereas cowards are pale by nature; cf. *Macb.* 5. 3. 11, 'thou cream-faced loon'.

242. *you starveling* etc. P. Henry 'exceeded the meane stature of men...his necke long, body slender and leane, and his bones small' (Stow, *Annals*, 1615, p. 342, drawing upon the fifteenth-century chronicler Tito Livio). It was to contrast with this lean prince, I suggest, that Sh. made his Fal. fat.

eel-skin (Hanmer) Q. 'elfskin', F. 'Elfe-skin'. All Fal.'s other 'base comparisons' exemplify Hal's thinness, to which 'elf-skin' (? meaning) seems irrelevant. But twice elsewhere Sh. uses 'eel-skin' to describe a man very tall and thin (*K. John*, 1. 1. 141; *2 Hen. IV*, 3. 2. 325). Lastly, Arden notes an obvious echo of the passage in Field, *Woman is a Weathercock*, 1. 2 ('that little old dried neat's tongue, that eel-skin') which goes far to confirm Hanmer's emendation.

245. *standing tuck* a blade that has no pliancy and is therefore 'vile', i.e. worthless. Cf. O.E.D. 'standing' 8, Arden (ed. 1930), and *M.W.W.* 3. 5. 101, 'to be compassed, like a *good* bilbo, in the circumference of a peck, hilt to point'.

246. *breathe* v. G.

247. *base comparisons* Cf. notes 1. 2. 79, 3. 2. 67.

253. *with a word* in a word.   *out-faced* bluffed.

256. *dexterity* agility.

257. *as ever…bull-calf* Fal. 'run and roared' like a young bull pricked in the haunches by swords or goads at a bull-baiting. Cf. *2 Hen. IV*, 3. 2. 177–8, 'Come, prick me Bullcalf, till he roar again', *3 Hen. VI*, 2. 5. 126, and below, 4. 1. 103.

263. *now* At this point, acc. to an American stage-tradition (v. B. Matthews, *Sh. Stage Traditions*, p. 11), Fal., who has been hiding his head in apparent shame behind a settle or chair, slowly lifts his sunlike face in triumph above it. Cf. *Fortunes*, p. 55. Garrick seems to have used his shield for a similar purpose (Sprague, p. 86, discussing this 'business').

268–9. *the lion…true prince* A notion that goes back to Pliny. Edward III dared Philip of Valois to prove his kingship by entering a lion's den (v. Einstein, *Italian Renaissance in England*, p. 239).

the true prince Hudson, *Sh.'s Life* etc. 1872 (ii. 86), suggests a sly allusion here to Henry IV's usurpation.

273–4. *Watch…to-morrow* Cf. *Matth.* xxvi. 41. Sanctimony again; but with Fal. 'watch' = sit up all night (cf. note, 4. 2. 56–7), and 'to-morrow'—never comes!

276. *a play extempore* Cf. note, ll. 106–7. In the old *Henry IV* Oldcastle and Hal seem to have rehearsed the scene in court when Hal strikes the L. Chief Justice. In *F.V.* sc. v, this is enacted by two clowns.

286–7. *a royal man* Promotion for 'a noble man'; a 'royal'=10s., a 'noble' only 6s. 8d. Cf. note, 1. 2. 135–6.

301. *he hacked...dagger* Cf. *Ado*, 5. 1. 182.

305–6. *tickle...spear-grass* Acc. to Harman, *Caveat for Common Cursetors*, 1579, beggars used speargrass to produce artificial sores. Cf. *F.V.* xix. 17–22 (Derrick tells how he won the name of a 'bloodie souldier' at Agincourt):

Euery day when I went into the field I would take a straw and thrust it into my nose, and make my nose bleed, etc.

307. *the blood of true men* i.e. of their victims; cf. note 2. 1. 91 and G. 'true'.

311. *with the manner* in the act, v. G. 'manner'.

316. *meteors...exhalations* Much the same thing, v. G.

319. *Hot livers, and cold purses* 'Drunkenness and poverty' (Johnson). Cf. *Ant.* 1. 2. 23, and Nashe parallel p. 193.

320–1. *Choler...halter* Double quibble: (i) 'choler'—'collar', (ii) 'rightly taken'=(a) properly understood, (b) justly laid by the heels. Based on the proverb 'After a collar cometh a halter' (Jente, No. 68).

327. *crept into* Cf. *M.W.W.* 3. 5. 133.

thumb-ring Worn by 'grave persons, citizens and aldermen' (Singer, ed. 1826).

327–8. *sighing and grief* (Monsieur Remorse's, cf. 1. 2. 109). The jest is that grief was supposed to impoverish the blood and so lead to emaciation and decline. Cf. *2 Hen. IV*, 4. 4. 58.

329. *Sir John Bracy* 'No trace...in the histories of the period' (Clar.).

332–34. *gave Amaimon...hook* Jocular allusions to
the dealings of 'conjurors' with demons. *Amaimon*
(Capell) Q., F. 'Amamon'. Cf. *M.W.W.* 2.2.274,
'Amaimon' and R. Scot, *Discoverie of Witchcraft*,
1594, xv, iii. One of the principal devils.

333–4. *upon...Welsh hook* Glend. is, Fal. implies,
(i) a rustic soldier, fighting with a billhook, (ii) a black
magician, swearing his men upon a hiltless weapon;
cf. note l. 203.

335. *Owen Glendower* (Dering MS.) Q., F. 'O
Glendower'. As Halliwell notes, Fal. catches up and
repeats the name.

341. *pistol* 'Pistols were not known in the age of
Henry. They were, in our author's time, eminently
used by the Scots' (Johnson).

348. *ye cuckoo* Because Hal 'had echoed...the
words "rascal" and "running"' (Elton).

352. *too* (Q2) Q. 'to'. *Mordake* v. note 1.1.
71–2. *blue-caps* Contemptuous for 'Scots', v. G.

370–3. *Do thou...my crown* Cf. note l. 276, and
F.V. v. 10–12:

thou shalt be my Lord chiefe Iustice, and thou shalt sit
in the chaire, and Ile be the yong prince, and hit thee a
boxe on the eare.

374–6. *Thy state* etc. 'The P. speaks with exag-
gerated solemnity, as if he were a prophet. Cf. *Isaiah*,
xxii. 19' (Kittredge). For 'state', 'joined-stool',
'leaden dagger', v. G. *taken for*=reckoned as (O.E.D.
48 *b*).

378. *Give me...sack* Cambyses' maudlin 'vein'
was an effect of drink.

380. *passion* grief; cf. ll. 409–11, and G.

380–1. *in King Cambyses' vein* i.e. in the style of
*A Lamentable Tragedy, mixed full of Plesant Mirth,
containing The Life of Cambises, King of Percia*, 1569,
by Thomas Preston. But Johnson questioned

if Sh. had ever seen this tragedy; for there is a remarkable peculiarity of measure, which, when he professed to speak in King Cambyses' vein, he would hardly have missed, if he had known it.

And all who read this play in fourteeners (v. J. Q. Adams, *Chief pre-Shakespearian Dramas*) must agree. I suspect that quotations from Preston figured in the old *Henry IV*, and that Sh. rewrote them to burlesque the more up-to-date style of Kyd or Greene (cf. notes ll. 385, 388). By 1596–8 Preston and fourteeners were *vieux jeux*.

385. *Weep not...vain* At l. 1029 Preston has a S.D. 'At this tale tolde, let the Queene weep'; but for the style Arden quotes Greene, *Alphonsus*, 2. 1. 573: 'Nay, then, Albinius, since that words are vain.'

386. *O, the father* A profane ejaculation.

387. *tristful* (Dering MS.) Q., F. 'Truſtfull'. Cf. *Ham.* 3. 4. 50 (F.).

388. *For tears...eyes* Cf. Preston, l. 1030: ' *Queene*. These words to heare makes stilling teares issue from christall eyes'; and, for style, Kyd's *Soliman and Perseda*, 4. 1. 94–5:

> How can mine eyes dart forth a pleasant looke,
> When they are *stopt* with *flouds* of flowing teares?

389. *harlotry* v. G.

394–6. *though the camomile...wears* A recognized parody of Lyly's *Euphues* (Lyly, i. 196), cf. Tilley, No. 68.

396. *yet youth* (Q3, F.) Q. 'ſo youth'. Q3 is almost cert. right, though it must be a guess-emendation.

398. *trick* v. G. and *All's Well*, 1. 1. 98.

402. *blessed...heaven* A jesting allusion to the sun as symbol of royalty. Cf. notes 1. 2. 189; 3. 2. 79.

407. *ancient writers* i.e. *Ecclus.* xiii. 1. Cf. Lyly, i, 250.

408–12. *for, Harry...name* Euphuistic antithesis and alliteration.

419–20. *If then...fruit* Cf. *Matth.* vii. 16–20.

'Fal. is the tree, and his virtuous looks the fruit' (Clar.).

428–9. *hang me...hare* i.e. baffle me. Cf. G. 'baffle'. For the absurd comparison of Fal., hanging upside down, with a baby rabbit or the long body of a skinned hare in a shop, cf. 'bunch of radish' (l. 183), 'shotten herring' (l. 126) and *Fortunes*, p. 31.

436. *tickle you for* 'divert you in the role of' (Arden).

438. *violently...grace* For Nashe parallel v. p. 194.

441–2. *bolting-hutch of beastliness*=accumulation of physical grossness, from which all the finer elements of human nature have been abstracted; v. G.

444. *roasted Manningtree...belly* Cf. G. 'Manningtree' and *Fortunes*, p. 30. For Nashe parallel v. p. 194. The 'pudding'=stuffing of sausage-meat.

445–6. *vice...iniquity...vanity* 'The Vice, Iniquity, and Vanity were personages...in the old moralities' (Malone), and 'Ruffian' was a cant word for the Devil, e.g. in the Chester miracle plays (cf. O.E.D. 'ruffin').

447. *cleanly* deft.   448. *cunning* skilful.

451. *take...you* explain yourself.

471. *I do, I will.* Cf. 1.2.187 ff. and *2 Hen. IV*, 5.5.64.

471 and 475. S.Ds. Q. and F. provide no previous exits for Bar. and Hostess. Camb. and mod. edd. supply at l. 471 'A knocking heard. Exeunt Hostess, Francis, and Bardolph'. This (i) would leave the stage silent for several moments, which is absurd, and (ii) is unnecessary, since Bard. and Host. can exit any time unnoticed by the audience.

472–73. *most monstrous watch* enormous posse of police.

477. *Heigh, heigh!* etc. Q4–5, F. and some edd. assign to '*Falst.*' It is an accident of the press.

the devil...fiddle-stick v. G. 'fiddle-stick', Apperson, 'Devil' 78.

481–3. *never call...seeming so* For much commentary and many emendations v. Hemingway. No change needed. Fal., cornered, humorously pleads for the P.'s help, saying, 'Don't let me down by calling a true-mettled fellow a false thief. Appearances are deceptive; you, for example, are really, though you don't look it, gold.' His next speech implies that he is bound to be hanged, unless the P. refuses the sheriff entry. The sheriff enters, but a thumping lie is forthcoming. Cf. *Fortunes*, pp. 57–8.

482. *essentially made* (Q + F) = the real thing, really made of gold. See *T.L.S.*, 6 Oct. 1945.

485. *your major* i.e. your major premiss (with a quibble on 'mayor', spelt 'major' by Jonson, v. iii. 400, l. 43). The quibble links with the old play; cf. *F.V.* iii. 3, 'Enter the Maior and the Sheriffe'. *deny*=refuse to admit.

486–7. *If I become...another man* i.e. I have no 'natural coward's' fear of death; I can play my part on the way to Tyburn as stoutly as anyone.

488. *as soon be strangled* etc. His weight would ensure that.

490. *arras* i.e. the curtain before the inner stage.

493. *their date is out* the lease has run out. Cf. *Son.* xviii. 4; Jonson, *Barth. Fair*, 5. 4. 97.

494. S.D. Q. omits. F. 'Exit'. For 'and Poins' cf. note l. 519.

495. S.D. For 'the Carrier' cf. note 2. 1. 44.

496–501. *Now, master...fat man* Q., F. as prose; Pope arranged as verse. Cf. pp. 112–13.

496. *sheriff* A monosyllable; cf. note 2 *Hen. IV*, 4. 4. 99.

497. *hue and cry* Cf. *F.V.* i. 19–20, 'the Towne of Detford is risen, With hue and crie after your man, Which...robd a poore Carrier'.

505. Cf. note l. 496.

511. *three hundred marks* Cf. note 2. 1. 54.

512–13. *It may be so...farewell* By this, I take it, Fal.'s snores are becoming audible to the whole theatre; hence the brusque dismissal. Cf. *Fortunes*, pp. 58–9.

519. *Falstaff* etc. Q., F. assign this and the speeches at ll. 524, 540 to Peto, reading 'Peto' for 'Poins' also in l. 539 and again at 3. 3. 195, with which Camb. and most mod. edd. concur. Following Johnson and Malone, I print Poins in all instances; 'Po' and 'Pe' might easily be confused in the copy. As Johnson asks:

What had Peto done that 'his place should be honourable' [l. 535], or that he should be trusted with the plot against Falstaff? Poins has the P.'s confidence and is a man of courage....[Moreover,] having only robbed the robbers, [he] had no need to conceal himself from the travellers.

Malone adds that Poins suits the metre of 3. 3. 195. I may also add (i) that it would be strange for Poins to disappear altogether after l. 466 and yet turn up later in *2 Hen. IV* with all his old vivacity, (ii) that Johnson has the support of the Dering MS. (v. p. 107), and (iii) that, as Johnson himself notes, Peto appears in 4. 2 not in the P.'s retinue but as Fal.'s 'lieutenant'.

526. *Item, A capon* etc. Q. omits prefix; F. assigns to *Peto* (v. note l. 519).

529. *Anchovies and sack* Anchovies were eaten to provoke thirst.   530. *ob.* i.e. obolus, halfpenny.

536–7. *his death...score* i.e. 'It will kill him to march so far as twelve-score yards' (Johnson). Cf. 2. 2. 12–14.

3. 1.

Citing Hol., Theobald heads this 'The Archbishop of Bangor's House in Wales', and all edd. follow; but Bangor is not mentioned by Sh., and 'the archdeacon' only once, casually (v. note 3. 1. 70). It is a family party (v. ll. 85–90, 188); Glend. behaves like a host; and Sh. prob. imagines his castle as the venue.

3–5. *Lord Mortimer...map* F. and mod. edd. arrange as verse, which softens Hot.'s bluntness; cf. pp. 112–13.

6–9. *No, here it is...heaven* Pope and mod. edd. arrange as verse.

10–11. *And you...spoke of* And this too is very nearly verse, e.g. if read:

> And you in hell, as often as he hears
> Owen Glendower spoke of.

12–16. *at my nativity* etc. Hol. (iii. 521; Stone, p. 137) speaks of 'strange wonders...at the natiuitie of this man', and (iii. 519; Stone, p. 137) of 'a blasing starre', which appeared in March 1402, when Glen. first attacked the English, and 'lifted the Welshmen into high pride, and increased meruelouslie their wicked and presumptuous attempts'.

14. *cressets* v. G. The most brilliant kind of artificial light known to Sh.

26–32. *Diseased nature...towers* The accepted explanation of earthquakes.

30. *enlargement* v. G. Hot. hints that Grandam Earth brought forth a windbag. Cf. *Isaiah*, xxvi. 17, 18.

34. *passion* v. G.

44. *chides* thunders upon (cf. *Shrew*, 1. 2. 94).

45. *read to* lectured, instructed.

47–8. *trace...experiments* follow me in the painful paths of science, or rival me in abstruse experiments. Science ('art') was then half magic, and 'experiment' mostly alchemical.

49. *better Welsh* i.e. more nonsense; a quibble. Cf. G. 'Welsh' and l. 118 below.

52. *vasty deep* 'abyss or depth of space' (O.E.D. 'deep' sb. 3c). Cf. *Par. Lost*, vii. 166–9.

54. *But will...them?* For Nashe parallel v. p. 194 and cf. Rabelais, 'Ils invoquent les Diables....Vray

est que ces Diables ne viennent tousjours a souhait
sur l'instant' (*Œuvres*, bk. v, ch. 10, cit. W. F. Smith,
'Rabelais et Sh.,' *Rev. Études Rabelaisiennes*, 1903).

57. *Tell...devil* Cf. Apperson, 'Truth', 3, and
Jente, No. 97. "Truth shames the Devil because he is
"the father of lies"'' (Kittredge).

61. *Come...chat* Pope arranged as 'Come, come/
No...chat'. Cf. pp. 112–13.

62–5. *Three times...back* Hol. (iii. 520, 530;
Stone, p. 138) notes two repulses owing to bad weather
caused by magic. Hardyng (ed. 1812, p. 359) seems
the only chronicler to record all three, occasioned by
'wethers foule' (v. Clar.).

65. *Bootless* (F.) Q. 'Booteles'. Perhaps a tri-
syllable, though disyllabic at 1. 1. 29.

68. *here's* (F) Q. 'here is'. Cf. p. 104. *right* rightful
territory.

70. *The archdeacon* What archdeacon? Cf. head-
note. Prob. more about him in the old play. Hall
and Hol. (iii. 521; Stone, p. 138) state that the conspirators '*by their deputies*, in the house of the archdeacon of Bangor, diuided the realme amongst them';
C.W. iii. 91 implies a meeting between the principals.

72. *hitherto* to this spot (on the map).

78–9. *indentures tripartite...interchangeably* Cf.
Hol. *op. cit.* 'a tripartite indenture...sealed with their
seales'. Each conspirator kept one part of the indenture
(v. G.) and each part was sealed by all. Cf. *Ric. II*,
5. 2. 98.

98. *cantle* (F.) Q. 'ſcantle'. All edd. follow F.,
which 'half-moon' seems to confirm (cf. also *Ant.*
3. 10. 6), while 'scantle' (=a builder's term for a
portion of wood or stone) does not give the meaning
required. Cf. p. 107. Clar. notes:

The Trent, turning northwards after leaving Burton till
it joins the Humber, cuts out a good part of Notts. and the
whole of Lincs. from what would have been Hot.'s share
if it had continued its easterly course.

100. *smug* v. G.   105–9. *Yea but...from you*
Q. as prose. F. gives ll. 109–10 as verse, and Capell
rearranged the rest. Cf. pp. 112–13.

112. *And then...even* A short line.

118. *Welsh* Cf. note l. 49.

119. *lord* 'Glen. is losing patience and becomes
formal. He no longer calls Hot. "cousin Percy"'
(Clar.).

120. *I was...court* Cf. Hol. (iii. 518; Stone,
p. 105):

This Owen Glendouer...was first set to studie the lawes
of the realme, and became an vtter barrester, or an appren-
tise of the law (as they terme him), and serued king Richard
at Flint castell, when he was taken by Henrie duke of
Lancaster; though other haue written that he serued this
king Henrie the fourth, before he came to atteine the
crowne, in room of an esquier.

123–4. *gave...you* One of the chief duties of
patriots in this age being to 'garnish' their native
tongue esp. in the realm of poetry, and the marrying
of verse to music being an acknowledged means thereto,
Glen. claims to be a better Englishman than Hot. who
hates both. Cf. Sidney, *Apologie*, passim, and Renwick,
Edmund Spenser, pp. 109–16.

128. *ballad-* (F.) Q. 'ballet'.

129. *turned* Alluding to the 'loathsom noise' of
copper candlesticks being turned on the lathe by
founders in Lothbury; cf. Stow, *Survey* (ed. Kingsford, i. 277).

132. *mincing* An affected way of walking upon
'feet'.

133. *forced...nag* jerky steps of a hobbled horse.
Cf. *A.Y.L.* 3.2.112, and Ascham, *Schoolmaster* (ed.
Arber), p. 112, 'varying a sentence in Hitching
(=hobbling) schole'.

147–51. *the moldwarp...ramping cat* App. based
on Hall, who relates (ed. 1809, p. 28) that 'a Welch
Prophecier' persuades the conspirators that

King Henry was the Moldwarpe, cursed of Goddes owne
mouth [cf. *Lev.* xi. 30; *Isai.* ii. 20], and that they thre
were the Dragon, the Lion and the Wolffe, which shoulde
deuide this realme betwene them, by the deuiacion and not
deuination of that mawmet Merlin.

Hol. repeats, but omits Merlin. The dragon=the
badge of Glen.; the lion, the crest of Percy; the white
wolf that of Mort. (G. R. French). Hot.'s 'couching'
and 'ramping' are contemptuous perversions of the
heraldic 'couchant' and 'rampant', while 'clip-winged'
suggests the domestic fowl.

153. *from my faith* i.e. as a Christian; cf. *Tw.Nt.*
3. 2. 68–70.

158–9. *a railing wife...house* 'A prov. sentence
common in the middle ages' (Jente, No. 290; Apperson,
p. 629); cf. Chaucer, *W. of Bath's Prol.* 278–80, and
v. *Prov.* x. 26; xix. 13; xxvii. 15.

160–2. *windmill...summer house* The quietude,
size, and freshness of a country house ('summer house')
are contrasted with the cramped, noisy, dusty quarters
of the windmill. Cf. Jonson, *Silent Woman,* 5. 3. 61–3.

164–5. *profited...concealments* v. G.

175. *too wilful blame* (Q.) v. G. 'too blame', and
cf. *K. John*, 5. 2. 124, 'too wilful opposite'.

177. *beside* (Q2) Q., F. 'befides'.

183. *opinion* v. G. and cf. *L.L.L.* 5. 1. 5.

184–7. *The least...commendation* The germ of
Ham.'s soliloquy on 'particular faults' (*Ham.* 1. 4. 23–
38).

188. *good manners...speed!* i.e. on the battle-field.

192. *she will* (Pope, and later edd.) Q., F. 'fheele'.

194. *my aunt Percy* Cf. table on p. 129. The Mort.
who married Glen.'s daughter *was* nephew to L. Percy,
but at 1. 3. 80, 156 and 2. 3. 83 he is Hot.'s brother-
in-law.

195. S.D. The boy playing L. Mort. was prob.
Welsh, as he sings a Welsh song; and as Glen. 'speaks

to her in Welsh', he also was prob. played by a Welshman, who perhaps acted Fluellen in *Hen. V* and Sir H.
Evans in *M.W.W.*

196. *here* i.e. on this point (Clar.).

196–7. *a peevish...harlotry* a perverse hussy, v. G.
Cf. *Rom.* 4. 2. 14.

197. *that no...good upon* A line of verse.

198. *That pretty Welsh* i.e. her tears.

199. *pourest down* Seymour's conj. 'down-pourest'
would ease the metre.

swelling heavens The rain-clouds of her brimming
eyes.

203. *a feeling disputation* i.e. an interchange of
feelings, if we cannot interchange words.

206. *highly penned* in lofty style. Cf. Bacon,
Masques and Triumphs, 'the Ditty High and Tragicall,
not nice or Dainty'. (Essay xxxvii.)

208. *division* v. G.

211. *wanton* fresh green; cf. *M.N.D.* 2. 1. 99.

214. *crown* i.e. give absolute power to. Cf. *Tw.Nt.*
1. 1. 36–8; 5. 1. 127. The image of a person or
personification sitting crowned upon another person's
head or in his mind is frequent in Sh. Cf. *Son.*
114. 1; *Rom.* 3. 2. 92–4; *Hen. V*, 2. 2. 5–6; *Ric. II*,
3. 2. 160–2.

216–19. *such...the east* i.e. 'a state partaking of
sleep and wakefulness, as the twilight of day and night'
(Johnson).

223–5. *those musicians...here* Glen. is clearly a
genuine magician, like Prospero.

224. *in the air* i.e. from the music-gallery in the
third story of the tiring-house; cf. J. C. Adams, *Globe
Playhouse*, p. 311.

230. *so humorous* i.e. only a very queer fellow would
learn such a tongue.

232–4. *Then should...Welsh* Q., F. as verse, and
'Lie still...lady sing' is a verse line. Cf. pp. 112–13.

235. *Lady, my brach* Cf. *Lear*, 1. 4. 125.

236. *in Irish* i.e. like an Irish wolf; cf. *A.Y.L.*
5. 2. 104–5.

240. *'tis a woman's fault* Ironical. 'still' (l. 239)=
silent.

241. *Now God help thee!* 'For *I* give thee up'
(Kittredge).

247–56. *Not yours...citizens* Note the mingling
of prose and verse. Cf. pp. 112–13. For the sentiments
cf. *A.Y.L.* 4. 1. 183–5. Puritans condemned swearing,
and many citizens were puritans; cf. *2 Hen. IV*, 1. 2. 35
note.

251–6. *And givest* etc. Note the sudden return to
verse.

252. *Finsbury* Finsbury Fields, the resort of citizens
and their wives on Sunday afternoons and holidays.

256. *velvet-guards* i.e. city dames in their best,
v. G. 'guard'.

259–60. *'Tis the next...teacher* i.e. You might as
well turn tailor or one who makes a living by teaching
little birds to sing.   *next*=nearest.

263. *hot* (F.) Q. 'Hot.'

3. 2.

The chroniclers record two meetings between K. and
the P., both in 1412–13, (i) in which the P. clears himself
of suspicions, excited by slanderers, that he sought the
K.'s life and crown; (ii) the death-bed scene, in which
the P. takes away the crown and the K. gives him his
dying advice. In *F.V.* the two follow each other
closely; but Sh. fixes the date of (i) before Shrewsbury,
leaving (ii) until act 4 of *2 Hen. IV*. Cf. *Library*, pp. 15–16.

5–11. *For some...mistreadings* A guilty conscience
speaks. Cf. *2 Hen. IV*, 4. 5. 183–5 and Introd.
pp. xxii–xxiii.

13. *bare...lewd...attempts* v. G.
17. *hold...level* v. G.
22–8. *Yet such...Find pardon* 'Let me beg so
much extenuation that, upon confutation of many false

charges, I may be pardoned some that are true' (Johnson).

25. *pickthanks* A word taken directly or indirectly from Hol. iii. 539 (Stone, p. 140).

28. *submission* v. G.   30. *affections* v. G.

31. *from* contrary to.

32–3. *Thy place...supplied* Alluding to the L. Chief Justice story; cf. note 1. 2. 83–6, and *Library*, p. 7.   ˙ *rudely lost* Cf. 2 *Hen. IV*, 1. 2. 190–1, 'For the box of the ear that the prince gave you, he gave it like a *rude* prince', etc.

36. *The...time* Your hopeful and promising youth; v. G. 'time'.

38. *do* (Q., F.) 'The soul of every man' is thought of as plur.

42. *Opinion* v. G.   43. *to possession* i.e. to Richard.

50. *stole all courtesy from heaven* i.e. assumed a Christ-like meekness. The phrase is repeated by Massinger, *Great Duke of Florence*, 2. 3. 156 ff.

56. *robe pontifical* Only worn on special occasions by specially important persons.

58–9. *Seldom...solemnity* Cf. 1. 2. 196–9.

59. *wan* Common form of pret.

60. *skipping* v. G.

61. *rash bavin* v. G. 'rash' and 'bavin', and cf. parallel from Nashe, p. 194.

62. *carded his state* lowered his prestige, v. G. 'card'.

67. *comparative* Cf. 1. 2. 79; 2. 4. 247, and G.

69. *Enfeoffed* sold outright.

71–2. *began...taste* (Pope) Q., F. 'began to loath The taſte'.

79. *sun-like majesty* Cf. notes 1. 2. 189; 2. 4. 402.

82. *aspect* looks.

83. *As cloudy...adversaries* As ill-tempered men give to those they dislike, v. G. 'cloudy'.

84. *Being...glutted* Arden cites the following from

North's *Plutarch* (Pericles), 1595, p. 170, which may be the germ of this passage, ll. 46–59 above, and 1.2.189 ff.:

Pericles nowe to preuent that the people should not be glutted with seeing him too oft...neither came abroade among them, but reserued him selfe...for matters of great importance.

84. *gorged* (F.) Q. 'gordge'.

91. *Make blind* etc. Cf. Hol. iii. 539, 'shedding teares' (not in Stone); *F.V.* vi. 114, S.D. 'He weepes'.   93. *Be more myself* Cf. 1.3.5.

98–9. *He...succession* He has a better title to govern the country than you have to the mere succession.   102. *the lion's* i.e. the king's.

103. *no more...thou* Cf. note 1.1.78–90.

105. *bruising* crushing, v. G.

107. *renownèd* (Q4) Q. 'renowmed'—the old sp.

112. *Thrice* The battles were (i) on 19 Aug. 1388 at Otterburn, which Douglas won, after great slaughter on both sides, (ii) on 22 June 1402 at Nisbet, and (iii) on 14 Sept. 1402 at Holmedon, v. 1.1.55 ff.

115. *Enlargèd* (Q2) Q. 'Enlarg'd'.

116. *To fill...up* i.e. to add one last insult to his gross defiance. The mouth is thought of as (*a*) shouting, (*b*) being crammed with food. Arden quotes Barnes, *Devil's Charter* (ed. McKerrow, ll. 2745–6):

Thus doth one hideous act succeed an other,
Vntill the mouth of mischeife be made vp.

123. *dearest* (*a*) direst, (*b*) best beloved, v. G.

125. *start of spleen* fit of ill-temper.

147–8. *factor...To engross up* agent...to buy up, v. G. 'engross up'. With a quibble in 'deeds'.

151. *worship of his time* honour of his life.

152. *the reckoning* i.e. the factor's account.

154 *if He...perform* (Q) F. 'if I performe, and doe suruiue'.

156. *intemperature* (F.) Q. 'intemperance'. Cf.
p. 107. A quibble, with a medical connotation (re-
flecting 'salve' and 'wounds') which 'intemperance',
of moral reference only, lacks.

157. *the end...bands* i.e. 'death squares all
accounts'. Apperson, p. 140; cf. *Temp.* 3. 2. 129;
2 Hen. IV, 3. 2. 237–8, etc.

164. *Lord Mortimer of Scotland* A mistake for
George Dunbar, the Scottish Earl of March, i.e. of
the borders between England and Scotland, who figures
prominently in Hol.'s account of the battle of Shrewsbury, etc. Mortimer was the name of the earls of the
borders between England and Wales. Only a very casual
reader of Hall or Hol. could commit such an error.
Cf. also *Mirror for Magistrates* (ed. L. Campbell), p. 131,
where the two earls are carefully distinguished.

173–8. *On Wednesday...shall meet*. Edd. try to
mend the metre by rearrangement. Two textual strata
seem discernible: (i) 'our meeting Is Bridgenorth'
(174–5) is repeated in l. 178. (ii) Other repetitions
are 'march' (174, 175), 'business' (177, 179). I suggest that 'by which account...meet' (176–8) was
intended to be deleted, and that 'On Wednesday...
Gloucestershire' is a prose passage written to replace
it. Cf. *Library*, pp. 14–16.

175. *Bridgenorth* About 23 miles from Shrewsbury.
180. *feeds him* feeds himself.
men Moore Smith suggests 'we', misread 'mẽ'.

3. 3.

S.D. As Fal. has his captain's truncheon (v. note
l. 87, and S.D. l. 88), he should perhaps be in battle-
dress (cf. note 4. 2. 47). For 'early morning' v. note
l. 196.

2. *this last action* i.e. the tense moments at the
end of 2. 4.

3. *loose gown* v. G.

4. *apple-John* v. G., and cf. *2 Hen. IV*, 2. 4. 2.

4–10. *I'll repent* etc. Cf. *Fortunes*, pp. 32–5.

5. *in some liking* (*a*) in the mood, (*b*) relatively plump, in fairly good condition; cf. *L.L.L.* 5. 2. 268.

6. *out of heart* (*a*) dispirited, (*b*) out of condition.

8. *peppercorn* At once minute, shrivelled, and worthless. Cf. notes 2. 4. 183, 428–9.

brewer's horse typifies stupidity in the extreme (cf. note 2. 4. 191), since horses past other service were sold to brewers as dray-horses.

9. *villainous company* Cf. *F.V.* vi. 112, 133, 'this vilde and reprobate company'.

10. *spoil* ruin.

11. *so fretful* etc. Cf. notes 2. 2. 2, 2. 4. 324–5, and G. 'fretful'.

13. *there is it* that's the trouble.

17–18. *quarter...three* (Q.) Hanmer and mod. edd. 'quarter—of an...borrowed—three'.

19–23. *compass...compass...compass* v. G.

25. *thou bearest* I conj. 'that bears'; and suggest that 'thou' was repeated by the compositor, and 'beares' afterwards corrected to 'bearest'. This would give: you are our flagship, which carries its lantern at the stern, though *you* carry yours in your nose.

26–7. *Knight...Lamp* Parodying Amadis, Knight of the Burning Sword, as does *The Knight of the Burning Pestle* (Moore Smith).

30. *death's-head...mori* Fashionable on seal-rings. Cf. *2 Hen. IV*, 2. 4. 232–3.

32. *Dives...purple* Cf. *Luke* xvi. 19–31, and note 4. 2. 25.

34–5. *By this fire...angel* i.e. Bard.'s face is (i) a memento mori, (ii) the flaming messenger of death. Cf. *Exod.* iii. 2; *Ps.* civ. 4; *Heb.* i. 7, 'Who maketh his ministers a flame of fire'. F. P. Wilson (*Sh. and the Diction of Common Life*, Brit. Acad. 1941) cites

Misogonus (*c.* 1570), 3. 1. 240, 'By this fier that
bournez, thats gods aungell'.   *that's* (Q3) Q. 'that'.

39. *wildfire* A quibble, v. G.

40. *triumph* torchlight procession.

46. *salamander* For Nashe parallel v. p. 194.

48–9. *I would...belly* 'A prov. curse on a bore
or an impertinent talker' (Kittredge), i.e. Enough of
my face! Stow it!

52. *Dame Partlet* Traditional name for a hen (cf.
Reynard for a fox); hence a hen-pecking woman (cf.
Wint. 2. 3. 76). Quickly, I think, flutters and fusses
like a hen, as she speaks.

56. *my husband* Cf. ll. 94, 171. A widow in *2 Hen.
IV* (v. 2. 1. 70, 83), she is married to Pistol in *Hen. V.*

57. *tithe* (Theobald) Q., F. 'tight'.

59. *shaved...hair* A poss. allusion to the 'French
disease'; cf. *M.N.D.* 1. 2. 89–90.

69–70. *Dowlas...bolters,* v. G. The linen was so
coarse that it could be used as a sieve.

72–3. *eight...an ell* A high price (Linthicum,
p. 98). No doubt she exaggerates, and so raises a
laugh; v. G. 'holland'.

74. *diet and by-drinkings* board and odd drinks.
Fal. is her lodger.

79. *let them coin his nose* etc. Cf. *Err.* 3. 2. 133,
'her nose, all o'er embellished with rubies, carbunckles,
sapphires'. For Nashe parallel v. p. 194.

80. *Will you...of me?* i.e. Am I to be robbed, like
the Prodigal Son, by strumpets? Cf. *3 Hen. VI,*
2. 1. 24; *M.V.* 2. 6. 14–19; *Fortunes,* pp. 34–5; and G.

81. *take mine...inn* Prov. 'inn' orig.=house.
Apperson, 'take' 28; Jente, No. 120.

86. *sneak-up* (O.E.D.) Q. 'sneakeup' (the second *e*
worn and resembles *c*). Q3–5, F. 'Sneake-Cuppe'
which most edd. follow; v. G. 'sneak-up'.

87. *cudgel* With the truncheon. Cf. *2 Hen. IV,* 2.
4. 137.

88. S.D. For 'Poins' v. notes 2. 4. 519 and l. 195 below.

89. *is the wind* etc. Prov. Cf. Apperson, p. 690; Jente, No. 348; *Ado*, 2. 3. 101.

91. *two and...fashion* 'As prisoners are conveyed to Newgate, fastened two and two together' (Johnson). Virtually a S.D.

105. *eight-penny* tuppeny-ha'penny.

114. *stewed prune* bawd, v. G.

114–15. *drawn fox* dragged fox (v. O.E.D. 'drawn', 1). A living fox is false enough; a dead one, dragged to lay a false trail, is doubly so.

115. *Maid Marian* A highly indecorous figure in the morris dance, usually played by a man. A 'deputy's wife' was, of course, eminently respectable; v. G. 'deputy'.

118. *a thing to thank God on* i.e. she is as God made her.

119. *nothing* (Q.) F. 'no thing'—which spoils the fun.

127. *neither fish nor flesh* Cf. Apperson, p. 219.

133–4. *this other day* the other day; cf. *Lear*, 1. 2. 153.   *ought* owed.

136–7. *Thy love...million* Cf. *Fortunes*, p. 104.

147. *the lion's whelp* Cf. *Prov.* xix. 12; xx. 2; *Hen. V*, 1. 2. 109; but Fal. is impertinent.

151. *pray God...break* Prov. Cf. Apperson, p. 659 'ungirt, unblest'; Jente, No. 158, and Browne (*Pseudodoxia*, v, xxii) who notes that a girdle symbolises truth, resolution and readiness unto action, and moreover divides the heart and parts which God requires from the inferior organs.

156–7. *embossed rascal* A retort to 'lion's whelp'; a double quibble, v. G.

159. *pennyworth of sugar-candy* Cf. 2. 4. 21–2 (note). Sugar was given to fighting-cocks to prolong their breath (Clar.)

161. *injuries* Lit. insults; hence, contemptible objects.

171. *husband* v. note l. 56.

172. *guests* (Q 2–5, F.) Q. 'gheſſe'.

173. *pacified still* always ready to make it up. Cf. Derrick in *F.V.* ii. 57, 'Nay, I am quickly pacified'.

175. *answered* accounted for.

176. *sweet beef* Cf. *Fortunes*, pp. 25–31, 'martlemas', in *2 Hen. IV*, 2. 2. 100 (v. G.) and below G. 'beef'. A pregnant epithet.

182. *Rob...exchequer* The 'receivers' theme'; cf. *Library*, p. 7.

183. *with unwashed hands* illotis manibus, straight away.　　　188–9. *heinously unprovided* disgracefully ill-equipped.

189. *God...rebels* Cf. *Fortunes*, p. 84.

193–8. *Go bear...afternoon* I follow the lining of Q. and F. N.B. omit 'yet' and 'Jack' in ll. 196–7 and we get three lines of verse, while 'Go bear this letter to my brother John' gives another. Cf. pp. 112–13 above, and *Library*, pp. 14–16.

195. *Go, Poins* (Johnson) Q., F. 'Go Peto'. Cf. note 2. 4. 519.

196. *thirty...time* This fixes the time of the scene as early morning; cf. l. 203.

197. *Temple hall* i.e. Inner Temple Hall, a common rendezvous; cf. *1 Hen. VI*, 2. 4. 3.

198. *o'clock* (F. 'a clocke') Q. 'of clocke'. Cf. p. 104.

200. *order...furniture* directions for their uniforms and equipment.

204. *O...drum* Hitherto unexplained. Fal. quibbles on 'tavern' (Lat. 'taberna') and 'tabern' or 'tabor' (v. O.E.D. 'taborn'). Cf. *Tw.Nt.* 3. 1. 3 (note) for the same quibble. The drum is a martial instrument, the tabor not; cf. *Ado*, 2. 3. 13–15, 'no music with him but the drum and fife, and now had he rather hear the tabor and the fife'.

S.D. F. 'Exeunt omnes'. Q. omits, makes no break between 3. 3. and 4. 1, and gives no entries for 4. 1.

4. 1.

S.D. from F. Q. omits, v. previous note.

1. *Well said* etc. Q prints *Per.* as prefix for Hotspur here and down to l. 93, but *Hot.* everywhere else.

2. *fine* v. G.　　　3. *attribution* v. G.

4. *of...stamp* minted in this age; cf. *Meas.* 2. 4. 46.

5. *go...current* pass as sterling.

6. *defy* v. G.　　　7. *soothers* v. G.

9. *task...word* 'challenge me to be as good as my word' (Clar.).

13. *I can but thank you* For this characteristically delayed reply to l. 10 cf. 2. 4. 105; 2. 3. 92.

20. *bear* (Q7, Rowe) Q., F. 'beares'. Since 'letters'=letter, the sing. may be intended.

my lord (Capell) Q., F. 'my mind'. The compositor repeats himself.

24. *feared by* v. G. 'fear' and cf. *Ric. III*, 1. 1. 137.

31. *inward sickness*—'Hot. is only quoting the material portions of the letter' (Clar. citing *Lear*, 2. 2. 172).

35. *removed* not directly concerned.

37. *conjunction* united body.

44. *want* absence.　　　46. *set* stake.

exact total. Accent 'éxact'.

47–8. *main...hazard* Elaborate quibble, v. G.

49–52. *for therein...fortunes* i.e. had North. been here, we should go to battle knowing that defeat if it came would be final, whereas his absence leaves open the possibility of retreat and re-formation. Cf. G. 'read', 'list' (a quibble) and *2 Hen. VI*, 5. 2. 78–9.

50. *soul* With a quibble on 'sole'.

53. *reversion*, (Q.) F. 'reuersion.' Most edd. 'reversion:' (taking 'Where' as 'Whereas'). The Q.

comma gives the sense: When an heir has a fair in-
heritance in prospect, he may boldly spend in advance.

55. *Is* (F.) Q. 'tis'.

56. *comfort in retirement* 'support to which we may
have recourse' (Johnson).

58. *look big* v. G.

59. *maidenhead...affairs* our yet untried arms.

61. *hair* v. G.

69. *the off'ring side* the insurgent party; the side
making the attack; cf. 3. 2. 169 and *2 Hen. IV*,
4. 1. 219.

70. *strict arbitrement* 'judicial enquiry' (Schmidt).

74. *fear* i.e. on our part.

77. *opinion* v. G.   78. *dare* v. G.

95. *nimble-footed* The quotation from Stow in
note 2. 4. 242 continues:

> He was of maruellous great strength, and passing swift
> in running, insomuch that hee with two other of his Lords,
> without hounds, bow or other engine, would take a wilde
> bucke, or Doe, in a large parke.

But Hot. is sarcastic; 'nimble-footed' suggests cowardice.

96. *daffed* Past tense because they have now
changed [J.C.M.].

97. *bid it pass* From the drinking-song refrain 'Let
the world pass'.

97–103. *All furnished...bulls* 'A more lively
representation of young men ardent for enterprise,
perhaps no writer has ever given' (Johnson). Sh. was
clearly inspired by Daniel's description of the P. at
Shrewsbury, i.e. *C.W.* iii. 110:

> There lo, that new-appearing glorious starre,
> Wonder of Armes, the terror of the field,
> Young Henrie, laboring where the stoutest are,
> And euen the stoutest forces backe to yeild.

98–9. *All plumed...bathed* The chief crux of the
text. Q. reads:

> All plumde like Estridges that with the wind
> Baited like Eagles hauing lately bathd,

and F. follows. Rowe conj. 'wing' for 'with', which
Johnson and Malone accepted; an emendation graphi-
cally plausible, *ing* and *ith* being easily confused in
'English' script. But a misunderstanding of 'baited',
gen. emended 'bating' or 'bated', has hitherto pre-
vented mod. endorsement. It means 'refreshed' or 're-
newed', cf. G., Sidney, *Astrophel and Stella* (1598), 39,
'Come sleep. . . .The baiting-place of wit, the balme of
woe', and *Ham.* 3.3.79 (note). If we accept 'wing', the
sense therefore is: The P. and his comrades, with
casques and chargers decked out in P. of Wales's
feathers, seem like ostriches sailing before the wind, or
like fresh-plumed eagles newly risen from the sea. And
that this is what Sh. intended is confirmed by the discovery of passages which furnished him with the two
images involved: (i) The description of the Earl of
Surrey riding to tilt in Nashe's *Unfortunate Traveller*
(McKerrow, ii. 272), cited by G. R. Coffman, *Mod.
Lang. Notes*, xiii. 318:

> The trappings of his horse were pounced and bolstered
> out with rough plumed silver plush, in full proportion
> and shape of an Estrich. . . .His wings, which he neuer
> vseth but running, beeing spread full saile, made his lustie
> stead as proud vnder him as he had bin some other Pegasus,
> & so quiueringly and tenderly were these his broade winges
> bounde to either side of him, that as he paced vp and
> downe the tilt-yard in his maiesty ere the knights were
> entered, they seemed wantonly to fan in his face and make
> a flickering sound, such as Eagles doe, swiftly pursuing
> their praie in the ayre. On either of his wings, as the
> Estrich hath a sharpe goad or pricke wherewith he spurreth
> himselfe forward in his saile-assisted race, so this artficiall
> Estrich. . .

A close connexion is indisputable. In both we have
plumes fanned by the wind, a horse like Pegasus, eagles
as well as ostriches, while Nashe's 'wings. . .spread full
saile' and 'saile-assisted race' give us the clue to Sh.'s
'estridges that wing the wind'. (ii) Spenser's descrip-

tion of the Red Cross Knight rising, lusty as an eagle, from the Well of Life (*Faerie Queene*, 1. xi. 34), cited Arden ed.:

> At last she saw where he upstarted brave
> Out of the well, wherein he drenchéd lay:
> As Eagle, fresh out of the Ocean wave,
> Where he hath lefte his plumes all hoary gray,
> And deckt himselfe with feathers youthly gay,
> Like Eyas hauke up mounts unto the skies,
> His newly budded pineons to assay,
> And marveiles at himselfe still as he flies:
> So new this new-borne knight to battell new did rise.

Here is the source of 'baited like eagles', and of the introduction of the P. of Wales's feathers, while the notion of moral regeneration is implicit in both Sh. and Spenser. For previous attempts at solution, v. Hemingway. Many gloss 'estridge' (v. G.) as 'goshawk', but the evidence for this is weak, while goshawks do not yield P. of Wales's feathers.

100. *images* i.e. of saints, decked out on holy days.

104. *beaver* i.e. helm; the part for the whole, v. G.

106. *feathered Mercury* Alluding to his winged cap.

107. *vaulted* Malone conj. 'vault it', to accord with 'rise'.

108. *dropped* (Q2, F.) Q. 'drop'.

110. *witch...horsemanship* Cf. *Ham.* 4. 7. 83 ff.

111–12. *worse than...agues* Kittredge notes:

Malarial fever (fever and ague) was prevalent in Sh.'s time on account of the undrained marshes. It was thought to be caused by vapours drawn up from marshland by the sun, esp. in early spring. Cf. *Lear*, 2. 4. 168–70.

113. *like...trim* like beasts decked out for sacrifice.

114. *fire-eyed maid* Bellona. Cf. 'fire-eyed fury', *Rom.* 3. 1. 129.

116. *altar* (Q4, F.) Q. 'altars'.

118. *reprisal* v. G. Cf. *2 Hen. IV*, 3. 1. 101, and Cheyney, i. ch. xxi.

124–7. *O, that Glendower...of yet* Hall and Hol.

(Stone, p. 146) state, 'The Welshmen...hearing of this battell toward, came to the aid of the Persies'. Sh. seems to follow *C.W.* iii. 99, which relates that the K. marched too quickly for the Welsh to arrive in time. This is historically correct (v. J. E. Lloyd, *Owen Glendower*, pp. 70–1); but whence did Daniel learn it?

126. *cannot* (Q5, F.) Q. 'can'.

127. *yet* (Q5, F.) Q. 'it'. Prob. 'yet' misread 'yt'.

135–6. *out of fear...year* Is Douglas, Macbeth-like, relying on some soothsayer's prophecy?

4. 2.

S.D. For 'jack-coat' v. note l. 47 and G. 'Jack'. The route of Fal.'s march to Bridgenorth is discussed in T.L.S. 1931, Jan. 8, 15, 22, 29, Feb. 5. I cannot think it ever engaged Sh.'s mind, except perhaps for a moment at ll. 44–5.

3. *Co'fil'* (Camb.) Q., F. 'cop-hill', i.e. 'Coldfield', which Sh. spelt 'Cophil' and pron. 'Cofil'.

5. *Lay out* Take it out of expenses, v. G. 'lay out'. Bard. is quartermaster (cf. *Fortunes*, p. 84).

6. *makes an angel* brings your debt to me up to 10s. Fal. pretends in reply that 'makes'=will bring in, i.e. that Bard. proposes to raise money on the bottle.

8. *answer* be answerable for. Alluding to the illegality of private minting.

9. *lieutenant Peto* 'This passage proves that Peto did not go with the P.' (Johnson); cf. note 2. 4. 519.

12. *gurnet* v. G. A small fish with a head as large as its body. When soused prob. a cheap substitute for anchovy (v. note 2. 4. 529). It is as if Fal. calls himself a pickled tadpole.

the king's press i.e. his captain's commission to impress recruits.

13–22. *I have...services* Complaints of such malpractices are frequent. Cf. *Sh. Eng.* i. 112, 122–5; *Fortunes*, pp. 84–5; and *2 Hen. IV*, 3. 2. 96 ff.

14–15. *press...inquire* Collier reads 'pressed...inquired'. Cf. l. 20. Poss. an *e: d* misprint, v. MSH. p. 109.

15–16. *contracted* i.e. in marriage.

17. *commodity...slaves* parcel of well-to-do cowards; v. G. 'commodity', 'warm'.

23–4. *ancients...companies* The ragamuffins do not rank as privates, though Fal. pays them as such. By securing promotion for the orig. 'warm' recruits, Fal. made more money as they sold out, and now pockets the difference between their pay and that of the new recruits. 'Gentlemen of companies' were something more than ordinary soldiers with a little more pay (O.E.D. 'gentleman' 1 *c*); cf. *Hen. V*, 4. 1. 39.

25. *painted cloth* v. G. For the Glutton cf. *2 Hen. IV*, 1. 2. 33 ff.

27. *unjust serving-men* Cf. *Luke* xvi. 8, 'the unjust (=dishonest) steward'.

28. *revolted* runaway prentices; cf. 2. 4. 45–7.

29. *cankers...peace* For Nashe parallel, v. p. 195.

30. *dishonourable* dishonourably.

old feazed ancient (Q.) F. 'old-fac'd Ancient'. Almost all edd. follow F., and suppose a man referred to. Vaughan reads 'feazed' for 'fazed'. Either word= frayed, worn thin, and 'ancient'=a standard. Fal.'s 'ensigns', etc., are ten times more *dis*honourably ragged than a battle-tattered flag. Cf. 'full of holes like a shot antient' 1. 2. 29, *Puritan Widow*, 1607 (T. Brooke, *Sh. Apocrypha*).

31. *as have* (Q.) F. 'that haue'.

33. *tattered* (F.) Q., F. 'tottered'—a variant sp.

33–4. *prodigals...husks* Cf. *Fortunes*, pp. 34–5, and Nashe parallel p. 195.

36. *gibbets* Common on the highway, petty theft being a capital offence down to the nineteenth century. Cf. 1. 2. 37–8 (note).

40. *out of prison* The Privy Council emptied the London prisons in 1596 to furnish recruits for the Cadiz expedition, v. Cheyney, ii. 49–50.

41. *not a shirt...and the half* Arden compares
2. 4. 126, 'not three good men...and one of them',
and 5. 3. 36, 'not three...left alive, and they are', etc.
Most edd. follow Rowe and read 'but' for 'not'.

44–5. *Saint Alban's...Daventry* On the road to
Coventry; cf. head-note.

46. *linen on every hedge* Cf. *Wint.* 4. 3. 5–7, 24.
The stealing of washing from hedges was common,
v. my *Life in Sh.'s England*, pp. 241–2.

S.D. Fal.'s evident surprise suggests an unexpected
approach, while his 'mad wag' may be his response
to a prod in the jack-coat.

47. *blown Jack...quilt* Cf. 2. 4. 320, 'bombast'.
Refers quibblingly to the leather-quilted jack Fal.
wears; v. G. 'jack', *Sh. Eng.* i. 128, and Spenser,
State of Ireland, Globe ed. p. 639/1; ed. Renwick, p. 90.

48–51. *what a devil...Shrewsbury* He forestalls
censure for his own delay by expressing shocked surprise at theirs.

55. *away all night* i.e. travel all night. (Q.) F.
'away all tonight'. Fal.'s 'vigilant' supports Q.

56. *fear me* worry about me.

56–7. *as vigilant...cream* as ready to be up all
night as a cat waiting to steal the cream. Cf. 2. 4. 273–4
(note) and G. 'vigilant'.

63–4. *toss* Cf. *3 Hen. VI*, 1. 1. 244.
food for powder Cf. 5. 3. 35–8 (note).

67. *bare* threadbare.

71–2. *three fingers* three finger-breadths.

77–9. *Well...guest* (Pope) Q., F. print as prose.
Cf. *Fortunes*, p. 85–6. Prov. Cf. Jente, No. 128.

4. 3.

S.D. Malone first read 'The Rebel Camp near
Shrewsbury'.

1. *We'll fight...to-night* etc. Cf. the dispute before
Actium, *Ant. & Cleo.* 3. 7. 28–9, before Philippi, *Jul.
Caes.* 4. 3. 196, and of the rebels in 1. 3. of *2 Hen IV*.

3. *supply* reinforcements.

7. *fear and cold heart* Cf. 2. 3. 31.

10. *well-respected* v. G., i.e. as understood by wise campaigners, not mere fire-eaters.

16–17. *Come...you are* (Pope) Q., F. 'come... not be/I wonder...you are'.

19. *drag...expedition* impede our progress.

21. *horse* (Q 5, F.) Q. 'horses'. Cf. 'horse' in l. 19.

22. *pride and mettle* Cf. G. and *V.A.* 419–20.

24. *half himself* (Steevens) Q., F. 'halfe of himſelfe'.

26. *In general* (Rowe, etc.). Kittredge places the comma after 'enemy' (l. 25).

journey-bated (F 3) Q., F. 'iourney bated', v. G. 'bate'.

28. *ours* (F.) Q. 'our'; Q. is poss. correct; cf. note 5. 4. 158 and v. Jespersen, *Mod. Eng. Gram.* ii. 16.27.

29. S.D. 'The trumpet'=the trumpeter of the theatre. The K.'s offer 'was really conveyed by Thomas Prestbury, Abbot of Shrewsbury' and by a clerk of the Privy Seal (Clar.).

39. *out of...rule.* o'erstepping the bounds of obedience and good government, v. G. 'limit'.

51. *suggestion* v. G. Not a pleasant word.

54–88. *My father* etc. See *Ric. II*, 2. 3. 113–36; 148–51; 3. 3. 101–20; and above, pp. xxiii–iv.

62. *sue his livery* Cf. *Ric. II*, 2. 3. 129, and G.

68. *more and less* great and small.

with cap and knee kneeling cap in hand.

70. *Attended...lanes* Cf. Berners, *Froissart*, II, ccxvii, 672, 'The people...made a lane for him to pass thorough'.

72. *heirs as pages,* (Malone) Q., F. 'heires, as Pages'.

as pages i.e. as hostages for their fathers' loyalty.

73. *golden multitudes* jubilating crowds, v. G. 'golden'.

76. *while...poor* while his stock was low; v. G. 'blood'.

78–80. *to reform...commonwealth* Cf. Hol. iii. 498 (Stone, p. 101):

Moreouer, he vndertooke to cause the paiment of taxes and tallages to be laid downe, and to bring the king to good gouernment.

81. *Cries out upon* v. G. and cf. *A.Y.L.* 2. 7. 70.

82. *country* (Q.); for attrib. use v. *O.E.D.* 'country 13' [J.C.M.].

87. *In deputation* Cf. 4. 1. 32, and G.

92. *in the neck of* v. G. 'neck'.   *tasked* v. G.

95. *engaged* held as hostage; cf. 'impawned', l. 108.

98. *intelligence* spies. Perhaps the popinjay (1. 3. 30 ff.) is meant.

103. *head of safety* force for our protection.

105. *indirect* Even less pleasant than 'suggestion' (l. 51). Both Bol.'s title and the means he employed to enforce it were 'indirect'. Cf. *2 Hen. IV*, 4. 5. 184, and *C.W.* iii. 87, 'The Percyes...conspire, vnder pretence to right / The crooked courses they had suffered long'.

107. *Not so* etc. Hot.'s sudden change of tone is remarkable and emphasizes 'the desperate state of the rebels' (Hemingway).

4. 4.

S.D. Q. 'Enter Archbishop of Yorke, sir Mighell.' The uncommon sp. 'Mighell', not found elsewhere in Sh., occurs twice in Nashe (McKerrow, iii. 88, ll. 17, 26). Edd. assume Sir Michael to be a priest; 'Sir' (=dominus) standing for mod. 'Rev.' He is almost as shadowy as 'the archdeacon' (3. 1. 70), and appears in no other scene.

2. *lord marshal* Thomas Mowbray, Earl of Norfolk.

3. *cousin Scroop* The only other Scroop mentioned in the play is York's 'brother', executed at Bristol (1. 3. 268), who oddly enough actually was his cousin.

15. *in the first proportion* the largest of all. The sense 'proportion'=size is not found elsewhere in Sh., but cf. 'in full proportion' in the passage from Nashe cited note 4. 1. 98–9.

16. *Glendower's absence* This point must be taken from Daniel (cf. note 4. 1. 124–7), unless there is some hitherto undetected source for the Glendower-Hotspur plot (v. note 2. 3. 89–90).

17. *rated* 'on which we reckoned' (Johnson).

18. *o'er-ruled by prophecies* Nothing of this in Hol. Cf. note 4. 1. 135–6.

5. I.

S.D. Q., F. give 'Weſtmerland' among the entries; as he is the 'surety' impawned with the rebels (5. 2. 30, 45) he cannot be 'on' here. Critics are at pains to account for Fal.'s presence at the K.'s council of war. Sh. needed him for the speech on Honour at the end, and, I conj. with Morgan, only added him in his second draft. N.B. except for the brief impertinence at l. 28 he has nothing to say until the K. goes out. Cf. *Fortunes*, p. 88 and Morgan, p. 34.

Pope read 'Shrewsbury' and Capell 'The king's Camp near Shrewsbury'.

1–3. *How bloodily* etc. An appropriate opening for a battle-scene. *busky* (F.) Q. 'bulky'.

8. S.D. Theobald added Vernon to the entry.

9. *How now*, etc. Q., F. print a fresh prefix *King* before this line.

17–21. *move...times* Cf. *K. John*, 5. 7. 74; *M.N.D.* 2. 1. 153; *Troil.* 1. 3. 85–124.

19. *exhaled meteor*, v. G. and 'exhalations', 2. 4. 316. Not moving in an 'obedient orb', comets were 'dis-astrous' and therefore ill-omened.

25. *do* (F.) Q. omits.

26. *dislike* discord. A rare use.

28. *lay...found it* The thief's excuse when discovered in possession of stolen goods.

34. *my staff...break* Cf. *Ric. II.* 2. 2. 58–60; 2. 3. 26–7.

42. *Doncaster* Cf. Hol. iii. 498 (Stone 100); not mentioned in Sh.'s *Ric. II.*

50. *injuries...time* evils of a time of disorder.

59–66. *being fed...your sight* Cf. Pliny, *Naturalis Historia*, x. ch. 9. T. W. Baldwin argues (*Parrott Presentation Volume*, 1935, pp. 157–63) that, since Holland's trans. only appeared in 1601, Sh. must have gone to Pliny direct. Cf. *Lear*, 1. 4. 235–6.

60. *gull* nestling.   *bird* chick.

64. *swallowing* being swallowed.

67–8. *Whereby...yourself* i.e. so that you are your-self the cause of our appearing against you.

71. *younger enterprise* Cf. 'infant fortune', 1. 3. 252, and v. 4. 3. 75 ff.

74–5. *face...colour* Quibbles, v. G. 'face', 'guard' and l. 80.

77. *rub the elbow* i.e. rub their hands; cf. *L.L.L.* 5. 2. 109–10. Fashions in gesture change; even rub-bing one's hands being now out of date.

78. *hurlyburly innovation* riotous insurrection.

80. *water-colours* thin pretexts, not intended to last beyond victory.

83. *our armies* (F.) Q. 'your armies'. Common type of misprint, cf. MSH. 119, 241. Most mod. edd. follow Q.; but the point of the P.'s speech is that a single combat will 'save the blood *on either side*' (l. 99).

87. *hopes* i.e. of salvation. Cf. *Ric. II*, 1. 1. 68.

88. *This...head* Apart from his responsibility for this present enterprise; v. G. 'set off', 5. 2. 21, and 2 *Hen. IV*, 4. 1. 145.

90. *active-valiant...valiant-young* Theobald sup-plies the hyphens.

100. *a single fight* This challenge, Sh.'s invention, is in keeping with Eliz. ideas; cf. Essex's challenge at Rouen, Jan. 1592 (Cheyney, i. 275).

102. *Albeit* Were it not that.

105. *cousin's* nephew's.   111. *wait on us* attend us.

114. *take it advisedly* you will do well to accept.

120. S.D. Q., F. 'Exeunt: manent Prince, Falſt.' Morgan suggests that the 'Exeunt' orig. closed the scene; cf. head-note.

122. *bestride me* The attitude of one defending a wounded man; cf. *2 Hen. IV*, 1. 1. 207.   *so*=good!

125. *I would...bed-time* 'Suggested by the P.'s "say thy prayers"' (Elton).

126–7. *thou...death* Prov.; cf. *2 Hen. IV*, 3. 2. 235. Prob. a pun on 'debt'.

128–9. *forward...on me* v. G. 'forward', 'call on'.

129–40. *Well, 'tis no matter*, etc. Cf. *Fortunes*, pp. 70–3. Stoll (*Sh. Studies*, p. 459) compares Basilisco's 'catechism before action' (v. Boas, *Kyd's Works*, pp. 223–4 and *K. John*, 1. 1. 244, note). It is difficult to believe that Fal.'s speech on Honour owes nothing to Montaigne's almost equally famous essay on Glory (v. Florio's trans. II, xvi).

130. *prick me off* Lit. tick me off. Cf. G., *2 Hen. IV*, 3. 2. 114; *Jul. Caes.* 3. 1. 216. The idea of the little hole (made by a bullet or rapier as by the pin on the paper list) is prob. also present.

135. *A trim reckoning!* A pretty balance sheet!

137. *insensible* imperceptible.

138. *will it* (Q2) Q. 'wil'.

140. *a mere scutcheon* nothing but a cheap piece of heraldry to grace funerals; v. G. 'scutcheon'.

catechism i.e. confession of faith, in the form of question and answer.

5.2.

S.D. Pope read 'Percy's Camp': Malone, 'The Rebel Camp'.

1–26. *O, no...the king* This explanation of Worc.'s treachery has no basis in the sources.

3. *undone* (Q5, F.) Q. 'vnder one'. Perhaps Sh.

wrote 'und one' (cf. Pollard in *Companion to Sh. Studies*, p. 274), and the Q. printer 'corrected'.

8. *Supposition* (Q., F.) 'Suspicion' (Rowe and most edd.). But 'Supposition' (=Rumour=Virgil's Fama) is the sense required. Cf. *2 Hen. IV*, Ind. 'Enter Rumour painted full of tongues', and *Aen.* iv. 181–3:

> cui, quot sunt corpore plumae,
> tot vigiles oculi subter (mirabile dictu),
> tot linguae, totidem ora sonant, tot subrigit aures.

9. *Of eyes* Q., F. print with l. 8.

11. *ne'er* (F.) Q. 'neuer'.

12. *a wild...ancestors* a taint of inherited insubordination.

19. *an adopted...privilege* i.e. the nickname 'Hotspur' licenses a number of misdeeds.

21. *live* Cf. note 1. 2. 182, and G.

23. *ta'en* caught (by infection).

30. *Deliver...Westmoreland* We have not yet been told that West. is the 'pawn' (4. 3. 108; cf. head-note 5. 1); and this command can hardly be theatrically intelligible. The obscurity may be the result of revision.

36. *mercy* A word selected to goad the hearer.

40. *forswearing* falsely denying on oath. Cf. *C.W.* iii. 92.

49–51. *O, would...Monmouth!* Cf. 5. 1. 83–100. A touch of tragic irony.

52. *tasking* Cf. l. 54 and G.

57. *duties* dues of respect, v. G.

61. *still...with you* i.e. constantly asserting that he could not find words good enough for you. This does not tally with the P.'s speech (5. 1. 83 ff.), but serves to heighten the audience's admiration for him.

63. *cital* v. G. The P. summons himself, as 'truant to chivalry' (5. 1. 94), to witness to Hot.'s chivalry.

66. *instantly* v. G.   68. *envy* v. G.

69. *owe* v. G.   72. *Upon* (Pope) Q., F. 'On'.

73. *a liberty* (Q.) F. 'at liberty', Capell 'a libertine', which most edd. now read. Cf. G. 'liberty', 'wild'.

76. *shrink* v. G.

78–80. *Better...persuasion* Better spend time taking thought for battle than wait for my lame words to stir your blood to action. Elton notes here: 'Sh., like Thucydides, does not so much break through grammar, as live before it.'

83–90. *O gentlemen...just* Stow, Hol., and Daniel all give Hot. a speech of this kind before the battle.

89. *for* as regards.

98. *Esperance!* Cf. Hol. iii. 523 (Stone, p. 145), and note 2. 3. 73. The final *e* is pronounced.

101. *heaven to earth* the odds are as heaven to earth.

102. S.D. Q., F. 'Here they embrace, the trumpets found, the king enters with his power, alarme to the battel, then enter Douglas, and fir Walter Blunt', i.e. neither Q. nor F. give an 'exeunt' or make a scene-division here. Yet the stage must be cleared for a moment before the K. passes across at the opening of 5. 3.

5. 3.

S.D. See end of previous scene and p. 111, *Acts and Scenes*.

1–3. *What is...head?* (Hanmer) Q., F. divide 'What...croffeft me, / What...head?'.

1. *the battle* (Hanmer) Q., F. 'battel'.

7. *Stafford* In Hol. (iii. 523; Stone, p. 146) he leads the vanguard, and is among the slain. It is Daniel (*C.W.* iii. 97) who speaks of an encounter with Douglas. Sh. alone makes him one of those who wears the K.'s coats.

11. *I was...Scot* (Q.) Q5. 'I was not born to yield, thou proud Scot'. F. 'I was not borne to yeeld, thou haughty Scot'. Cited in Malone's Preface (1790) as an example of progressive textual degradation. Cf.

Pollard, *Sh's. Fight with the Pirates* (2nd ed.),
pp. 73–4.

15. *triumphed* As at 5. 4. 14 and *Ric. III*, 3. 4. 91,
accented on second syllable.

16. *won! here* F. 'won, here'; Q. 'won here,'.

22. *A fool* (Capell) Q., F. 'Ah foole'. The compositor takes 'A' for 'Ah'. An Eliz. gibe='may the
name "fool" cling to thy soul!'.   25. *coats* v. G.

29. *stand...day* look like doing well to-day.

30. *shot-free* without paying; v. G.

31. *scoring* Cf. 2. 4. 26 and *Err.* 1. 2. 65, 'score
your fault on my pate'. A quibble.

33. *here's no vanity!* Ironical. Here's a fine proof
of the truth of my catechism!

35–8. *I have led...during life* Cf. 4. 2. 63–4.
Fal. leads his 'charge' to a hot corner, and then himself
takes cover, in order that he may pocket the pay of
those killed. Cf. *Fortunes*, p. 85, and Arden for contemporary quotations showing this was a not uncommon practice.

36. *ragamuffins* Q., F. 'rag of muffins'. Prob. compositor's expansion, cf. p. 104.

38. *town's end* v. G.

39–55. *What...dally now?* Lining as in Q. This
seems to me a clear example of verse prosified in
revision. Cf. pp. 112–13 and *Library*, pp. 14–16.

39. *stand'st* (F.) Q. 'ftands'. Cf. MSH. p. 291.

42. *are yet* (Q.) F. 'are'.

45. *Turk Gregory* Usually identified, unconvincingly,
with Gregory VII (Hildebrand). The context de-
mands a bloodthirsty tyrant (v. G. 'Turk'), credited
with some great massacre, such as Fal. pretends to
have executed upon the rebels. Pope Gregory XIII
(1572–85), inveterate foe of England, who blessed if
he did not instigate the Massacre of St Bartholomew,
and promised plenary indulgence to anyone who would
murder Elizabeth, fills the bill. And in 1579 he was

figuring with Nero and the Grand Turk as one of 'The Three Tyrants of the World' in coloured prints sold on the streets of London (v. Neale, *Qu. Eliz.* pp. 225, 248; Black, *Reign of Eliz.* pp. 144, 304).

47. *paid Percy* killed Percy. Fal.'s imagination is already playing with the idea.

sure harmless. Hal takes it as='safe', 'untouched'.

51. *get'st* (Q2, F.) Q. 'gets'. Cf. note l. 39.

52. *What...case?* It should have been primed for instant use and not in the holster. Fal. pretends he has put it up to cool after much firing.

56. *Percy...pierce* 'Pierce' was pron. 'perse'; cf. *L.L.L.* 4. 2. 87–8. The aside is suggested by Steevens. For 'so' v. note 5. 1. 122.

58. *a carbonado* a rasher, v. G.

61. *an end* Of (*a*) my words, and (*b*) my life.
unlooked for beyond my expectations, cf. Son. 25.4.

5.4.

S.D. F. heads this 'Scena Tertia'; cf. note 5. 2. 102
S.D. For 'wounded in the cheek', cf. note ll. 1–2 below.

1–3. *I prithee...with him* (Steevens and mod. edd.) Q. prints 'I prithee' with l. 2; F. as prose. Cf. note ll. 7–8, the prose ll. 5, 9, and *Library*, pp. 14–16.

1–2. *Harry...too much* Cf. Hol. iii. 523 (Stone, p. 146):

The prince that daie holpe his father like a lustie yoong gentleman; for although he was hurt in the face with an arrow, so that diuerse noble men that were about him would haue conueied him foorth of the field, yet he would not suffer them so to doo, least his departure from amongst his men might happilie [=haply] haue striken some feare into their harts.

6. *retirement...amaze* v. G.

7–8. *I will...tent* Q. as prose, F. and mod. edd. as verse. Cf. note ll. 1–3 above.

15. *breathe* v. G.   22. *maintenance* v. G.

24. S.D. Q. gives Douglas no entry.

34. *thee: so* (F.) Q. 'thee, and'. Cf. p. 107 and for a similar verbal substitution note 2. 4. 396.

38. S.D. et seq. Sh. takes the details of Hal's prowess from Daniel, who, developing Hol.'s hint, cited in note ll. 1–2 above, adds the rescue of the K., the defeat of Douglas, the encounter with Hot. (but not his overthrow) to his laurels (cf. Moorman, *Sh. Jahrbuch*, XL. 78 and *Library*, pp. 4–6). In Hol. the K. is the hero of the battle; cf. iii. 523 (Stone, p. 147).

41. *Shirley* Q., F. 'Sherly', i.e. 'Sir Hugh Shirley, Master of the Hawks to Henry IV' (Clar.). Cf. *C.W.* iii. 113, 8: 'valiant Shorly', in context with 'magnanimous Stafford' and 'couragious Blunt'.

43. *pay* A quibble, v. G.

45. *Gawsey* In Hol. 'Gausell', i.e. 'Sir Nicholas Goushill of Hoveringham, co. Notts' (Clar.).

46. *Clifton* 'Sir John Clifton...of Nottingham' (Clar.).

48. *opinion* v. G.   49. *tender* v. G.

51–7. *O God...your son* This is the only direct reference in the play to suspicions, explicit in *F.V.* and the chronicles, that the P. had designs upon his father's life.

54. *insulting* v. G.

65. *Two stars...sphere* A separate sphere was assigned to every moving star in the old astronomy. Cf. 5. 1. 17–21.

68. *Nor* (F.) Q. 'Now'. Cf. MSH. pp. 106–7.

74. *vanities* empty boasts.

75. *Well said* Well done! Cf. *A.Y.L.* 2. 6. 14.

76. S.D. As L. G. Knights (p. 130, *Determinations*, ed. Leavis) points out, 'It is important to realise...

that when Fal. feigns death, he is meant to appear actually dead in the eyes of the audience'.

81–3. *But thought...stop* But thought depends on Life, and Life's the sport of Time, and Time though it rule the whole world must have an end. v. G. 'survey'.

81. *slave* (Q2, F.) Q. 'flaues'.

time's fool Cf. *Son.* 116, 9; *Meas.* 3. 1. 11.

83. *prophesy* The dying were supposedly gifted with prophetic power; cf. *Ric. II,* 2. 1. 5–16; *Ham.* 5. 2. 353.

88. *Ill-weaved ambition* Such is the quality of Hot.'s ambitions (cf. note 1. 3. 208); and such the language of Sh., the wool-dealer's son, who well knew that cloth loosely woven was specially apt to shrink.

90–2. *A kingdom...enough* Cf. *Ric. II,* 3. 3. 153–4.

92. *thee dead* (Q7) Q., F. 'the dead'.

94. *sensible* able to feel.

95. *dear...zeal* heartfelt...affection or admiration.

96. *favours* H. Hartman (*Pub. Mod. Lang. Ass. America,* 1931) suggests that these are feathers from the P.'s helm. 'Favour' (v. O.E.D. 7)=any kind of badge or token worn in the helmet, not merely a lady's favour, as edd. usually interpret. Cf. 3. 2. 142; 4. 1. 98, 106; 5. 4. 72–3; and *Fortunes,* p. 66.

102–10. *What! old...lie* The audience imagine this epitaph spoken over a dead man; cf. note l. 76. S.D.

105. *heavy* grievous (with a pun on 'heavy'= weighty).

107–8. *Death...fray* Cf. *Jul. Caes.* 3. 1. 204 ff. and *Ham.* 5. 2. 362–5 (note).

109. *Embowelled* i.e. disembowelled for embalming.

112. *powder* v. G. Steeping in brine was a method of embalming (Hotspur's corpse was thus treated; v. Wylie, i. 364), while 'the deer having been disembowelled...the venison is reserved for the powdering

tub', i.e. the pickling vat (Madden, p. 65). Cf.
'Martlemas' (G. *2 Hen. IV*), and *Fortunes*, pp. 25–31.

114. *paid*, v. G.

scot and lot v. G. A quibble on 'Scot'.

119–20. *The better part...discretion* Here 'part' =
quality. Arden quotes Saviola, *Of Honour*, 1595,
'Without wisdome and discretion...a man is not to
be accounted valiant, but rather furious'. Cf. Apperson, p. 153. Fal.'s cynical misinterpretation of a wise
maxim is now generally accepted as its true meaning!

121. *gunpowder* i.e. both explosive and highly inflammable; cf. *2 Hen. IV*, 4. 4. 48, and above 3. 2. 61.

125–6. *Why may...I?* i.e. If the 'dead' Fal. rises,
who will deny that the dead Hot. might have risen?

127. S.D. Capell reads 'Giving him a stab'.

129. *fleshed* v. G.

133–6. *Art thou alive?* etc. Cf. notes l. 76, S.D.,
ll. 102–10. Spirits were supposed to appear in cor-
poreal form, v. C. S. Lewis, *Preface to Par. Lost*,
ch. xv.

137. *double-man* wraith, v. G. With Hot. on his
back, Fal. quibbles.

138. *Jack* knave, trickster; cf. *Ado*, 1. 1. 174.

139. S.D. Capell reads 'Throwing down his load'.

146. *at an instant* simultaneously.

156–7. *For my part...have* Had the promise been
given in P. John's hearing it would have lost all
point. Ll. 154–5 seem carefully phrased to support
Fal.'s 'strangest tale'.

156. *a lie* i.e. this lie of yours.

do...grace get thee favour. There is irony here
and 'grace' has a double meaning. Cf. *Fortunes*,
pp. 71, 88 ff. Fal.'s lie is his undoing.

157. *gild...have* trick it out with the most specious
arguments I can command, v. G. 'gild'.

158. *ours* (F.) Q. 'our'. Cf. note 4. 3. 28.

159. *let's* (F.) Q. 'let vs'. Cf. p. 104.

161. *I'll follow...reward* Cf. *2 Hen. VI*, 2. 3. 108,
'Come, fellow, follow us for thy reward'. In hunting,
the hounds 'follow' and are given 'reward', i.e. portions assigned to them at the 'breaking-up of the deer'
(v. Turbervile, *Booke of Hunting*, 1576, pp. 135,
244–5). Fal. claims to have brought the great quarry
down; app. his 'reward' is a 'pension' (*2 Hen. IV*,
1. 2. 242, and *Fortunes*, pp. 90–2).

163. *purge* (*a*) confess and repent, (*b*) take purga-
tives. Cf. *Ham*. 3. 2. 306.

164. *nobleman* He is already 'either earl or duke'
in imagination.

5. 5.

1. *rebuke* v. G.　　4. *turn...contrary* misconstrue.

5. *Misuse...trust* misrepresent the terms entrusted
you for Hot.

29–30. *valours...Have* (Q.) F. 'valour...Hath'
which all edd. read. But as Franz, § 196, notes,
'Older Mod. Eng. shows a strong tendency to express abstractions in a plur. form'; cf. 'shames',
3. 2. 144, and 'behaviours', *Ado*, 2. 3. 9, 100, etc.

32–3. *I thank...immediately* Q5, F. omit. 'I
suspect that these lines were rejected by Sh.' (Johnson).

36. *bend, you with* (Q.) F. 'bend you, with'—
which all edd. follow.

PARALLELS FROM NASHE

NOTE. *Henry IV*, especially Part 1, contains a large number of parallels with the writings of Nashe, some of them rather striking; and it seemed best to bring them together in tabular form, though it will be observed that the ed. of the Arden *1* and *2 Henry IV* has noted many of them. I have no explanation to offer, though making a few general observations on the problem in *The Library*, June 1945.

PART I

1. 2. 6–12. *What a devil hast thou to do with the time of the day?* etc.

What haue we to doe with scales and hower-glasses, except we were Bakers or Clock-keepers? I cannot tell how other men are addicted, but it is against my profession to...keepe any howers but dinner or Supper. It is a pedanticall thing to respect times and seasons.   Arden

Summers Last Will, 1600—produced 1592 (McKerrow, iii. 247, ll. 425–30).

1. 2. 102–3. *Why, Hal, 'tis my vocation, Hal, 'tis no sin for a man to labour in his vocation.*

He held it as lawful for hym (since al labouring in a mans vocation is but getting) to gette wealth as wel with his sword by the High-way side, as the Laborer with his Spade or Mattocke, when all are but yron.

Arden

Christes Teares, 1593 (McKerrow, ii. 64).

1. 2. 106–7. *the most omnipotent villain.* **178–9.** *the incomprehensible lies* Cf. **2. 2. 87,** *gorbellied knaves*

O, tis an vnconscionable vast gorbellied Volume, bigger bulkt than a Dutch Hoy, & farre more boystrous and cumbersome than a payre of Swissers omnipotent.

galeaze breeches. But it shuld seeme he is asham'd of the incomprehensible corpulencie thereof... Arden

Have with you, 1596 (McKerrow, iii. 35).

2. 1. 94. *Go to, 'homo' is a common name to all men*

Newgate, a common name for al prisons, as Homo is a common name for a man or a woman.

Pierce Penilesse, 1592 (McKerrow, i. 187–8).

2. 2. 11–35. *The rascal hath removed my horse...Eight yards of uneven ground is threescore and ten miles afoot with me...I'll not bear mine own flesh so far afoot again.*

The Romane Censors, if they lighted vpon a fat corpulent man, they straight tooke away his horsse, and constrained him to goe a foote: positiuely concluding his carkasse was so puft vp with gluttonie or idlenesse. If we had such horse-takers amongst vs, and that surfit-swolne Churles, who now ride on their foot-cloathes, might be constrained to carrie their flesh budgets from place to place on foote, the price of velvet and cloath would fall with their belies...Plenus venter nil agit libenter. Arden

Pierce Penilesse, 1592 (McKerrow, i. 201).

2. 2. 43–4. *An I have not ballads made on you all and sung to filthy tunes*

Ignominious Ballads made of you, which euery Boy woulde chaunt vnder your nose.

Christes Teares, 1593 (McKerrow, ii. 103–4).

2. 2. 87–8. *gorbellied knaves...fat chuffs*

I lighted vpon an old straddling Vsurer...a fat chuffe it was.

Pierce Penilesse (McKerrow, i. 162–3).
you gorbellied Mammonists
Christes Teares (McKerrow, ii. 163).
rich Chuffes *ibid.* (McKerrow, ii. 107).

2. 2. 104–5. *Each takes his fellow for an officer*

A theefe, they saie, mistakes euerie bush for a true man.

Unfortunate Traveller, 1594 (McKerrow, ii. 319).

2. 3. 113. *Thou wilt not utter what thou dost not know*

. Who will commit anything to a woman's tatling trust, who conceales nothing that shee knowes not?

Malone, Arden

Anatomie, 1589 (McKerrow, i. 14).

2. 4. 25. *Anon, anon, sir!* [and the episode that follows.]

Mine host...start vp, and bounst with his fist on the boord so hard that his tapster ouer-hearing him, cried, anone, anone, sir, by and by, and came and made him a low legge and askt him what he lackt. Hee was readie to haue striken his tapster for interrupting him... but for feare of displeasing mee hee moderated his furie, & onely sending for the other fresh pint, wild him looke to the barre, & come when he is cald with a deuils name.   Arden

Unfortunate Traveller, 1594 (McKerrow, ii. 212).

The best meanes I could imagine to wake hym out of his traunce, was to crie loud in his eare, Hoe, hoste, whats to pay? will no man looke to the reckoning here? And in plaine veritie it tooke expected effect, for with the noyse he started and bustled, lyke a man that had beene scarde with fire out of his sleepe, and ran hastely to his Tapster, and all to belaboured him about the eares, for letting Gentlemen call so long and not looke in to them.

Ibid. (McKerrow, ii. 214).

2. 4. 319. *Hot livers and cold purses*

Hot liuered drunkards.

Unfortunate Traveller, 1594 (McKerrow, ii. 247).

2. 4. 438–9. *Thou art violently carried away from grace, there is a devil haunts thee...*

the Diuell...violently carries him away to vanitie, villanie, etc.

Pierce Penilesse, 1592 (McKerrow, i. 220)

2. 4. 444–5. *that roasted Manningtree ox with the pudding in his belly*

All the rest of his inuention is nothing but an oxe with a pudding in his bellie, not fit for any thing els, saue only to feast the dull eares of ironmongers, plough-men, carpenters, and porters.   Arden

Christes Teares, 1593 (McKerrow, ii. 180).

3. 1. 54. *But will they come when you do call for them?*

Heauens bare witnes with vs it was not so, (heauens will not alwayes come to witnes when they are cald)

Unfortunate Traveller, 1594 (McKerrow, ii. 259).

3. 2. 61–2. *shallow jesters and rash bavin wits, soon kindled and soon burnt*

Weomen...hauing naturally cleere beauty, scortch-ingly blazing, which enkindles any soule that comes neere it, and adding more Bauines vnto it of lasciuious embolstrings etc.

Christes Teares, 1593 (McKerrow, ii. 136).

3. 3. 45–7. *I have maintained that salamander of yours with fire etc.*

3. 3. 78–9. *What call you rich? let them coin his nose etc.*

Should I tell you how manie Pursueuants with red noses, and Sergeants with precious faces, shrunke away in this Sweate, you would not beleeue me. Euen as the Salamander with his very sight blasteth apples on the trees, so a Pursueuant or a Sergeant at this present, with the verie reflexe of his fierie facies, was able to spoyle a man a farre of.

Unfortunate Traveller, 1594 (McKerrow, ii. 230).

4. 1. 98. *All plumed like estridges that wing the wind*
[See passage quoted in note 4. 1. 98–9 (ii)]

Unfortunate Traveller, 1594 (McKerrow, ii. 272).

4. 2. 28–9. *the cankers of a calm world and a long peace*
    64. *food for powder*, etc.

There is a certaine waste of the people for whome there is no vse, but warre: and these men must haue some employment still to cut them off.

Pierce Penilesse, 1592 (McKerrow, i. 211).

The cankerwormes that breed on the rust of peace.

ibid. (McKerrow, i. 213).   Arden

4. 2. 33–4. *tattered prodigals, lately come from swine-
            keeping, from eating draff and husks*

[of an academic performance of *Acolastus*] The onely thing they did well was the prodigall childs hunger, most of their schollers being hungerly kept... Not a ieast had they to keepe their auditors from sleeping but of swill and draffe.

Unfortunate Traveller, 1594 (McKerrow, ii. 250)

Part II

2. 4. 60–2. *there's...stuffed in the hold.*

An vnconscionable vast gorbellied Volume, bigger bulkt than a Dutch Hoy.

Have with you, 1596.   (McKerrow, iii. 35).

4. 2. 11–12. *That man...favour.*

Assemble the famous men of all ages, and tel me

which of them sate in the sun-shine of his Soueraignes grace.... Arden

Pierce Penilesse, 1592 (McKerrow, i. 186).

4. 3. 88–92. *There's none of these demure boys...they get wenches*

[Bacchus curses one who denies wine-drinking] I beseech the gods of good fellowship, thou maist fall into a consumption with drinking smal beere. Euery day maist thou eate fish etc. Arden

Summers Last Will, 1600, produced 1592 (McKerrow, iii. 268).

4. 3. 110–13. *So that skill in the weapon...act and use*

So, I tell thee, giue a soldier wine before he goes to battaile...it makes him forget all scarres and wounds, and fight in the thickest of his enemies, as though hee were but at foyles amongst his fellows. Giue a scholler wine, going to his booke, or being about to inuent, it sets a new poynt on his wit, it glazeth it, it scowres it, it giues him *acumen*.

Summers Last Will, 1600, produced 1592 (McKerrow, iii. 265).

5. 3. 75–7. *Do me right,*
   And dub me knight,
    Samingo

  Mounsieur Mingo for quaffing did surpasse
   In Cup, in Can, or glasse.
   God Bacchus doe him right,
    And dubbe him Knight. Arden
Summers Last Will (McKerrow, iii. 267).

5. 5. 51. *surfeit-swelled*

surfit-swolne Churles [cf. above, *1 Hen. IV*, 2. 2. 11–35]. Arden

Pierce Penilesse, 1592 (McKerrow, 1. 201).

GLOSSARY

Note. Where a pun or quibble is intended, the meanings are distinguished as (*a*) and (*b*)

ADMIRAL, flagship; 3. 3. 25

ADVANTAGE, 'at more advantage' = at a more favourable opportunity; 2. 4. 533

ADVERTISEMENT, (i) news; 3. 2. 172, (ii) counsel; 4. 1. 36

ADVISEDLY, 'take advisedly' = consider carefully; 5. 1. 114

AFFECTIONS, inclinations. Often in a bad sense (cf. *Lucr.* 500; *2 Hen. IV*, G.); 3. 2. 30

AGATE-RING, ring with seal cut in agate (cf. *Rom.* 1. 4. 55); 2. 4. 69

ALARUM (or ALARM) to battle. From O.Fr. 'alarme' (= to arms), but erroneously interpreted = 'all arml'; 5 3 1 (S.D.), 30 (S.D.), 5. 4. 1 (S.D.)

AMAZE, dismay, perplex; 2. 4. 77 (S.D.); 5. 4. 6

ANCIENT, ensign-bearer, flag; 4. 2. 23, 30

ANGEL, gold coin = 10s.; 4. 2. 6

ANSWER (vb.), discharge, defend, guarantee; 1. 3. 185; 3. 3. 175; 4. 2. 8

ANTIC, ridiculously old-fashioned person; 1. 2. 60

APPLE-JOHN. Ripened about St John's Day (midsummer), and was eaten two years later when shrivelled and wrinkled; 3. 3. 4

APPOINTMENT, detail of dress; 1. 2. 168

APPROVE, put to the test; 1. 1. 54; 4. 1. 9

ARBITREMENT, scrutiny; 4. 1. 70

ARGUMENT, theme; 2. 2. 93; 2. 4. 277

ART, science, magic; 3. 1. 47

ARTICULATE, set out in articles, tabulate; 5. 1. 72

ASPECT, (*a*) respect, (*b*) Astrol. position of one heavenly body in relation to another; 1. 1. 97

ATTEMPT, escapade; 3. 2. 13

ATTRIBUTION, credit, honour; 4. 1. 3

AUDITOR, royal official who examined the accounts of receivers, sheriffs, etc. (Minshew); 2. 1. 56

BACON, (*a*) bumpkin, (*b*) fat man; 2. 2. 89

BAFFLE, degrade (a knight) by hanging him up by the heels (cf. note 2. 4. 428–9, *Ric. II*, G., and Spenser, *F.Q.* vi, vii. 27); 1. 2. 99

BAITED. Lit. 'refreshed as at an inn' (cf. note and *Euphues*, Bond i, 323, 'A pleasant companion is a bayte in a journey'); 4. 1. 99

BALKED, (*a*) ploughed in ridges, (*b*) defeated; 1. 1. 69

BAND, bond, debt; 3. 2. 157

BARE, (i) beggarly; 3. 2. 13;
(ii) (*a*) thread-bare, (*b*) lean;
4. 2. 67–9, (iii) patent; 1. 3.
108

BASE-STRING, lowest note; 2.
4. 5–6

BASILISK, largest type of cannon, called after the fabulous
reptile (cf. *culverin*); 2. 3. 55

BASTARD, a common Sp. wine,
brown or white; 2. 4. 26, 72

BASTINADO, cudgelling. Sp.
'bastonada'; 2. 4. 332

BATE, diminish in weight or
number or energy; 3. 3. 2;
4. 3. 26

BATTLE, battle-array; 4. 1. 129

BAVIN. Lit. fire-wood; 3. 2. 61

BEAR, convey meaning; 4. 1.
20

BEAR (a point), take up a
fencing position; 2. 4. 192

BEAR HARD, resent; 1. 3. 267

BEAST, fool, idiot (O.E.D. 5);
3. 3. 123

BEAVER. Lit. part of helmet
guarding mouth and chin;
4. 1. 104

BEEF, fat ox; 'sweet beef' =
unsalted beef; 3. 3. 176

BELDAM, grandam (disrespect-
ful); 3. 1. 31

BIRD, chick; 5. 1. 60

BLOOD, spirit, vigour; 3. 1. 179;
4. 3. 76

BLOWN, inflated; 4. 2. 47

BLUE-CAPS, blue bonnets. A
term of contempt for Scots.
Lit. 'servants' (who wore
blue caps in England); 2. 4.
352

BOLTER, cloth for sifting flour
from bran; 3. 3. 70

BOLTING-HUTCH, bakers' bran-
bin (v. *bolter*); 2. 4. 441–2

BOMBARD, large leather vessel
to hold liquor; 2. 4. 443

BOMBAST, padding (for clothes);
2. 4. 323

BOOK, legal document; 3. 1.
221, 263

BOOTS, booty (a quibble); 2. 1.
81; 3. 1. 66

BOTS, worms. A horse disease;
2. 1. 9

BOW-CASE, i.e. for a fiddler's
bows; 2. 4. 245

BRACH, bitch-hound; 3. 1. 235

BRAVE, fine, glorious; 1. 1. 53;
1. 2. 63; 5. 2. 88

BRAWN, fatted boar-pig; 2. 4.
107

BREAK WITH, tell, reveal to;
3. 1. 142

BREATHE, (i) utter; 1. 1. 3;
(ii) pause; 1. 3. 102; 2. 4.
15, 246; 5. 4. 15

BRIEF, letter; 4. 4. 1

BRING ON, bring out; 1. 3. 275

BRISK, smartly dressed; 1. 3. 54

BRUISE, crush (cf. *Meas.* 2. 1.
5–6); 3. 2. 105

BUFFETS, 'go to buffets' = fall
to blows; 2. 3. 33

BULL'S-PIZZLE, bull's penis,
'formerly a much-used in-
strument of flagellation'
(O.E.D.); 2. 4. 243

BUSKY, bushy; 5. 1. 2

BY-DRINKING, drink between
meals; 3. 3. 74

BY-ROOM, side-room; 2. 4. 28

CADDIS, worsted tape, used for
cheap garters; 2. 4. 69

CALIVER, light musket; 4. 2. 19

CALL ON, demand payment
from; 5. 1. 129

CAMBYSES (son of Cyrus), K.
of Persia 529–522 B.C.; 2.
4. 381

CAMOMILE, creeping plant, often covering the paths of Eliz. gardens; 2. 4. 395

CANKER, (i) wild rose (with quibble on ii), (ii) ulcer; 1. 3. 176; 4. 2. 29

CANK'RED, malignant; 1. 3. 137

CANSTICK, candlestick; 3. 1.129

CANTLE, 'projecting corner of land' (O.E.D.); 3. 1. 98

CAPITULATE, draw up articles of agreement; 3. 2. 120

CARBONADO, rasher; 5. 3. 58

CARD, adulterate (esp. of drink); 3. 2. 62

CARRY AWAY, transport (figur.); 2. 3. 77

CASE (sb.), suit of clothes; 1. 2. 172

CASE (vb.), cover the face or body; 2. 2. 51

CAST, a throw at dice; 4. 1. 47

CATERPILLAR, blood-sucker (cf. Ric. II, 2. 3. 166); 2. 2. 83

CESS. Aphetic f. 'assess'; 'out of all cess' = beyond computation; 2. 1. 7

CHAMBER-LYE, urine; 2. 1. 20

CHAMBERLAIN, bedroom attendant (cf. Macb. 1.7.63); 2. 1. 46, 49

CHANGELING, renegade; 5. 1. 76

CHARGE, (i) valuables; 2. 1. 45, 57; (ii) cost; 3. 1. 110, 113; (iii) military command; 1. 1. 35; 2. 4. 536; 3. 2. 161; 4. 2. 23; 5. 1. 118; (iv) mandate; 4. 3. 41

CHARLES' WAIN, the Great Bear. Orig. Charlemagne's Wain; 2. 1. 2

CHEAP (sb.), v. good cheap; 3. 3. 44-5

CHEWET, jackdaw, chatterbox; 5. 1. 29

CHIMNEY, fireplace; 2. 1. 20

CHOPS, or CHAPS, (a) fat cheeks, (b) butcher's 'chops'; 1. 2. 131

CHUFF, close-fisted churl (cf. Nashe, p. 192); 2. 2. 88

CITAL, summons (cf. Hen. VIII, 4. 1. 29); 5. 2. 63

CLEANLY, deft; 2. 4. 447

CLIPPED IN, embraced; 3. 1. 43

CLOAK-BAG, portmanteau; 2. 4. 440

CLOSE (sb.), encounter. Fencing term; 1. 1. 13

CLOSE (adj. and adv.), hidden, secret; 2. 2. 3, 74, 95; 2. 3. 112; 2. 4. 530

CLOUDY, gloomy (cf. Macb. 3. 6. 41); 3. 2. 83

COAT, coat-armour, i.e. 'a vest of rich material embroidered with heraldic devices worn …over armour' (O.E.D.); 4. 1. 100; 5. 3. 25, 26

COCK-SURE, with perfect safety; 2. 1. 85

COLOUR (sb.), pretext, semblance; 3. 2. 100; 5. 1. 75, 80

COLOUR (vb.), disguise; 1. 3. 109

COLT (vb.), (a) befool, (b) mount (cf. Cymb. 2. 4. 133); 2. 2. 36-7

COME AWAY, come along. Still colloq. in Scotland; 2.1.22, 23

COME ON, enter the field; 5. 1. 131

COMFORT, succour; 4. 1. 56

COMMAND, authority; 4. 4. 32

COMMODITY, lit. packet of goods upon which money could be raised at the usurers (v. Meas. G.); 1. 2. 82; 4. 2. 17

COMMON-HACKNEYED, vulgarised, prostituted; 3. 2. 40

COMMUNITY, over-familiarity; 3. 2. 77

COMPARATIVE, abusive, personal (cf. *L.L.L.* 5. 2. 840); 1. 2. 79; (as sb.) 3. 2. 67

COMPASS, (*a*) moderation; 3. 3. 19, 20; (*b*) circumference; 3. 3. 22, 23

CONCEALMENT, secret art; 3. 1. 165

CONDITION, disposition; 1. 3. 6 *

CONFEDERACY, conspiracy; 4. 4. 38

CONFOUND, consume; 1. 3. 100

CONJUNCTION, joint force; 4. 1. 37

CONTAGIOUS, pestilential; 1. 2. 190

CONTINENT, river bank; 3. 1. 108

CORINTHIAN, gay dog, 'wencher' (Johnson); 2. 4. 11

CORRIVAL, partner; 1. 3. 207; 4. 4. 31

COURSE, phase; 3. 1. 41

COZEN (vb.), cheat; 1. 2. 119

COZENER (sb.), cheat; 1. 3. 254

CRANK (vb.), wind, double (cf. *V.A.* 682); 3. 1. 96

CRESSET. Lit. an iron basket upon a pole in which pitched rope, etc. was burnt for illumination, e.g. of playhouses (v. Cotgrave, 'Falot'); 3. 1. 14

CRISP, curling; 1. 3. 106

CRY OUT UPON, denounce (cf. *A.Y.L.* 2. 7. 70); 4. 3. 81

CULVERIN, small cannon (from Fr. *couleuvrin* = adderlike); 2. 3. 55

CURRENT (sb.), vicissitude; 2. 3. 57

CURRENT (adj.), accepted as true or fashionable; 1. 3. 68; 2. 1. 53; 2. 3. 96

CUSHES, armour for the thighs; 4. 1. 105

CUT, short for 'curtal', a horse with docked tail; 2. 1. 5

DAFF, stand aside from, ignore. A variant of 'doff'; 4. 1. 96

DARE, daring; 4. 1. 78

DAY, 'by the day' = o'clock; 2. 1. 1

DEAR, precious, estimable, heartfelt; 1. 1. 33; 4. 1. 34; 4. 4. 31; 5. 4. 95

DEAREST, utmost, direst; 3. 1. 180; 3. 2. 123; 5. 5. 36

DEEP (v. note); 3. 1. 52

DEFY, renounce, despise; 1. 3. 228; 4. 1. 6

DENIER. Fr. coin = $\frac{1}{12}$ of a sou; 3. 3. 80

DENY, (i) refuse; 1. 3. 25, 29, 77; (ii) refuse to admit; (quibble) 2. 4. 485

DEPUTATION, 'by d.' = through substitutes; 4. 1. 32; 'in d.' = as viceregents; 4. 3. 87

DEPUTY, or 'Deputy of the Ward', who acted as magistrate in the absence of an alderman; 3. 3. 116

DETERMINATION, mind; 4. 3. 33

DIRECTLY, without evasion; 2. 3. 88

DISDAINED, disdainful; 1. 3. 183

DISLIKE, discord; 5. 1. 26

DISPUTATION, conversation; 3. 1. 203

DITTY, the words of a song; 3. 1. 122, 206

DIVISION. Musical term = melodic passage; 3. 1. 208

DOUBLE-MAN, wraith (v. O.E.D. 'double' adj. C. 2c, sb. 2c); 5. 4. 137

DOWLAS, coarse linen; 3. 3. 69

DRAFF, pig-wash; 4. 2. 34

DRAWER, tapster; 2. 4. 7, etc.

DRAWN FOX i.e. false trail; 3. 3. 114

DRENCH, dose (for a horse); 2. 4. 104

DURANCE, (a) stout cloth; (b) imprisonment; 1. 2. 43

DUTY, due; 5. 2. 57

DYE SCARLET, drink deep; 2. 4. 14–15

EMBOSSED, (a) swollen, (b) at bay; 3. 3. 156

EMBOWEL, disembowel (a) a corpse for embalming, (b) a deer after the kill; 5. 4. 109, 111

ENFEOFF, sell with absolute possession; 3. 2. 69

ENGAGE, give as a hostage; 4. 3. 95; 5. 2. 45

ENGROSS UP. Lit. buy up wholesale; 3. 2. 148

ENLARGEMENT, release from confinement; 3. 1. 30

ENVY (sb.), ill-will; 1. 3. 27; 5. 2. 68

ENVY (vb.), begrudge; 4. 3. 35

ESSENTIALLY MADE, i.e. gold by nature; 2. 4. 482

ESTRIDGE, ostrich. The usual Eliz. meaning 4. 1. 98

EXHALATION, exhaled meteor (q.v.); 2. 4. 316

EXHALED METEOR, comet, meteor (q.v.) supposedly engendered from vapours drawn up by the sun (cf. *Rom.* 3. 5. 13); 5. 1. 19

EXPEDIENCE, enterprise; 1. 1. 33

EXPEDITION, progress; 4. 3. 19

EXTREMITY, severity; 1. 2. 181

FACE, trim (v. *guard*); 5. 1. 74

FALL OFF, revolt; 1. 3. 94

FAT, 'Of a room: full of dense air' (O.E.D.); hence—stuffy; 2. 4. 1

FAT-WITTED, dull (cf. *L.L.L.* 5. 2. 268, and Chapman, *Ovid's Banquet*, st. 115, 'fat and foggy brains'); 1. 2. 3

FAVOUR, (i) feature; 3. 2. 136; (ii) token or badge worn in the helmet; 5. 4. 96

FEAR (vb.) fear for; 4. 1. 24; 4. 2. 56

FEAZE, fray, wear thin; 4. 2. 30

FEELING (adj.), affecting; 3. 1. 203

FIDDLE-STICK, 'the devil rides upon a fiddlestick'=what a fuss about a trifle!; 2. 4. 477

FINE, refined, subtle; 4. 1. 2

FINGER. A measure = ¾ inch; 4. 2. 72

FLESH (vb.), blood (cf. *2 Hen. IV*, 4. 5. 132); 5. 4. 129

FOOL, plaything (cf. *Rom.* 3. 1. 141; *Son.* 116. 9); 5. 4. 81

FOOT-LAND-RAKER, foot-pad (rake = roam); 2. 1. 72

FORM, 'the essential principle' (O.E.D.); 1. 3. 210

FORSWEAR, (i) swear to abandon; 2. 2. 15; (ii) (a) deny on oath, (b) swear falsely; 5. 2. 40

FORWARD, (a) eager, (b) premature; 5. 1. 128

FRANKLIN, 'landowner of free but not noble birth' (O.E.D.); 2. 1. 54

FRETFUL, (a) given to worry, (b) wearing away; 3. 3. 11

FRONTIER, (i) frontier fortress (cf. *Ham.* 4. 4. 16); 1. 3. 19; (ii) rampart, 2. 3. 54

FUBBED or FOBBED, cheated; 1. 2. 59

FURNISHED, equipped (horse and man); 4. 1. 97; 5. 3. 21

FURNITURE, military equipment; 3. 3. 200

GIB CAT, tom cat (Gib = Gilbert); 1. 2. 73

GILD, give specious lustre to; 5. 4. 157

GOD DEFEND, God forbid; 4. 3. 38

GOD SAVE THE MARK! 'Prob. orig. a formula to arrest an evil omen, whence used in way of apology when something horrible, disgusting, indecent or profane had been mentioned' (O.E.D.). Here expresses impatient scorn; 1. 3. 56

GOD'S ME = God save me; 2. 3. 96

GOLDEN, auspicious, flattering (cf. *A.Y.L.* 1. 1. 6); 4. 3. 73

GOOD CHEAP, bon marché, cheap; 3. 3. 44–5

GORBELLIED, pot-bellied; 2. 2. 87

GOVERNMENT, (i) conduct, self-control (cf. *3 Hen. VI*, 1. 4. 132); 1. 2. 27; 3. 1. 182; (ii) military command; 4. 1. 19

GRACE, 'do g. to' = bring credit to; 2. 1. 70; 5. 4. 156 (with quibble on 'grace' = salvation)

GRIEF, (i) bodily pain; 1. 3. 51; 5. 1. 132; (ii) grievance; 4. 3. 42, 48

GRIFFIN. Fabulous animal, with eagle's head, forelegs and wings, and lion's body, hind legs and tail; 3. 1. 150

GUARD, ornamental band or border, different in colour and material from the rest of the garment; unfashionable by end of 16th c. (Linthicum); 3. 1. 256

GULL, unfledged nestling; 5. 1. 60

GUMMED, stiffened with gum; 2. 2. 2

GURNET, gurnard, marine fish of genus *Trigla* (v. note); 4. 2. 12

GUTS, (i) belly, intestines, (ii) butcher's offal, (iii) skin for sausages and black puddings, (iv) greed, gluttony, (v) a corpulent or gluttonous person; 2. 4. 224, 255, 443; 3. 3. 152, 155

HA?, eh? 1. 1. 75; 1. 3. 278

HABITS, clothes; 1. 2. 168

HAIR. 'Of one hair' = of one colour and appearance, hence 'hair' came to mean 'sort, kind, character' (O.E.D.); 4. 1. 61

HALF-FACED. Lit. as of a face on a coin, hence = thin, wretched, half-and-half (cf. *K. John*, 1. 1. 92); 1. 3. 208

HAPPY MAN BE HIS DOLE. Prov. phrase for wishing good luck (Apperson, p. 284). Lit. may his lot ('dole') be that of a happy man; 2. 2. 75

HARDIMENT, prowess; 1. 3. 101

HARLOTRY (adj. and sb.), 'A term of playful contempt, without any thought of the origin of the word' (Clar.); 2. 4. 389; 3. 1. 197

HARNESS, armour; 3. 2. 101

HAZARD, (a) a game at dice (v. *Sh. Eng.* ii. 470), (b) chance; 4. 1. 48

HEAD, (i) current driven against a bank; 1. 3. 106; (ii) armed force; 1. 3. 281; 3. 2. 102, 167; 4. 3. 103; 4. 4. 25; 5. 1. 66. Cf. *make head*

HEADY, impetuous; 2. 3. 57

HEARKEN FOR, wait or long for (cf. *Shrew*, 1. 2. 250); 5. 4. 52

HEART!, by God's heart!; 3. 1. 247

HEART (out of), (a) dispirited, (b) in poor condition; 3. 3. 6

HEAVY, ominous, grievous; 2. 3. 65; 5. 4. 105 (quibble)

HEST. Meaning doubtful (v. note); 2. 3. 64

HOLD IN, keep counsel; 2. 1. 76

HOLD LEVEL, claim equality; 3. 2. 17

HOLD PACE, keep up, rival; 3. 1. 48

HOLD WELL, be apt; 1. 2. 30

HOLD A WING, keep a course; 3. 2. 30

HOLIDAY (adj.), gay, dainty (cf. *Wives*, 3. 2. 62; 'festival' *Ado*, 5. 2. 40); 1. 3. 46

HOLLAND, fine quality linen, first made in Holland; 3. 3. 72

HOLY-ROOD DAY, Sept. 14th; 1. 1. 52

HOPE, (i) expectation; 1. 2. 203; (ii) promise; 3. 2. 36

HOSE, trunk hose (mod. 'breeches'); 2. 4. 212

HUMOROUS, moody, odd; 3. 1. 230

HUMOUR, (i) physiol. the four fluids of the human body (here, in an excessive quantity); 2. 4. 441; (ii) inclination, fancy, mood; 1. 2. 69, 188; 2. 4. 91; 3. 1. 170

IMPAWN, give as a hostage; 4. 3. 108

INCOMPREHENSIBLE, infinite; 1. 2. 178

INDENT (sb.), indentation; 3. 1. 102

INDENT (vb.), enter into a formal agreement; 1. 3. 87

INDENTURE, sealed agreement (made in duplicate with indented edges that fit together); 2. 4. 46; 3. 1. 78, 139, 260

INDIRECT, (a) not directly derived, (b) crooked, unjust; 4. 3. 105

INDIRECTLY, off-hand, evasively; 1. 3. 66

INDUCTION, first steps; 3. 1. 2

INDUSTRIOUS, zealous; 1. 1. 62

INJURY, (i) insult; 3. 3. 161; (ii) evil; 5. 1. 50

INNOVATION, rebellion (usual sense in Sh.); 5. 1. 78

INSENSIBLE, not to be seen or felt; 5. 1. 137

INSTANTLY, simultaneously; 5. 2. 66

INSULTING, scornfully triumphant; 5. 4. 54

INTELLIGENCE, espionage; 4. 3. 98

INTEMPERATURE, (a) 'distempered condition of the body' (O.E.D.), (b) unbridled licentiousness; 3. 2. 156

INTEND, purpose to travel; 4. 1. 92

INTERCEPT, interrupt; 1. 3. 151

INTEREST, title; 3. 2. 98

INWARD, internal; 1. 3. 58; 4. 1. 31

IRON, pitiless (cf. *2 Hen. IV*, 4. 2. 8); 2. 3. 50

ITERATION, the repetition of the Scriptures etc. in worship (cf. Hooker, *Ecc. Pol.* bk. 5, xxxvii. 2, 'why we iterate the Psalms'); 1.2.89

JACK, (i) knave. A term of contempt; 2. 4. 11; 3. 3. 86, 138; 5. 4. 138; (ii) a sleeveless jacket 'formerly worn by foot-soldiers...usually of leather quilted' (O.E.D.); 4. 2. 47

JOINED-STOOL, stool made by a joiner. Often the subject of some obscure jest now lost; 2. 4. 374

JORDAN, chamber-pot; 2. 1. 19

JUMP WITH, agree with; 1.2.68

JUSTLING, jostling; 4. 1. 18

KEEP, dwell; 1. 3. 244

KENDAL GREEN, coarse green cloth, in 16th c. only worn by labourers, but perhaps traditionally associated with Robin Hood; 2. 4. 219

KNOTTY-PATED, block-headed; 2. 4. 224

LAY BY, stand and deliver. Orig. doubtful; 1. 2. 35

LAY OUT, disburse; 4. 2. 5

LAY THE PLOT, organize, direct; 2. 1. 51

LEADEN DAGGER. A theatrical property, 'type of ineffectual weapon' (O.E.D.); 2. 4. 375

LEAPING-HOUSE, brothel; 1.2.9

LEASH, set of three (dogs); 2. 4. 6

LEG (sb.), bow; 2. 4. 379

LET SLIP, unleash; 1. 3. 277

LEWD, vile; 3. 2. 13

LIBERTY, licence (cf. *Meas.* 1. 3. 29); 5. 2. 73

LIE, assume a fencing posture; 2. 4. 192

LIKING, (*a*) inclination, (*b*) good bodily condition; 3. 3. 5

LIMIT, (i) 'limits of the charge' = distribution of commands in an army; 1. 1. 35; (ii) division, district; 3. 1. 71; (iii) prescribed bounds (of allegiance); 4. 3. 39

LINE (sb.), degree, category. Lit. series; 1.3.168; 3.2.85

LINE (vb.), reinforce; 2. 3. 85

LIQUOR, v. note; 2. 1. 84

LIST, extremity; 4. 1. 51

LIVE, lie, exist; 1. 2. 182; 4. 1. 56; 5. 2. 21

LIVERY, v. *sue his livery*; 4. 3. 62

LOACH, small fresh-water fish; 2. 1. 21

LOOK BIG, threaten; 4. 1. 58

LOOP, loop-hole (e.g. in a castle-wall); 4. 1. 71

LOOSE GOWN or 'loose-bodied gown'. Hung, without waist, from neck to foot, 'so that any deformity, however monstrous, remains hidden' (Linthicum, 183); 3. 3. 3

LUGGED, baited (of bears or bulls); 1. 2. 73

MAID MARIAN, v. note; 3. 3. 115

MAIN, (*a*) army, (*b*) stake at 'hazard' (q.v.); 4. 1. 47

MAINLY, mightily; 2. 4. 197

MAINTENANCE, bearing; 5. 4. 22

MAJORITY, pre-eminence; 3. 2. 109

Make up, move forward; 5.
4. 5, 58

Malt-worm, drunkard; lit.
weevil that breeds in malt;
2. 1. 74

Mammet, doll, puppet; orig.
'mawmet' (Mahomet) =
idol; 2. 3. 94

Manage, horsemanship; 2. 3.
51

Manner (with the), in the act.
From 'mainour' = stolen
property found upon a thief
at arrest; 2. 4. 311

Manningtree, Essex town
'famous for the revelry in-
dulged in at its fairs, and for
the fatness of its oxen'
(Clar.); 2. 4. 444

Mark, 13s. 4d. or two nobles.
A sum of money, not a coin; 2.
1. 55; 2. 4. 511; 3. 3. 42, 83

Master, possess (cf. Son. 106.
8); 5. 2. 65

Match (sb.), plot, device;
2. 4. 88; 'set a match', lit.
make an appointment, (in
thieves' cant) arrange a
meeting between highway-
men and victims; 1. 2. 104

Match (vb.), join, associate;
1. 1. 49; 3. 2. 15

Mean, instrument; 1. 3. 260

Medicine, drug (of any kind);
2. 2. 18

Melt, take pity on (cf. 2 Hen.
IV, 4. 4. 32); 2. 4. 117

Memento mori, ring with a
death's head; 3. 3. 30–1

Meteor, atmospheric pheno-
menon of any kind, e.g.
'airy' = wind, 'watery' =
rain, snow, etc., 'fiery' =
lightning, shooting stars, etc.
(cf. Errors, 4. 2. 6 and G.);
1 .1. 10; 2. 4. 316; 5. 1. 19

Mettle, natural vigour; 2. 4.
12, 344; 4. 3. 22; 5. 4. 24

Micher, truant; 2. 4. 402

Midriff, diaphragm; 3. 3. 155

Milliner, dealer in gloves,
bands, etc., which were per-
fumed to make them more
marketable. Orig. 'of Milan';
1. 3. 36

Mince, walk with affected
delicacy; 3. 1. 132

Minion, darling, favourite; 1.
1. 83; 1. 2. 26

Misprision, mistake; 1. 3. 27

Misquote, misread; 5. 2. 14

Mistreading, going astray;
3. 2. 11

Misuse (sb.), abuse; 1. 1. 43,
(vb.) misrepresent; 5. 5. 5

Mo, more; 4. 4. 31

Moiety, share; 3. 1. 94

Moldwarp, mole; 3. 1. 147

Moor-ditch, section of old
city moat, draining the fen
of Moorfields, seldom if ever
cleaned out; 1. 2. 77

More and less, high and low;
4. 3. 68

Mouthed, gaping; 1. 3. 97

Move, urge, appeal to; 2. 3. 33

Muddy, filthy (O.E.D. 7); 2.
1. 96

Muster (take a), call troops
together; 4. 1. 133

Mutual, shared in common;
1. 1. 14

Naked, desolate; 4. 3. 77

Neat (adj.), spruce; 1. 3. 33

Neat (sb.), ox; 2. 4. 243

Neck, 'in the n. of' = following directly upon. A
race-course expression (cf.
Son. 131. 11); 4. 3. 92

Netherstocks, stockings; 2.
4. 112–13

NEW-FALL'N, recently acquired; 5. 1. 44

NOT-PATED, close-cropped; 2. 4. 69

OFFER, offer battle (cf. 3. 2. 169); 4. 1. 69

OLD LAD OF THE CASTLE, roisterer or wencher (cf. G. Harvey, ed. Grosart, i. 225, ii. 44; and Nashe, ed. McKerrow, iii. 5, l. 18); 1. 2. 42

OMNIPOTENT, almighty (jocular; cf. Nashe, p. 191); 1. 2. 107

ONYER, ? clerk to Exchequer (v. note); 2. 1. 75

OPINION, (i) arrogance; 3. 1. 183, (ii) public opinion (cf. *Oth.* 1. 3. 225); 3. 2. 42; (iii) reputation; 4. 1. 77; 5. 4. 48

OUT-FACE, bluff, browbeat; 2. 4. 253

OWE, own; 5. 2. 69

PAINTED CLOTH, cheap wall-hanging (cf. *2 Hen. IV*, G. 'waterwork'); 4. 2. 25

PARCEL, (i) detail, item; 2. 4. 98; 3. 2. 159; (ii) set, lot (contemptuous); 2. 4. 442

PARTICIPATION, fellowship; 3. 2. 87

PASSAGE, action (cf. *Tw. Nt.* 3. 2. 70); 3. 2. 8

PASSION, grief, pain; 2. 4. 380, 410; 3. 1. 34

PAY, settle, kill; 2. 4. 189, 215; 5. 3. 47; 5. 4. 43, 114

PAY HOME, deal effectively with; 1. 3. 285

PEPPER, make it hot for; 2. 4. 188

PEPPER-GINGERBREAD, a cheap

kind made with pepper instead of ginger; 3. 1. 255

PHANTASY, hallucination; 5. 4. 134

PICKTHANK, obsequious tale-bearer; 3. 2. 25

PINCH, worry; 1. 3. 229; 3. 1. 28

PISMIRES, ants; 1. 3. 240

PLAY OFF, toss off (a bumper); 2. 4. 16

POCKET UP, swallow (an insult); 3. 3. 162

POINT, (i) pommel of saddle; 2. 1. 6; (ii) (*a*) sword-point, (*b*) one of the tagged laces suspending the hose from the doublet; 2. 4. 211

POLICY, craft in public affairs; 1. 3. 108

POLITICIAN, intriguer; 1. 3. 241

POMGARNET, pomegranate; 2. 4. 37

POPINJAY, parrot, chattering overdressed coxcomb; 1. 3. 50

POPULARITY, keeping company with common people; 3. 2. 69

PORTLY, stately; 1. 3. 13

POSSESSED, informed; 4. 1. 40

POST (sb.), courier; 1. 1. 37

POST (vb.), travel express; 5. 1. 35

POULTER, poulterer; 2. 4. 429

POUNCET-BOX, small perfume-box with perforated lid; 1. 3. 38

POWDER (vb.), salt for pickling; 5. 4. 112

POWER, army; 1. 1. 22, *et passim*

PRECEDENT (v. note); 2. 4. 32

PREDICAMENT, category, lit. that which is predicated (logic); 1. 3. 168

PRICK (vb.), (a) spur; (b) finish off, lit. tick off (by pricking a hole on a list; cf. *Jul. Caes.* 4. 1. 1–3); 5. 1. 129–30

PRIDE, (i) height; 1. 1. 60; (ii) mettle; 4. 3. 22

PRIVILEGE, (i) pre-eminence; 3. 2. 86; (ii) 'of privilege' = which confers immunity; 5. 2. 19

PROFITED, proficient; 3. 1. 164

PROPORTION, size; 4. 4. 15

PRUNE, preen; 1. 1. 98

PUDDING, stuffing for a roast; 2. 4. 444

PUKE-STOCKINGS, cheap stockings made of dyed cloth; 2. 4. 69

PUNY, novice; 2. 4. 29

PUPIL AGE, minority (orig. 'pupil' = minor); 2. 4. 92

PURCHASE, (i) plunder (cant); 2. 1. 91; (ii) purchasing power; 3. 3. 40

PURGE, (i) clear; 3. 2. 20; (ii) amend one's life, (b) take aperient; 5. 4. 163

PUSH (stand the), become the butt of; 3. 2. 66

QUALITY, party; 4. 3. 36

QUESTION (sb.), discussion; 1. 1. 34; (vb.) talk with; 1. 3. 47

QUIDDITY, subtle jest (cf. *Ham.* 5. 1. 96); 1. 2. 45

RABBIT-SUCKER, sucking rabbit; 2. 4. 429

RASCAL, (a) scoundrel, (b) lean deer; 3. 3. 157

RASH, quickly inflammable; 3. 2. 61

RAZE or Race, root of ginger; 2. 1. 24

READ, (i) act as tutor; 3. 1. 45; (ii) learn, discover; 4. 1. 49

REBUKE, violent check; 5. 5. 1

REMOVED, not directly concerned; 4. 1. 35

RENDEZVOUS, refuge (cf. *Hen. V*, 2. 1. 18; 5. 1. 88); 4. 1. 57

REPRISAL, prize, lit. prize at sea; 4. 1. 118

REPROOF, disproof; 1. 2. 182; 3. 2. 23

REWARD, portions of the deer thrown to the hounds at the end of a chase (v. note); 5. 4. 161

RIOT, wantonness; 1. 1. 85

RIVO. A toper's exclamation of doubtful meaning; Arden cf. *Jew of Malta*, 4. 6. 10, 'Rivo Castiliano', which it translates 'Castilian stream', i.e. liquor; 2. 4. 108

ROUNDLY, plainly; 1. 2. 22

ROYAL, coin worth 10s.; 1. 2. 136

SACK, v. note; 1. 2. 3–4, *et passim*

SAD, serious; 1. 1. 56

SAINT NICHOLAS' CLERKS, v. note; 2. 1. 60

SARCENET, soft thin silk material (fig.); 3. 1. 251

SAVING YOUR REVERENCE. An apology for mentioning something unpleasant; 2. 4. 460

SCANDALIZED, disgraced; 1. 3. 154

SCHOOLED, admonished; 3. 1. 188

SCORE (vb.), (i) chalk up a reckoning; 2. 4. 26, (ii) make cuts or notches (with quibble on i); 5. 3. 31

SCOT (v. note); 1. 3. 214

SCOT AND LOT, full and final payment; 5. 4. 114

SCUTCHEON or escutcheon, shield or hatchment of arms painted on wood and used at funerals; 5. 1. 140

SEASON, age, period; 4. 1. 4

SECOND, subordinate (v. *2 Hen. IV*, G.); 1. 3. 165

SEMBLABLY, in like fashion; 5. 3. 21

SENSIBLE, capable of feeling; 5. 4. 94

SERVE, suffice for; 4. 1. 132

SET (vb.), stake; 4. 1. 46, 47

SET OFF (his head), not reckoned (to his account); 5. 1. 88

SET TO, set (a limb); 5. 1. 131

SETTER, 'one employed by robbers...to spy upon their intended victims' (O.E.D.); 2. 2. 49

SHAPE, conception, conjecture; 1. 1. 58

SHAVE, (*a*) fleece, (*b*) have the head shaved; 3. 3. 59

SHOT, (*a*) payment for drink, (*b*) i.e. from a gun; 5. 3. 30—1

SHOTTEN, (of a herring) that has shed its roe, (hence) emaciated, good-for-nothing; 2. 4. 126

SHRINK, shiver (cf. *A.Y.L.* 2. 1. 9); 5. 2. 76

SKIMBLE-SKAMBLE, scamped together anyhow; 3. 1. 152

SKIPPING, flighty; 3. 2. 60

SMUG, smooth, trim; 3. 1. 100

SNEAK-UP, a mean, creeping scoundrel; 3. 3. 86

SNUFF (take in), (*a*) snuff up and sneeze, (*b*) take umbrage at; 1. 3. 41

So, good! very well!; 5. 1. 122; 5. 3. 57, 60

SOFT, wait a bit!; 1. 3. 155; 2. 1. 35; 5. 4. 130

SOOTHER, flatterer; 4. 1. 7

SOUSED, pickled in salt; 4. 2. 12

SPANISH POUCH, cheap pouch of Spanish leather; 2. 4. 70

SPEAR-GRASS or spear wort; 2. 4. 305—6

SPLEEN, supposed the organ of sudden action or impulse, (hence) irritability, caprice, ill-humour, impetuosity; 2. 3. 80; 3. 2. 125; 5. 2. 20

SPOIL (sb.), ruin; 3. 3. 10

SQUIER, foot-rule; 2. 2. 12

STAMP, mintage, begetting; 4. 1. 4

STAND FOR, (*a*) be good for, (*b*) represent; 1. 2. 136

STANDING, gone stiff (v. note); 2. 4. 245

START, sudden fit; 3. 2. 125

STARTING-HOLE, bolt-hole (for a hunted animal); 2. 4. 260

STARVE, die of cold; 1. 3. 159; 2. 2. 20

STATE, (i) state-chair, throne; 2. 4. 372, 374; (ii) dignity; 3. 2. 62; (iii) kingdom, estate, fortune; 3. 2. 98, 169; 4. 1. 46

STEWED PRUNE, bawd (because a brothel commonly displayed a dish of prunes in the window); 3. 3. 114

STIR, be up and about (cf. *Jul. Caes.* 2. 2. 110); 3. 2. 46

STOCK-FISH, dried cod or ling; 2. 4. 243

STOMACH, appetite; 2. 3. 43

STORE, capital, savings; 2. 2. 88

STRAPPADO, torture by disjointing the limbs; 2. 4. 234

STRIKER, foot-pad (cf. Ger. *Landstreicher*); 2. 1. 73

STUDY, pursuit; 1. 3. 228

SUBMISSION, confession; 3. 2. 28

SUDDENLY, soon; 1. 3. 291

SUE A LIVERY, make legal claim
for delivery of land; 4. 3. 62

SUFFERANCE, suffering; 5. 1. 51

SUGGESTION, instigation; 4. 3.
51

SUPPLY, reinforcements; 4. 3. 3

SURE. (a) harmless' (b) safe;
5. 3. 47; 5. 4. 125–6

SURVEY, oversight, control
(O.E.D. 2); 5. 4. 82

TAFFETA, light lustrous silk
fabric; 1. 2. 11

TALL, doughty; 1. 3. 62

TALLOW, animal fat of any
kind, dripping from a roast
(cf. *Errors*, 3. 2. 98); 2. 4.
108

TALLOW-CATCH, dripping-
pan (?); 2. 4. 225

TARGET, buckler; 2. 4. 199

TASK, (i) challenge; 4. 1. 9;
5. 2. 52, (ii) tax; 4. 3. 92

TASTE, test; 4. 1. 119

TEMPER, brightness (cf. *Ric. II*,
4. 1. 29); 5. 2. 95

TEMPT, try; 3. 1. 172

TENDER (make tender of), have
regard for; 5. 4, 49

TERMAGANT, imaginary Mo-
hammedan deity of turbu-
lent character, belonging to
morality plays; 5. 4. 114 .

THEREFORE, for that purpose;
1. 1. 30

THICK, dim; 2. 3. 48

TICKLE-BRAIN, strong liquor
(slang); 2. 4. 391–2

TILT, contend. Often used
equivocally; 2. 3. 94

TIME, (i) time of life, life; 3. 2.
36, 151; (ii) affairs; 4. 1.
25

TOO BLAME, too blameworthy.
A 16th and 17th c. mis-
understanding of the infin.

'to blame' used predica-
tively (O.E.D. 'blame' vb.
6); 3. 1. 175

TOASTS-AND-BUTTER, . . milksop.
Lit. eater of buttered toast;
4. 2. 20

TOSSED, vexed; 2. 3. 81

TOUCH, touchstone, 'bide the
touch' = stand the test; 4.
4. 10

TOWN'S END, outskirt of town
or village, where rubbish was
shot, stocks stood and beggars congregated (v. quots.
O.E.D.); 4. 2. 9; 5. 3. 38

TRACE, follow; 3. 1. 47

TRADE-FALLEN, out of work;
4. 2. 28

TRAIN, entice; 5. 2. 22

TRICK, trait; 2. 4. 398; 5. 2. 12

TRIM (sb.), trappings; 4. 1. 113

TRIM (adj.), fine, pretty
(ironical); 5. 1. 135

TRIM UP, deck out; 5. 2. 58

TRIMLY, elegantly; 1. 3. 33

TRIUMPH, torchlight procession; 3. 3. 40

TROJAN, boon companion (cf.
L.L.L. 5. 2. 674); 2. 1. 68

TRUE, honest; 1. 2. 107; 2. 1.
91; 2. 2. 22, 91; 2. 4. 307

TUCK, long narrow rapier; 2. 4.
245

TURK, ferocious person; 5. 3. 45

UNDER-SKINKER, under-drawer;
2. 4. 23

UNEVEN, untoward; 1. 1. 50

UNGRACIOUS, graceless; 2. 4.
437

UNSORTED, ill-chosen; 2. 3. 14

UNYOKED, uncurbed; 1. 2. 188

VALUED, taken into consideration; 3. 2. 177

VASSAL (adj.), base; 3. 2. 124

VELVET-GUARDS, wearers of velvet trimmings (v. *guard*); 3. 1. 256

VICE, buffoon clad as a fool and armed with a wooden dagger (v. Chambers, *Med. Stage*, ii. 203–5); 2. 4. 445

VIGILANT, wakeful; 4. 2. 56

VIZARD, visor, mask; 1. 2. 123, 171; 2. 2. 51

WAG, naughty boy. Often a term of endearment; 1. 2. 16, 23, 44; 4. 2. 48

WAIT, attend upon; 5. 1. 111

WANTON, (i) luxuriant; 3. 1. 211; (ii) sportive; 4. 1. 103; (iii) unruly; 5. 1. 50

WARM, well-to-do (O.E.D. 8); 4. 2. 17

WASP-STUNG, irritable; 1. 3. 236

WATERING, the act of drinking; 2. 4. 15

WELL-RESPECTED, well-considered; 4. 3. 10

WELL SAID!, bravo! well done!; 5. 4. 75

WELSH, gibberish (a quibble); 3. 1. 49, 118

WELSH HOOK, woodman's bill-hook; 2. 4. 334

WILD (sb.), weald; 2. 1. 54

WILD (adj.), (a) untamed, insubordinate; 5. 2. 12; (b) dissolute; 5. 2. 73

WILDFIRE, (a) highly inflammable preparation of gunpowder, (b) erysipelas; 3. 3. 39

WIND, wheel; 4. 1. 109

WORSHIP, honour; 3. 2. 151

WRING, gall; 2. 1. 6

WRITER, notary; 3. 1. 141

YOUNKER, prodigal son. Lit. 'younger' (brother); 3. 3. 80

ZEAL, loyalty, affection; 4. 3. 63; 5. 4. 95